T0305181

Globalisation, Agriculture and Development

Globalisation, Agriculture and Development

Perspectives from the Asia-Pacific

Edited by

Matthew Tonts

Professor of Geography, School of Earth and Environment, University of Western Australia, Perth, Australia

M.A.B. Siddique

Associate Professor of Economics, Business School at the University of Western Australia and Director, Centre for Trade, Migration and Development, University of Western Australia, Perth, Australia

Edward Elgar
Cheltenham, UK • Northampton, MA, USA

Published by
Edward Elgar Publishing Limited
The Lypiatts
15 Lansdown Road
Cheltenham
Glos GL50 2JA
UK

Edward Elgar Publishing, Inc.
William Pratt House
9 Dewey Court
Northampton
Massachusetts 01060
USA

A catalogue record for this book
is available from the British Library

Library of Congress Control Number: 2010932046

MIX
Paper from
responsible sources
FSC® C018575

ISBN 978 1 84720 818 7

Typeset by Servis Filmsetting Ltd, Stockport, Cheshire
Printed and bound by MPG Books Group, UK

Contents

Contributors

Neil Argent, Division of Geography and Planning, University of New England, Armidale, New South Wales, Australia.

J.N. (Nick) Callow, School of Geography, Planning and Environmental Management, University of Queensland, St Lucia, Queensland, Australia.

Srikanta Chatterjee, School of Economics and Finance, Massey University, Palmerston North, New Zealand.

Julian Clifton, School of Earth and Environment, University of Western Australia, Crawley, Western Australia, Australia.

Zhao Dingtao, University of Science and Technology of China.

Paul Huddleston, School of Earth and Environment, University of Western Australia, Crawley, Western Australia, Australia.

Kenneth E. Jackson, Centre for Development Studies, University of Auckland, Auckland, New Zealand.

Bill Pritchard, Division of Geography, School of Geosciences, University of Sydney, New South Wales, Australia.

Allan Rae, School of Economics and Finance, Massey University, Palmerston North, New Zealand.

Ranjan Ray, Department of Economics, Monash University, Clayton, Victoria, Australia.

Brian J. Shaw, School of Earth and Environment, The University of Western Australia, Crawley, Western Australia, Australia.

M.A.B. Siddique, Associate Professor of Economics, Business School and Director, Centre for Trade, Migration and Development, University of Western Australia, Crawley, Australia.

Matthew Tonts, Professor of Geography, School of Earth and Environment, University of Western Australia, Crawley, Australia.

Yanrui Wu, Business School, University of Western Australia, Crawley, Western Australia, Australia.

Acknowledgements

Without the help of a number of people this book would not be possible. All of the chapters in this book were double-blind refereed, and we would like to thank all of the referees for their assistance in this review process. We would also like to thank Ms Beena Anil Biswas, who proofread the manuscript and prepared the reference lists. Thank you also to staff at Edward Elgar for their ongoing support of this project.

Finally, we would like to express our gratitude to Professor Kadambot Siddique, the Director of the University of Western Australia's Institute of Agriculture. Without Siddique's encouragement and enthusiasm for all things related to agriculture this project would not have been possible.

1. Globalisation, agriculture and development: perspectives from the Asia-Pacific

Matthew Tonts and M.A.B. Siddique

THE GLOBALISATION OF AGRICULTURE

Agriculture across much of the Asia-Pacific is being rapidly reshaped as local farming systems become increasingly integrated into global networks of production, distribution, consumption, investment and finance (Robinson 2004; Murray 2006; Rigg 2006). While for much of the region agriculture has had a long colonial history of being linked into wider international networks of trade, it is generally accepted that since the 1970s and 1980s there has been an increase in the scope and depth of global integration in the sector (Murray 2001). The reasons for this have been discussed at length elsewhere (see Le Heron 1993; Robinson 2004; Lawrence 2005; Rigg 2006), but include the collapse of the Bretton Woods agreement in 1971, the economic upheaval experienced in the world economy during the 1970s and 1980s, and the subsequent process of neoliberal economic reform in both developing and developed economies.

Indeed, it is the emergence of this neoliberal policy agenda during the 1980s and the consequent moves to reduce trade barriers and deregulate national economies that is claimed to have facilitated the expansion of a more complex, globalised agri-food system (Murray 2006). In developed economies, such as Australia and New Zealand, the neoliberal policy reforms of the subsequent decades aimed to increase farmers' levels of exposure to competitive global forces, partly as a means of stimulating innovation, and partly as a means of facilitating flows of commodities and capital (Lawrence 2005). Over this period, protective institutional structures that had supported agriculture were gradually removed, largely on the grounds that they distorted market forces and stifled innovation and entrepreneurship. Governments removed import restrictions on agricultural commodities, reduced tariffs, removed various price support mechanisms, and deregulated statutory marketing authorities. This not only increased international trade, but also promoted greater corporate involvement in the sector through a more coordinated set of links between the different components of the supply chain (Tonts et al. 2003). Indeed, the proliferation of formalised contracting arrangements between farmers and other commercial entities, such as processors, distributors and supermarkets, is clear evidence of the development of these vertical ties.

In developing countries, the context was somewhat different, though the general objective of improving efficiency and productivity was much the same. As Murray (2006) has suggested, neoliberal policy frameworks were implemented (often at the insistence of international credit and aid agencies) as a means of attracting foreign investment and stimulating exports, particularly in agriculture. Considerable policy emphasis has also been placed on transforming agriculture from a largely subsistence or 'localised' economic activity, to one that is more globally oriented, and which thereby generated export earnings and foreign capital. As in the developed nations, this saw an increasing involvement by transnational corporations in the sector, and the emergence of vertically coordinated networks of production and consumption (Kirsten and Sartorius 2002).

AGRICULTURAL TRANSFORMATIONS

All of this raises questions about how processes of globalisation have transformed agriculture at the level of the farm and local area. In the case of developed nations, the transformation of farming has been rapid, but in part this is a continuation of longstanding processes of change, and is not necessarily entirely the result of more recent globalisation processes. These changes have received considerable attention in the literature (for example Lawrence 1987; Pritchard and McManus 2001; Gray and Lawrence 2001; Cocklin and Dibden 2005). Perhaps the most apparent trend is the worsening cost–price squeeze in agriculture, which has ultimately forced many farmers to leave the industry. In the pursuit of economies of scale, those farmers that remain have increased the size of their holdings, and invested heavily in technological advancements that have improved levels of productivity and efficiency. In essence, there has been an intensification of production as farmers have sought to maximise outputs per hectare (Robinson 2004). These processes have long been evident in Australian and New Zealand agriculture, but have arguably gathered pace under a more liberalised and globally integrated agricultural system. Moreover, farmers are increasingly engaged in direct relationships with corporate actors through contracts or other purchasing arrangements, and are now well attuned to the changing needs of global markets for agricultural commodities (Tonts et al. 2003; Pritchard et al. 2007).

In the developing economies of the Asia-Pacific, the transformation of farming systems has been even more radical (Rigg 2006). At its most simple, there has been a widespread shift from the production of food for family consumption and local trade, to farming systems focused on the production of cash crops (Robinson 2004). Driven in large part by prevailing development policy and practice, farmers have invested heavily in new technologies and techniques, including fertilisers, new seed varieties and innovative land management systems, with a view to improving income (Rigg 2005). The outcome has been a general reduction in the level of agricultural diversity, and a focus on intensification and improved productivity. These agricultural systems are geared towards national, regional and global markets, with the focus squarely on income generation. As in the developed world, many of the economic linkages are with transnational corporations, and often involve complex contracting arrangements (Kirsten and Sartorius 2002; Huddleston and Tonts 2007).

AGRICULTURE AND DEVELOPMENT

The links between agriculture and development are not straightforward. While the economic performance of agriculture across the Asia-Pacific has improved if measured by output or value of production, the distribution of any benefits, in both spatial and socio-economic terms, appears to be extremely uneven (World Bank 2005; Rigg 2006). At the national level, evidence exists to suggest that the level of export earnings and gross domestic product (GDP) per worker in agriculture has improved considerably under a more globalised system (for example Gollin et al. 2002). At the local scale, a more complex set of realities prevail. On the one hand, there is evidence indicating that across most of the developing nations of the Asia-Pacific a globalised agriculture has indeed improved incomes and helped to alleviate poverty (World Bank 2005). On the other hand, in places like Australia and New Zealand, research suggests that the gap between rich and poor farmers is widening, and that many farmers have extremely low real incomes and are struggling in the face of both difficult trading conditions and environmental stress, notably drought (Cocklin and Dibden 2005). Other issues that have emerged across the region include increasing levels of farmer dependency on corporations, rising cost–price pressures, and the impacts of agricultural systems of fragile environments.

STRUCTURE OF THIS BOOK

All of this brings us to the purpose of this book. That is, to (re-)explore the links between globalisation, agriculture and development in a selected number of Asia-Pacific contexts in the early twenty-first century. It draws on the perspectives of economists and geographers, and aims to paint a picture of the broad nature of agricultural transformation under conditions of globalisation, and how this might impact on development at a range of different spatial scales.

In Chapter 2, Neil Argent provides an examination of the influences of globalisation on Australian agriculture and farmers. He considers how complex and interdependent forces, including liberalised financial systems, neoliberal policies and transnational corporations, are reorganising the landscape of agriculture in Australia. Building on this, Chapter 3 by Bill Pritchard and Matthew Tonts, also in the context of Australia, critically examines the argument that a more liberalised and 'efficient' agricultural sector contributes to more prosperous regional economies. Drawing on a set of regional case studies, they suggest that Australia's pursuit of a globalised and more efficient agricultural sector has been problematic for many rural communities, and has not necessarily contributed to a sustainable pattern of regional development. Chapter 4 also considers a developed economy: New Zealand. In this chapter Kenneth E. Jackson explores the evolution of New Zealand agriculture, its role in that country's economy, and how policy reform has begun to reshape the industry. Importantly, he raises questions about New Zealand's level of dependence on agriculture, and the challenges that this presents the country under conditions of globalisation.

The next three chapters deal with two of the Asia-Pacific's most powerful economies: China and India. In Chapter 5, M.A.B. Siddique offers an overview of the structure and dynamics of agriculture in these countries. He demonstrates not only that they are both experiencing rapid increases in the volume of output, but also that levels of productivity and efficiency are improving rapidly. He also shows how agriculture is playing an increasing role in contributing to macro-level development in terms of both GDP and export earnings. Chapter 6, by Srikanta Chatterjee, Allan Rae and Ranjan Ray, examines the links between economic reform and agriculture in India, focusing on its external trade relations, particularly with Australia and New Zealand. They note that while agricultural trade linkages have increased, there remain major challenges for both farming systems and broader processes of rural social and economic development. In Chapter 7 the attention turns to China, where Yanrui Wu and Zhao Dingtao explore the links between global integration and agricultural productivity. They find that China's agricultural productivity has improved substantially over recent years, in part due to its integration with the international economy, and in part because of technological investment. However, they also note that this transformation has not been geographically even, and that there are considerable variations in both agricultural performance and levels of development.

Chapter 8 sees the book shift its focus to the Association of South East Asian Nations (ASEAN) region. Here M.A.B. Siddique provides a general overview of the structure of agriculture and its recent evolution in the ASEAN region. He notes considerable diversity in the productivity and performance of agriculture in this region, and suggests that the links between globalisation, agriculture and development in the ASEAN region are complex. This complexity is further elaborated in Chapter 9, where Brian J. Shaw explores the relationship between agriculture and the emergence of Southeast Asian megacities. He considers how changes in agriculture have fuelled processes of urbanisation, and the ways in which the economies and social structures of megacities are still closely tied to local agricultural systems. In Chapter 10, Paul Huddleston examines contract farming arrangements in the rapidly growing oil palm industry in the Philippines. This chapter notes the role of contracts in providing farmers with access to capital, market security and technology, and shows how this has contributed to improved local incomes and increased regional economic activity. However, he also suggests that contracts have the potential to become problematic where farmers become excessively dependent on processing firms for their technological needs and begin to lose autonomy over their operations.

In Chapters 11 and 12 the links between environmental problems and globalised agricultural systems are explored. In Chapter 11, Julian Clifton provides an analysis of an initiative in Indonesia designed to improve environmental conservation and, at the same time, improve rural economic and social well-being. He points out that globalisation is not simply a problematic economic process, but one that is socio-institutional and that can result in positive social and environmental outcomes. In Chapter 12, J.N. Callow and Julian Clifton offer a general overview of the ways in which globalised agriculture can affect environmental systems, and how this in turn affects development. Their analysis shows how economic and social processes are ultimately tied into ecological processes that, in turn, are important not only in terms of agricultural production, but also in terms of their capacity to offer broader 'environmental services'. Chapter 13 by M.A.B. Siddique and Matthew Tonts concludes the book, providing a synthesis of the key themes and offering a number of future lines of enquiry.

REFERENCES

Cocklin, C. and J. Dibden (eds) (2005), *Sustainability and Change in Rural Australia*, Sydney, NSW: University of New South Wales Press.

Gollin, D., S. Parente and R. Rogerson (2002), 'The role of agriculture in development', *American Economic Review*, **92**, 160–64.

Gray, I. and G. Lawrence (2001), *A Future for Regional Australia: Escaping Global Misfortune*, Cambridge: Cambridge University Press.

Huddleston, P. and M. Tonts (2007), 'Agricultural development, contract farming and Ghana's oil palm industry', *Geography*, **93**, 266–78.

Kirsten, J. and K. Sartorius (2002), 'Linking agribusiness and small-scale farmers in developing countries: is there a new role for contract farming?', *Development Southern Africa*, **19**, 503–29.

Lawrence, G. (1987), *Capitalism and the Countryside*, Sydney, NSW: Pluto Press.

Lawrence, G. (2005), 'Globalisation, agricultural production systems and rural restructuring', in C. Cocklin and J. Dibden (eds), *Sustainability and Change in Rural Australia*, Sydney, NSW: University of New South Wales Press, pp. 104–20.

Le Heron, T. (1993), *Globalized Agriculture: Political Choice*, Oxford: Pergamon Press.

Murray, W. (2001), 'The second wave of globalization and agrarian change in the Pacific Islands', *Journal of Rural Studies*, **17**, 135–48.

Murray, W. (2006), *Geographies of Globalization*, London: Routledge.

Pritchard, W., D. Burch and G. Lawrence (2007), 'Neither "family" nor "corporate" farming: Australian tomato growers as farm family entrepreneurs', *Journal of Rural Studies*, **23**, 75–87.

Pritchard, W. and P. McManus (2001), *Land of Discontent: The Dynamics of Change in Rural and Regional Australia*, Sydney, NSW: University of New South Wales Press.

Rigg, J. (2005), 'Poverty and livelihoods after full-time farming: a south-east Asian view', *Asia-Pacific Viewpoint*, **46**, 173–84.

Rigg, J. (2006), 'Land, farming, livelihoods and poverty: rethinking the links in the rural South', *World Development*, **34**, 180–202.

Robinson, G. (2004), *Geographies of Agriculture: Globalisation, Restructuring, Sustainability*, Harlow: Pearson Prentice Hall.

Tonts, M., D. Haplin, J. Collins and A. Black (2003), *Rural Communities and Changing Farm Business Structures*, Canberra: Rural Industries Research and Development Corporation.

World Bank (2005), *Agricultural Growth for the Poor: An Agenda for Development*, Washington, DC: World Bank.

2. Australian agriculture in the global economic mosaic

Neil Argent

INTRODUCTION

By any objective measure, Australian agriculture has undergone substantial change since the early 1980s (see Pritchard and McManus 2000; Gray and Lawrence 2001). In some respects, it seems something of a paradox to consider the past and current position of Australian agriculture under the rubric of globalisation. First, globalisation is itself still a contested and contentious idea. For many theorists, the phenomenon is more readily associated with industry sectors such as 'high-tech' and more basic heavy industrial manufacturing, finance and property services – the sectors in which flexible specialisation and accumulation, new international divisions of labour, space–time compression or convergence would appear to have had the greatest impact in terms of employment and production change. By contrast, agriculture, with its relatively constant temporal rhythms and real spatial fixity, seems relatively lacking in dynamism.

Although the development of the 'new political economy of agriculture' during the 1980s and the subsequent offshoot of agri-food restructuring studies have played major roles in correcting this misconception, doubts remain over the application of concepts borrowed from the post-Fordist or flexible specialisation literature to agrarian change (see Goodman and Watts 1994; Watts and Goodman 1997). Nevertheless, as Le Heron (1993) observes, the restructuring of the agri-food and fibre processing and farm input sectors of developed countries during the 1980s and 1990s cannot be understood in isolation from the reorganisation of capital markets, and financial and banking systems, together with the concomitant increase in merger and acquisition activity between corporate players. One of the key features of this corporate activity, aside from its capital intensity and rapidity, was the degree to which it wound farmers into much closer and more direct relations (financial and organisational) with other 'capital fractions', particularly the banking and related finance sectors, input providers, end processors and end markets themselves (for example super-market chains) (Le Heron 1993).

The second reason for regarding globalisation and Australian agriculture as perhaps a paradoxical coupling is that, as a nation, Australia has for much of its European-dominated history been heavily internationally oriented by virtue of its incorporation into the political and economic networks of the British Empire. As emphasised by dominion capitalism theorists (for example Ehrensaft and Armstrong 1978; Armstrong and Bradbury 1983; Schwartz 1989) and more recent observers (for example Barnes 1996), the political economy and the character of industrial development of settler societies like Australia, New Zealand and Canada have been moulded by their dependence upon the export of 'staples' – relatively untransformed primary commodities, such as lumber, pelts, wheat and gold – to the Imperial Centre, and imports of capital, manufacturing goods and labour. In all three nations this dependence became a historical legacy by which the primary production sectors (forestry and agriculture in Canada and New Zealand; agriculture and mining in Australia) continued to be regarded as the engines of macroeconomic strength and stability long after this role for other developed nations had passed to the manufacturing sector. Settler state economies were then characterised by a dual structure: a strong, dynamic and internationally oriented primary production sector given the task of providing macroeconomic stability, and a domestic economy dominated by industries and businesses that employed the vast majority of the labour force and operated behind a high tariff curtain (Emy and Hughes 1988).

However, globalisation involves significant qualitative changes to the strength and the nature of linkages between firms, communities, institutions and governments within and across national boundaries. Much social scientific discussion during the closing decades of the twentieth century and the first decade of the twenty-first century has been almost unanimously negative in its judgement of the consequences of globalisation for Australian farming. In this context, the purpose of this chapter is to explore the influences and impacts of globalisation on Australian agriculture and farmers. Admittedly, this is an ambitious exercise. Nevertheless, as I will argue below, much valuable light can be shed on the changing face of farming in contemporary Australia, with a nuanced approach to the topic that explicitly acknowledges the spatial and scalar-specific nature of globalisation processes, and that insists upon the dialectic of structure and agency in shaping globalisation as a set of tendencies.

The chapter is comprised of four subsequent main sections. First, I clarify the specific stance taken towards globalisation for this argument. Second, I consider the growing international body of literature on globalisation and agri-food restructuring before examining the role of 'globalising forces' in the shape of liberalised financial systems and banks, neoliberal states and transnational corporations – some of which emerged rapidly from humbler roots as national-scale firms – in reorganising Australian food and drink production, processing, marketing and distribution during the 1980s and 1990s. The final major section deals more explicitly with the primary purpose of this chapter: globalisation's role as a driver of major structural change in Australian farming. This is done through the examination of four key aspects of globalisation: (1) the rise of neoliberalism as an ideology of state management and as a rationale for the pursuit of global free trade; (2) the growing might of agri-food-based transnational corporations and their impacts upon regional farming structures; (3) the apparent looming of global environmental crises, and the closely related rise of global environmental movements; and (4) the spread of global finance and banking into the sector. A final section concludes.

GLOBALISATION

If nothing else, the interpretativist turn in human geography since the late 1980s has reminded us of the critical role that language plays in describing and shaping our understandings of, and interventions in, the 'real world' (Barnes, 1997). In particular, we have learned the dangers of the uncritical use of metaphors. Used carefully, these can be enlightening literary devices, sophisticated and powerful enough to form the basis of an entire research agenda because they can accurately reflect back to us a simplified and readily understandable version of the 'truth' of what they seek to encapsulate (Sayer 1992; Barnes 1997; Argent et al. 2008). Globalisation has been a key target of this deconstructionist effort, with Leyshon (1997) situating the supposed hegemony of globalisation discourse within the corporate boardrooms and parliamentary corridors whence it emits, Fagan (1997) challenging the 'steamroller' model of globalisation, and Massey (1994) critiquing overhyped claims concerning 'the end of geography' (O'Brien 1992).

Geographical scale provides a heuristic framework through which we can apprehend globalisation as a term, idea, discourse and real material process. An attentiveness to scale, and relations between scales, forces us to focus on the specific and usually highly complex and uneven ways in which, for example, free agricultural trade principles established at the global scale – at a (WTO) meeting, for example – are interpreted and translated into policy by national governments, and responded to by local farmers and rural communities. In other words, it concentrates attention on the radically complex power relations, and their effects, both between and within scale, thereby avoiding the reification of simplistic and dichotomous hierarchies such as 'global–local' (Murray 2006; Woods 2007). As Woods (2007, p. 11) notes: 'globalization is itself hybrid, involving many different strands that become knitted together, yet which may also elicit different responses from local actors. Second, globalization proceeds by hybridization, fusing and mingling the local and the extra-local to produce new formations'.

In other words, a nuanced conception of scale and scale relations allows us to see the complexity of globalisation as a process, a set of tendencies which may, or may not, be realised at any particular scale due to flawed acts of translation and/or acts of resistance (Dicken 2003; Murray 2006; Woods 2007). Key amongst these tendencies are:

1. the relative extensiveness of networks;
2. the relative intensity of network flows, together with their degree of interconnectedness;
3. the velocity of flows (of capital, people, commodities, information, and so on); and
4. the degree to which individual places (nodes in the networks) are susceptible to change driven by the first three processes (Murray 2006, p. 41).

The extent to which these factors draw together governments, firms, communities and individuals into an integrated system across and through international borders is fundamental to a robust conceptualisation of globalisation. However, there is more to globalisation than seamless flows of growing volumes of finance, people and products across the globe. The increasing international dissemination of cultural mores and ideals, consumption modes and the discourses of environmental concern are also major elements of what we experience as globalisation. The first two are obviously closely interrelated (though not mutually exclusive), and refer to the spread of consumer preferences across the globe and into societies: 'For example, large numbers of the world's young people enjoy wearing blue jeans and Nike shoes, consuming Coca-Cola and Pepsi, smoking Marlboro cigarettes, eating McDonald's hamburgers, listening to Madonna, or watching American action movies' (Stutz and Warf 2005, p. 15). The globalisation of the environment concerns the growing recognition of the global character of major environmental issues (for example global warming, biodiversity decline, ozone depletion) as well as the growth of truly global organisations (for example Greenpeace, the World Wide Fund for Nature) that campaign for solutions to these problems from the global to the local and all scales in between. This factor is germane to the changes under way in Australian agriculture, as will be made clear later in this chapter.

One of the ideas central to the development of globalisation is the rise and spread of neoliberal ideology, or neoliberalism for short. For many, neoliberalism is seen as providing the philosophical rationale for, and practical guidance in, the spread of globalisation from the expanding edifice of supranational bodies (for example the World Bank, International Monetary Fund, WTO) and transnational corporations (TNCs) to nation-states and local communities. Key elements of the toolkit are: the embrace of international free trade; the associated deregulation of product markets and regulatory systems; and the corporatisation and/or the privatisation of formerly state or state-owned enterprises or agencies (Harvey 2006). In some of the more 'hyperglobalist' accounts (Murray 2006), neoliberalism and globalisation have eviscerated the nation-state, reducing it to: 'a Janus-faced state . . . bifurcated between a dominant "entrepreneurial state", developing an active programme of deregulation, privatization and decentralization, and a subordinate "soup kitchen state" catering for the unemployed and those on the margins of the post-Fordist economy' (Tickell and Peck 1992, p. 204).

Here, too, caution needs to be exercised. Neoliberalism contains a solid philosophical core: Hayekian economics, Chicago School monetarism, social Darwinism and the rational sovereign economic subject at the heart of neo-classical economics, together with Ayn Rand's political philosophy (Peck 2004, p. 400); but it is nonetheless a contingent phenomenon (O'Neill and Argent 2005). Peck and Tickell (2002) identify two main strains: 'roll-back' and 'roll-out' neoliberalism. 'Roll-back' neoliberalism is associated with the deregulation and privatisation programmes of Western governments during the 1980s in which the Keynesian welfare state was gradually dismantled by the Reagan administration in the United States, the Thatcher government in the UK, the Lange Fourth Labour Government in New Zealand and the Hawke–Keating Labor Government in Australia. 'Roll-out' neoliberalism refers to the more human face of conservative and centrist politics seen in the 'Third Way-ism' of the Clinton and Blair administrations. This variant underscores neoliberalism's internal inconsistencies, for as it seeks to repair some of the damage done to social cohesion from earlier phases of macroeconomic 'reform' it nevertheless retains a tight focus upon the creation of economically rational citizens (Peck and Tickell 2002).

In summary, while there are a number of relatively incontrovertible structural tendencies at the heart of globalisation it is crucial to appreciate at least two things. First, policies and programmes of neoliberal globalisation do not necessarily issue forth from a Washington Consensus production line, ready for installation in subscribing nations and programmed to filter throughout each branch of society and economy (see Peck and Tickell 2002). We must be attentive to the variegated, partial spread of globalisation and neoliberalism, paying heed to the resistances they encounter at differing scales from the global to the local. Second, while the role of the nation-state (together with regional states and local states as found in federal polities such as Australia's and Canada's) has become somewhat circumscribed through the de- (and re-)regulation of markets, this does not mean that it has been 'hollowed-out' (Jessop 1993) or rendered a 'phantom state' (Thrift and Leyshon 1994). Governments, at a range of scales, continue to intervene in politically significant, even if sometimes contradictory ways, and sometimes even contrary to the hegemonic ideals of advanced liberal rule.

GLOBALISATION AND AGRICULTURE

For some, globalisation's impacts upon agriculture mark a distinct break with the entire international and national governance of agriculture that pertained throughout the period from the conclusion of the Second World War until the Organization of Petroleum Exporting Countries (OPEC) oil price 'hike' of 1973 (see Friedmann and McMichael 1989). The concept of 'food regimes' is pertinent here (see Table 2.1). It developed from Friedmann and McMichael's (1989) criticism of the prevailing wisdom that economic development, including agricultural trade, diffused from fully economically mature industrialised nations to developing nations. This account, according to Friedmann and McMichael, overemphasised the early development of autarkical nation-states and downplayed the importance of international relations of power, trade and investment in setting the foundations for the present agri-food and fibre system. Their account of the rise and fall of national agricultures formed the basis for subsequent analyses of the international farm crisis of the 1970s and 1980s and the reputed collapse of the second food regime.

The seeds of change that facilitated the transition to a putative third food regime were sown when corporate capital-sponsored or owned science and technology were applied to inert chemicals or basic agricultural outputs and by-products to create 'durable' foods during the second regime (Friedmann 1991; Le Heron 1993). Via this increased application of industrial capital and technology to agricultural products and processes, agriculture was brought into much closer and more intimate relationships with off-farm businesses, including corporate capital. Since this time, therefore, farming has increasingly been seen as merely one stage and entity in agri-commodity chains and complexes which bind producers,

Table 2.1   Food regimes: principal tendencies and historical features

Food regime	Principal tendencies	Main historical features
First (1780s–1945)	Centred on European imports of wheat and meat from settler states between 1910 and 1914 and imports by settler states of European manufactured goods, labour and capital.	Culmination of colonialism.
Second (1950s–1970s)	Extension of state system to former colonies. Transnational restructuring of agricultural sectors by agri-food firms. Productivism, corporatism, industrialism.	Based on strong state protection and organisation of world food economy under US hegemony after 1945.
Third (1980s–present)	Post-productivism and/or multifunctionality. Emphasis on quality alongside industrial scale of production. Advancing biotechnology.	Neoliberalism and monetarism become dominant ideologies in state economic management. Increasingly global character of world trade, and of trade regulation. 'Governance' instead of government.

Sources: Friedmann and McMichael (1989), Le Heron (1993), Murray (2006).

processors, packagers, marketers, distributors, regulators and, finally, consumers into increasingly long concatenated lines of power and responsibility (see Whatmore and Thorne 1997; Whatmore 2002; Pritchard et al. 2007). As Le Heron (1993, p. 47) reminds us:

> An agro-commodity chain rests on a distinctive ecology; involves a series of 'sites' of physical production at which natural, industrial and other inputs are variously transformed into potentially useful and exchangeable products; is sustained by equally distinctive social and cultural arrangements; and evolves in the wider context of capitalist political economy. Importantly, each site of physical production is also the site for the creation of value, through the application of labour. The abstract notion of agro-commodity chain thus highlights the interdependence of a range of investors at different stages in physical production; the direction of evolution of parts or the whole chain; competition

amongst interests; sources of conflict, around class, gender and ethnicity . . .
interconnections with multiple political constituencies, and the geographic
specificity of chains.

More specifically, this transition from the second to a third food regime
has seen tighter links develop between the farming sector and credit providers (with some farm input providers and processing firms becoming
more prominent farm lenders over time), farm input suppliers, marketers and supermarkets themselves (Le Heron 1993). This increased real
(or indirect) subsumption of farmers translated into the pursuit of ever-
increasing scales of operation, and created stark contrasts between those
'farming units' that could and could not keep up with the agricultural
treadmill. As Whatmore (2002, p. 65) observes, 20 per cent of European
farmers now account for 80 per cent of farm commodity production. For
Watts and Goodman (1997, p. 13) the third food regime, and globalisation, is associated with: 'the hegemonic role of global capital circuits
(transnational agro-capitals), the standardization of diets, new forms of
international division of labour, a distinctive social economy, regional spe-
cialization, global sourcing, the homogenization of production conditions,
and the undermining of state autonomy'. However, they also caution
against overgeneralised accounts of the globalisation of food and fibre
production and processing which emphasise the evisceration of the nation-
state as a regulatory power. Although national agricultural sectors have
experienced decreasing levels of direct state support through deregulatory
policies and reductions in protection, farmers are nonetheless increasingly
subject to the powerful reach of 'private global regulation' (Watts and
Goodman 1997, p. 13) in the form of the WTO, the North American Free
Trade Agreement (NAFTA), the Asia-Pacific Economic Cooperation
(APEC) and the like, and a re-regulation of other dimensions of farming
(for example food quality assurance; quarantine controls as a non-tariff
barrier to food and fibre imports).

   Having clarified the stance taken towards globalisation, and globalisation and agriculture, the analysis shifts focus and scale by considering the
specific ways in which globalising tendencies have been interpreted by
Australian governments, corporations and farmers.

AUSTRALIAN FOOD AND FIBRE PRODUCTION AND PROCESSING IN AN ERA OF GLOBALISATION

To the extent that globalisation, as defined here, has impacted upon
Australian agriculture, its direct effects are perhaps more readily seen in

the input and processing sectors upstream and downstream of farming. As shown by Fagan (1990, 1995), and Fagan and Webber (1999), it was in the turbulent reorganisation of the Australian food and beverage processing sectors that some of the strongest evidence emerged of Australia's incorporation into a global economy. Four key corporate strategies deployed by firms in this sector highlight the tenor of the times (Fagan and Webber 1999, pp. 105–6). First, merger and takeover activity increased, with large firms – including TNCs such as Nestlé and Cadbury-Schweppes – acquiring smaller domestic businesses. Some instructive examples include the merger between Carlton and United Breweries (CUB), Elders (a long established pastoral company but controlled by CUB) and IXL, a fruit processor in the late 1980s (Fagan 1990) and Nestlé's 1995 acquisition of the Petersville brand (best known for Peter's ice cream) (Pritchard 1999). Second, some of the country's more established businesses diversified into the higher cash flows then being achieved in the processed food sector, and away from comparatively less profitable activities. Again, Elders IXL is a useful example, with the expansion of its finance arm – once used primarily to offer short-term bridging finance to its once natural clientele, farmers – into merchant banking, stockbroking and trade financing (Fagan 1990; Fagan and Webber 1999, p. 109). Third, many of these corporations also diversified back into food production and processing in order to add more stable cash-flow enterprises to their high-risk portfolios. Good examples of this strategy were the failed corporate raiders, Adelaide Steamship and Bond Corporation, who both invested massive amounts of borrowed capital in order to develop substantial interests in local food processing and brewing (Fagan 1995; Fagan and Webber 1999). Fourth and finally, some corporations – the exemplar again being Elders IXL – used their established agribusiness interests to launch their international, or global, strategies. In these cases, the relative freedom and ease with which these conglomerates could leverage very large loans was a direct result of the deregulation of the Australian financial system and banking sector during the mid-1980s, together with the more generally liberalised conditions for finance around the world (Fagan and Webber 1999).

However, it is rather more difficult to find such compelling evidence of globalisation's influence (as defined above) on the Australian farm sector. This is not to say that globalisation processes and tendencies have not filtered down at all to local agriculture – they most certainly have – but the nature and strength of their effects have generally been much more indirect and muted than in the case of corporate-scale food, beverage and fibre processing and marketing. There are a number of reasons why this might be the case. As already noted, Australia's historical status post-European invasion as a colony of the British Empire and as an exporter of relatively untransformed primary resource commodities has meant that, like New Zealand's and Canada's primary resource sectors, Australian agriculture has generally possessed a strong export and, therefore, international orientation (Le Heron 1993). It has, then, been in a better position than some other national industry sectors, such as the heavily protected textile, clothing and footwear manufacturing sector, together with the farm sectors of other countries, to adapt to the more uncertain and highly competitive trading environment under globalisation.

Notwithstanding the earlier pointers regarding the historically international orientation of Australian agriculture, the sector has, at least until the mid-1980s, enjoyed strong and comprehensive government support – both state and federal – across a wide range of areas, from specific commodity sector support to rural settlement. From 1952, when the Federal Minister of Commerce and Agriculture and leader of the Country Party, 'Black Jack' McEwen, announced a new agricultural and rural policy, farming was installed as the nation's engine of economic growth and the bulwark behind which the manufacturing-based industrialisation of Australia in the post-Second World War era 'golden age' could be achieved. Truly a policy envisaged as 'a rising tide [which would] lift all boats' (Potter 1997, p. 80), the conservative coalition's policy involved, by contemporary standards and ideas, an impressive and ambitious array of instruments and plans to both modernise and expand the domestic farming sector. For instance, the introduction of a concessional farm loan programme, and the establishment of the Commonwealth Development Bank in 1959 and the Primary Industries Bank of Australia in 1978, facilitated the 'capital deepening' of the farm sector (Argent 1997, 2002b). In this way, a corporatist alliance developed between the commonwealth and state governments, finance capital and farmers, based on the mutual need for stable conditions for accumulation.

From the late 1970s and 1980s, though, the regulatory and institutional apparatus erected to help ensure agriculture's ongoing success and its contribution to solving Australia's persistent balance-of-payment problems was gradually dismantled. A series of reports, beginning with the 1974 Green Paper on Rural Policy (Working Group 1974), bore the hallmarks of the neoliberal monetarist approach to public sector management. In the context of an increasingly difficult international trading environment, borne out in the loss of preferential access to the British market in 1973, and the growing recognition of widespread poverty amongst some of Australia's small farm sector (McKay 1967; Lawrence 1987), governments began to feel that a vibrant, self-reliant farm sector, responsive to international market signals, would be best served by the removal of price-distorting arrangements and by the reform of structural inefficiencies within other macroeconomic sectors (for example banking, domestic shipping and the waterfront, industrial relations). As Wonder (1995, p. 2) observes, for the 1980s and 1990s: 'the orientation of Australia's agricultural policies is therefore towards facilitation of market responsiveness, risk management and self-reliance. There has been a deliberate move away from policies that distort market signals to producers'.

True to globalisation discourse, successive federal governments have argued that this domestic stance is essential to the success of their international campaign to bring down protection in the US and the EU and thereby provide Australian farmers with an opportunity to compete on the famed 'level playing field' (Le Heron 1993; Pritchard 2000; Gray and Lawrence 2001; Cocklin and Dibden 2002; Lockie et al. 2006). More importantly, though, it is vital to see the policy shifts of the 1980s and 1990s as a re-regulation of Australian agriculture and farm support (Le Heron 1993; Cocklin and Dibden 2002); a process that took agriculture from its relatively privileged public policy position – along with mining – during the post-Second World War era and thence placed it on the same footing alongside all other industry sectors.

AUSTRALIAN FARMING IN A GLOBALISING ENVIRONMENT

In this section of the chapter, I consider the salient features of contemporary Australian agriculture and the degree to which, if at all, globalisation can be said to have been responsible for major structural changes within it. My chief foci here are: the reregulation of farm trade; structural change in the farm sector; the increasing importance of environmental regulation in shaping agriculture's access to natural resources; and the globalisation of finance and Australian farmers.

Liberalisation of Farm Trade and the Re-regulation of Australian Agriculture

Perhaps one of the clearer examples of globalisation's impact on Australian agriculture lies in the management of the nation's trading links with the rest of the world, and the ways in which an aggressively free-trade stance has been translated to the organisation of farm commodity marketing arrangements within the country. As has already been noted, the drive for freer trade in all goods and services at the global scale, in which Australia has been in the vanguard individually as well as through its membership of the Cairns Group, has been replicated in the dismantlement or substantial restructuring of farm commodity marketing and trading arrangements within Australia (Pritchard 2000). This, as Pritchard (2000) demonstrates, is the two-edged sword of Australian governments' drive for trade liberalisation at the global level. Along one blade sits the often untested but grandiose claims of the national benefits to flow from farmers' access to hitherto protected markets. Along the other lies the frequently traumatic processes (for farmers and the local communities that serve them) of domestic market 'reform' required for the arguments of Australian trade negotiators before the WTO and similar institutions to appear as consistent as possible.

Farmer-owned co-operative marketing boards which once managed the marketing of a range of farm products from eggs, milk, butter, apples and pears, dried fruit, wine grapes, wool, wheat and other cereals by pooling returns and thereby hedging against the risk of price fluctuations on notoriously volatile markets, were virtually all abolished, corporatised or privatised during the 1980s and 1990s. On the positive side of the ledger, the removal of these monopoly marketing bodies opens up opportunities for individual farmers and private traders to pursue their own market strategies. To some extent this has been seen in the aftermath of the gradual dismantling of the Australian Wool Commission during 1993, with some wool growers establishing their own brands of knitwear and/or entering into direct relationships with international woollen millers. On the other hand, though, this requires the assumption of a great deal more risk on the part of the individual farmer as he or she becomes solely responsible for deciding who to sell farm products to, when and on what terms. One of the last remaining co-operative-based marketing 'boards' in Australian agriculture is the Australian Wheat Board (AWB), though this was deprived of its statutory monopoly in 1989 (Gray and Lawrence 2001, p. 59).

The potential for such dramatic regulatory reform to drive a wedge between farmers is highlighted by Pritchard (2000) and Cocklin and Dibden (2002). They highlight the contested and contentious nature of deregulation, with many farmers torn between the lure of the 'holy grail' of international free trade in farm commodities and the potential for increased Australian farm export returns, while on the one hand, the discomforting awareness that it may well be they who are forced out of farming due to structural change. Cocklin and Dibden's (2002) detailed research with Victorian dairy farmers in the months preceding and following the deregulation of the Australian dairy market highlights the decision-making 'knife edge' that many navigated prior to the plebiscite that provided the imprimatur for the official removal of regulated milk prices. Since deregulation there has been a dramatic loss of dairy farms from Queensland and New South Wales, and an increasing concentration of the sector in Victoria, as farm-gate prices for milk plummeted (Davidson 2001). Alongside the extreme financial stress placed upon dairy farmers, some have expressed a disenchantment with dairying as an occupation and way of life as declining real incomes, increased debt burdens and a loss of autonomy have hit home:

> Stricter requirements in terms of quality assurance have led some farmers to feel that one form of regulation – which benefited them financially – has been replaced by another form that limits the autonomy that made the physical hardships of dairying worthwhile; it has also inflated the debt burden of some farmers. (Cocklin and Dibden 2002, p. 39)

Globalisaton and Structural Change on Australian Farms

One of the dominant themes of the agrarian restructuring literature of the 1970s and 1980s focused on the persistence of kin-based production systems – commonly known as family farming – in an era of advanced capitalism. The key point of debate was whether or not farming families could resist the 'iron laws' of capitalism, which demand the attainment of ever-greater economies of scale and scope, or whether this type of producer would eventually be subsumed by corporate capital. Within a fully globalised, or globalising, agricultural sector one would expect to see a high level of vertical and horizontal integration within the sector, with transnational capital increasingly extending its reach from food and fibre processing, packaging and distribution backwards to actual production at the farm level.

Direct subsumption, whereby corporate capital owns the means of farm production as well as its downstream processing, marketing and distribution, is by no means a general trend. Lawrence (2005) has documented the widespread incidence of contract farming relations in intensive horticultural industries such as potatoes (Miller, 1996) and tomatoes (Pritchard and Burch 2003) where corporate, including transnational, capital has majority, even monopoly, control of the sector. For example, 95 per cent of Tasmanian potato production occurs under contract (Lawrence 2005, p. 108). Outside of these intensive farming sectors, though, there is at best mixed evidence for much vertical integration and direct subsumption of Australian farmers. First and foremost, Australian farms are overwhelmingly family-owned and -run affairs, even though there is a growing tendency for company and trust ownership and management structures to be used by farmers. In the late 1990s, virtually all farms were family-owned, with only 0.4 per cent owned by corporations (Garnaut and Lim-Applegate 1998).

Horizontal integration has been the topic of much more discussion and debate. Due in large part to that great constant (other than a harsh climate) of Australian farming – the cost–price squeeze – farm amalgamation has occurred at varying rates since the end of the Second World War. However, it is difficult to obtain reliable and robust time-series data on this issue. In New South Wales the total number of farms officially declined by 27 per cent between 1981 and 1996, from 56 798 to 41 444 (Garnaut and Lim-Applegate 1998), but most of this decrease can be attributed to the ninefold increase in the Australian Bureau of Statistics' (ABS) estimated value of operations (EVAO) threshold for inclusion in its published statistics, from $2500 to $22 500 in 1991–92. A more thorough analysis of farm structural change in Australia, which considered both rates of entry into as well as exits from farming, reveals that rates of exit reached a historical low of 0.44 per cent per annum between 1996 and 2001 after relatively high rates of exit during the 1980s and early 1990s (Barr 2004).

Geographically, trends in farm numbers have been far from uniform. Barr disaggregates farm turnover into four major regional types: (1) tightly held regions; (2) churning regions; (3) fragmenting regions; and (4) consolidating regions (Barr 2004, pp. 36–7). Those areas that have experienced consistently high rates of loss from the mid-1970s – known as 'churning regions' – are generally confined to the remoter rangelands, but also include the 'heartland' agricultural regions of the New South Wales Northern and Southern Tablelands, western Victoria, and the drier wheat and sheep belt of Western Australia. Critically, the deregulation of co-operative statutory marketing arrangements and the associated privatisation of formerly government-owned commodity marketing organisations has seen increased financial pressure placed on family growers as they are forced to purchase more land and machinery in order to raise their economies of scale. This has led to a substantial horizontal integration, thereby reducing overall farm numbers. In the case of tomato growers, over 300 growers exited the industry between 1984 and 2004 (Pritchard et al. 2007, p. 76). A similar magnitude of decline has been found in the number of Tasmanian potato growers (Burch and Rickson 2001, p. 174).

The Global Environment, Global Environmentalism and Australian Agriculture

Alongside the concern to remove structures and arrangements that might fetter the free operation of markets, farm policy has also been increasingly influenced by the rise and global spread of environmental consciousness since the 1970s and, more recently, by the quest for environmentally sustainable development (Argent 2002b). As the ecological impacts of land clearing, inland irrigation development and capital-intensive broadscale farming have gradually become more widespread and widely known, environmentalism has eroded farming's once pivotal and esteemed position within the Australian political economy. Since the mid-1990s, a panoply of federal and state agri-environmental policies have been introduced to combat, *inter alia*, soil erosion, groundwater depletion, dryland and irrigated land salinity, and habitat and biodiversity decline. These policies and programmes all bear the imprint of the ecologically sustainable development (ESD) protocols agreed upon by state and federal governments in 1992 (Aplin 1998). Of course, ESD principles are themselves the product of the international and, eventually, global debate over the long-term, potentially catastrophic environmental impacts of capitalist development, beginning with the landmark 1987 Brundtland report.

In Australia, the gradual 'greening' of political affairs has been increasingly allied with neoliberalism. The normative values of economic efficiency, individual self-reliance and ecological sustainability have been elevated as dominant precepts in agri-environmental policy (Lockie et al. 2006). For example, in the southeastern states, legislation regulating the use of inland waterways for irrigation use has, in accordance with the National Water Policy Reform Framework, reduced the total pool of water available for irrigation and stock dams as well as raising the price of tradeable water rights. In the context of one of the most serious droughts in recorded history, dairy farmers, fruit and vegetable growers and broadscale cropping farmers have been forced to expend large sums of money to purchase what little water is available to produce crops and/or keep stock alive.

Any discussion of globalisation, agriculture and the environment would be incomplete without reference to what Braun and Castree (1998) refer to as the construction of 'global nature' through the genetic manipulation (conscious and accidental) of plants and animals. Mercifully, Australia has avoided major biological crises such as bovine spongiform encephalitis (BSE) or foot-and-mouth disease by dint of its island continent status, relative remoteness and strong customs controls. However, the recent decision by the New South Wales state government to permit the cultivation of genetically modified (GM) canola from 2008 now potentially draws the nation's agriculture more tightly within a truly global network of gene technology research development and transfer, controlled by transnational corporations such as Monsanto. Again, this decision has divided the agricultural sector, with some broadacre farmers greatly concerned that their own crops may be cross-contaminated by GM canola pollen, thus ruining their ability to market their crops as 'GM-free'. Farmers may be caught in yet another powerful compromise: reject the promise of greater profitability from the planting of GM crops due to lower herbicide and pesticide use and give up a potential opportunity to beat (if only temporarily) the ongoing cost–price squeeze in Australian farming; or adopt biotechnology, potentially reduce costs and increase profits, but at the possible risk of neighbours' opprobrium and increased market risk (due to the widespread public uncertainty over the potential environmental and personal health dangers of GM consumption).

Finally, in a parallel trend, Australian farmers have been forced to mount an international campaign to defend their 'clean and green' image against the guerilla-style tactics of animal rights groups like People for the Ethical Treatment of Animals (PETA). In a highly successful and sustained offensive, PETA has highlighted to an international audience what it regards as the inhumane treatment of lambs in the 'mulesing' operation which is widely practiced amongst Australian sheep farmers. Mulesing is generally restricted to Merino lambs and involves the unanaestheticised removal of wrinkly skin from around the lamb's breech at marking times in order to reduce its risk of blowfly strike. However, such has been the success of PETA's campaign that high-profile US department store chain Abercrombie & Fitch removed all Australian wool apparel from their stores. Australian wool growers have responded with an intensive search for more humane treatments and a 2010 deadline for the abolition of mulesing.

Farm Credit in an Era of Global Finance

The Australian federal government's decision to float the Australian dollar in December 1983 and to deregulate the national financial and banking system emphatically shifted rural banking and farm credit into the global circuit of capital. The deregulation allowed the gradual stripping out of the many concessional aspects of the internal relations between Australian financial institutions (trading and savings banks and stock firms) and farm borrowers. For the first time in nearly 50 years, banks and stock firms could provide credit to farmers on fully commercial terms, with the market conditions for the various farm commodities, the price of funds and the lender's ability to choose investments that would return the average rate of profit unfixed by the nation-state. Such conditions obviously required new levels of expertise, placing new responsibilities upon the actors within the relationship and introducing new vulnerabilities.

The major trading and savings banks competed fiercely for market position in the immediate wake of the deregulation, particularly in the face of the prospect of the establishment of 16 foreign banks in the

Australian banking system after 1985 (Pauly 1987). Farming, for the first time in decades, stood on its own merits alongside all other sectors of the economy as an investment site. In the more competitive environment following deregulation, banks have been forced to become more autonomous in their management of their balance sheets, a trend which has manifested itself in: increased fees and charges for bank services as part of a sector-wide shift towards a full 'cost-recovery' philosophy; and attempts to rationalise the branch network (House of Representatives Standing Committee on Finance and Public Administration 1991, p. 271; Boyd and Mobbs 1993, p. 35; Argent and Rolley 2000; Argent 2002a).

While deregulation did not immediately alter the role of publicly owned institutions such as the Commonwealth Development Bank (CDB) in the farm credit market, it did facilitate the CDB's gradual commercialisation, allowing it to source its loan funds from international money markets. Since 1994 the CDB has been in full competition with all other financial institutions, including its parent, the Commonwealth Trading Bank. It was fully privatised in 1996 (Downey 1996, p. 23). The Primary Industry Bank of Australia (PIBA) was granted its own banking licence in 1987 (Powell and Milham 1990, pp. 242–3), but was sold to the Dutch agri-business bank, Rabobank Nederland, in 1994. Other smaller public lenders attached to state departments of agriculture have also been abolished (Argent 2000). 'In the light of these developments it can be argued that farm finance in Australia in the 1980s has been essentially "privatised" and "commercialised"' (Powell and Milham 1990, p. 234).

Overall, deregulation has greatly expanded farmers' access to finance, and from a wider range of sources. Often, these sources had direct links to global financial markets, as in the infamous case of the foreign currency loans offered by some Australian major trading banks during the mid- to late 1980s. Numerous small business owners, including farmers, took out substantial loans denominated in Swiss francs only to see the size of the debt rapidly expand as the Australian dollar underwent a sudden and dramatic devaluation on international currency markets. Spiralling domestic interest rates, with some farmers forced to pay up to 25 per cent interest on overdraft facilities (Argent 1997), further financially crippled many farm families. Although some families won potentially precedent-setting cases against banks for alleged prudential negligence (Gale 1995; Megalogenis 1995), many were not so lucky. The growth of Australian farm debt (Argent 1997; Jones 2002) cannot be blamed solely on the finance sector. The more sharply competitive nature of agriculture since the early 1980s, together with serious climatic and environmental problems, have made increased borrowings a basic fact of life for most farmers.

CONCLUSION

Australian agriculture has always operated in a more or less international context. The globalising tendencies inherent to capital flows, advanced information and communications technologies, modern firm hierarchies and networks, and environmental issues have helped reshape agricultural policy and the organisational structure and practice of farming in Australia. The extent to which such structural change has been brought about by globalisation is debatable, though as I have argued throughout this chapter, what one sees as the impacts of globalisation very much depends upon the understanding and conceptualising of globalisation that one begins with. Against some of the hyperbolic claims about the phenomenon, its reach and power, I have proposed that a scalar-sensitive concept of globalisation – one which precisely charts its networks of power and influence across space and through different places without necessarily privileging any particular scale (for example the global) – is key to appreciating the actual influence of globalisation upon nations, regions and localities, and disentangling its impacts from more sectoral trends and processes.

In this vein, it is possible to see both the increased corporate penetration of key sectors of Australian agriculture by global agri-food TNCs and the ongoing overwhelming dominance by farming families of the organisational structure of Australian farming. Neoliberalism, as the core ideology underpinning globalisation, has obviously had a dramatic impact upon Australia's political institutions and its broader political economy (see Beeson and Firth 1998; O'Neill and Moore 2005) and has obviously infiltrated farm policy and the nation's well-publicised stance on international trade. Its influence can be seen in the abolition or deregulation of statutory marketing authorities through the 1980s and 1990s as Australia sought to demonstrate its free trade 'honest broker' credentials to the rest of the world. As has been demonstrated in relation to the recent deregulation of the dairy industry, this process has driven substantial structural and spatial change, and introduced a great deal of uncertainty for individual farm families, towns and regions.

Similarly, the rapid and radical exposure of the once heavily regulated (and protected) banking sector to global competition from the mid-1980s brought substantial change to the range and type of financial 'products' (for example loans) that Australian farmers could access, but all with much inherently greater risk attached. Some institutions (for example the privatised PIBA and the former State Bank of South Australia) and a great many farmers did not survive this structural reform, as a combination of poor commodity prices, seasonal crises (for example droughts), declining terms of trade, spiralling domestic interest rates and lax lending policies and prudential management took their toll.

Lastly, emerging awareness of the global character of environmental issues, and the related rise of truly global networks of environmental activism, have shaped Australian agriculture in a number of ways. Government-mandated ecologically sustainable development principles are leading to a re-regulation of farm production, with the price mechanism acting as the chief regulatory tool. Farmers now confront higher costs for access to ecosystem services, such as water, together with tighter restrictions on their use. Parallel to this heightened scrutiny of the environmental externalities of farming practices is a growing international concern over the ethics of animal husbandry on Australian farms. The once omnipotent farm lobby, its political clout seriously weakened over recent decades, now faces highly organised, innovative and technologically sophisticated guerilla-style groups such as PETA which are able to take their claims to a global audience. These changes do not mean that the sector has been made over in the likeness of a global model, but they do suggest that the decision-making and actions of policy-makers, activists and farmers alike now takes place much more within increasingly global networks of power and influence.

REFERENCES

Aplin, G. (1998), *Australians and Their Environment: An Introduction to Environmental Studies*, Melbourne, VIC: Oxford University Press.

Argent, N. (1997), Global finance/local crisis: the role of financial deregulation in the geographical restructuring of Australian farming and farm credit, unpublished PhD thesis, Department of Geography, University of Adelaide.

Argent, N. (2000), 'Whither the lender of last resort? The rise and fall of public farm credit in Australia and New Zealand', *Journal of Rural Studies*, 16, 61–77.

Argent, N. (2002a), 'A global model or a scaled-down version? Geographies of convergence and divergence in the Australian retail banking sector', *Geoforum*, 33, 315–34.

Argent, N. (2002b), 'From pillar to post? In search of the post-productivist countryside in Australia', *Australian Geographer*, 33, 97–114.

Argent, N. and F. Rolley (2000), 'Financial exclusion in rural and remote New South Wales: a geography of bank branch rationalisation, 1981–1998', *Australian Geographical Studies*, 38, 182–203.

Argent, N., F. Rolley and D.J. Walmsley (2008), 'The sponge city hypothesis: does it hold water?', *Australian Geographer*, 39, 109–30.

Armstrong, W. and J. Bradbury (1983), 'Industrialisation and class structure in Australia, Canada and Argentina: 1870 to 1980', *Essays in the Political Economy of Australian Capitalism*, 5, 43–74.

Barnes, T. (1997), 'Theories of accumulation and regulation: bringing life back into economic geography', in R. Lee and J. Wills (eds), *Geographies of Economies*, London: Arnold, pp. 231–47.

Barr, N. (2004), *The Micro-Dynamics of Change in Australian Agriculture: 1976–2001*, Canberra: Australian Bureau of Statistics.

Beeson, M. and A. Firth (1998), 'Neoliberalism as a political rationality: Australian public policy since the 1980s', *Journal of Sociology*, **34**, 215–31.

Boyd, A. and R. Mobbs (1993), 'Banks may co-operate in moves to close branches', *Australian Financial Review*, 15 March, p. 35.

Braun, B. and N. Castree (1998), 'The construction of nature and the nature of construction: analytical and political tools for building survivable futures', in B. Braun and N. Castree (eds), *Remaking Reality: Nature at the Millennium*, London: Routledge, pp. 3–42.

Burch, D. and R. Rickson (2001), 'Industrialised agriculture: agribusiness, input-dependency and vertical integration', in S. Lockie and L. Bourke (eds), *Rurality Bites*, Sydney, NSW: Pluto Press, pp. 165–77.

Cocklin, C. and J. Dibden (2002), 'Taking stock: farmers' reflections on the deregulation of Australian dairying', *Australian Geographer*, **33**, 29–42.

Davidson, A. (2001), 'Dairy deregulation and the demise of dairying in New South Wales', *Rural Society*, **11**, 23 37.

Dicken, P. (2003), *Global Shift: Reshaping the Global Economic Map in the 21st Century*, 4th edn, London: Sage.

Downey, E. (1996), 'Farmers wary over CBD (sic) sale', *Land*, 31 June, p. 23.

Ehrensaft, P. and W. Armstrong (1978), 'Dominion capitalism: a first statement', *Australian and New Zealand Journal of Sociology*, **14**, 352–63.

Emy, H. and O. Hughes (1988), *Australian Politics: Realities in Conflict*, South Melbourne, VIC: Macmillan.

Fagan, R. (1990), 'Elders IXL Ltd: finance capital and the geography of corporate restructuring', *Environment and Planning A*, **22**, 647–66.

Fagan, R. (1995), 'Economy, culture and environment: perspectives on the Australian food industry', *Australian Geographer*, **26**, 1–10.

Fagan, R. (1997), 'Local food/global food: globalization and local restructuring' in R. Lee and J. Wills (eds), *Geographies of Economies*, London: Arnold, pp. 197–208.

Fagan, R. and M. Webber (1999), *Global Restructuring: The Australian Experience* (2nd edn), South Melbourne, VIC: Oxford University Press.

Friedmann, H. (1991), 'Changes in the international division of labor: agri-food complexes and export agriculture', in W. Friedland, F. Buttel and A. Rudy (eds), *Towards a New Political Economy of Agriculture*, Boulder, CO: Westview Press, pp. 65–93.

Friedmann, H. and P. McMichael (1989), 'Agriculture and the state system: the rise and decline of national agricultures, 1870 to the present', *Sociologia Ruralis*, **29**, 93–117.

Gale, J. (1995), 'NFF defends decision not to fund Copping court battle', *Stock Journal*, 4 May, p. 11.

Garnaut, J. and H. Lim-Applegate (1998), 'People in farming', ABARE research report 98.6, Canberra: Australian Bureau of Agricultural and Resource Economics.

Goodman, D. and M. Watts (1994), 'Reconfiguring the rural or fording the divide? Capitalist restructuring and the global agro-food system', *Journal of Peasant Studies*, **22**, 1–49.

Gray, I. and G. Lawrence (2001), *A Future for Regional Australia: Escaping Global Misfortune*, Cambridge: Cambridge University Press.

Harvey, D. (2006), *Spaces of Global Capitalism: A Theory of Uneven Geographical Development*, Stuttgart, Germany: Franz Steiner Verlag.

House of Representatives Standing Committee on Finance and Public Administration (1991), *A Pocketful of Change: Banking and Deregulation*, Canberra: Australian Government Publishing Service.

Jessop, B. (1993), 'Towards a Shumpeterian workfare state?', *Studies in Political Economy*, **40**, 7–39.

Jones, E. (2002), 'Rural finance in Australia: a troubled history', *Rural Society*, **12**, 160–80.

Lawrence, G. (1987), *Capitalism and the Countryside: The Rural Crisis in Australia*, Leichhardt, NSW: Pluto Press.

Lawrence, G. (2005), 'Globalization, agricultural production systems and rural restructuring', in C. Cocklin and J. Dibden (eds), *Sustainability and Change in Rural Australia*, Sydney, NSW: UNSW Press, pp. 104–20.

Le Heron, R. (1993), *Globalized Agriculture: Political Choice*, Oxford: Pergamon Press.

Lockie, S., G. Lawrence and L. Cheshire (2006), 'Reconfiguring rural resource governance: the legacy of neo-liberalism in Australia', in P. Cloke, T. Marsden and P. Mooney (eds), *Handbook of Rural Studies*, London: Sage Publications, pp. 29–43.

Massey, D. (1994), *Space, Place and Gender*, Cambridge: Polity Press.

McKay, D. (1967), 'The small farm problem in Australia', *Australian Journal of Agricultural Economics*, **11**, 115–32.

Megalogenis, G. (1995), 'Battlers in loan advice victory', *The Australian*, 17 June, p. 1.

Miller, L. (1996), 'Contract farming under globally-oriented and locally-emergent agribusiness in Tasmania', in D. Burch, R. Rickson and G. Lawrence (eds), *Globalization and Agri-Food Restructuring: Perspectives from the Australasia Region*, London: Avebury, pp. 203–18.

Murray, W. (2006), *Geographies of Globalization*, Abingdon: Routledge.

O'Brien, R. (1992), *Global Financial Integration: The End of Geography?* New York: Council of Foreign Relations.

O'Neill, P. and N. Argent (2005), 'Neoliberalism in Antipodean spaces and times', *Geographical Research*, **43**, 2–8.

O'Neill, P. and N. Moore (2005), 'Real institutional responses to neoliberalism in Australia', *Geographical Research*, **43**, 19–28.

Pauly, L. (1987), *Foreign Banks in Australia: The Politics of Deregulation*, Mosman, NSW: Australian Professional Publications.

Peck, J. (2004), 'Geography and public policy: constructions of neoliberalism', *Progress in Human Geography*, **28**, 392–405.

Peck, J. and A. Tickell (2002), 'Neoliberalizing space', *Antipode*, **34**, 380–404.

Potter, C. (1997), 'Environmental change and farm restructuring in Britain: the impact of the farm family life cycle', in B. Ilbery, Q. Chiotti and T. Rickard (eds), *Agricultural Restructuring and Sustainability: A Geographical Perspective*, Wallingford: CAB International, pp. 73–86.

Powell, R. and N. Milham (1990), 'Capital, investment and finance', in D. Williams (ed.), *Agriculture in the Australian Economy* (3rd edn), South Melbourne, VIC: Sydney University Press in association with Oxford University Press, pp. 215–47.

Pritchard, B. (1999), 'Switzerland's billagong? Brand management in the global food system and Nestle Australia', in D. Burch, J. Goss and G. Lawrence (eds), *Restructuring Global and Regional Agricultures: Transformations in Australasian Agri-Food Economies and Spaces*, Aldershot: Ashgate, pp. 23–40.

Pritchard, B. (2000), 'Negotiating the two-edged sword of agricultural trade liberalisation: trade policy and its protectionist discontents', in B. Pritchard and P. McManus (eds), *Land of Discontent: The Dynamics of Change in Rural and Regional Australia*, Sydney, NSW: UNSW Press, pp. 90–104.

Pritchard, B. and D. Burch (2003), *Agrifood Globalization in Perspective: International Restructuring in the Tomato Processing Industry*, Aldershot: Ashgate.

Pritchard, B., D. Burch and G. Lawrence (2007), 'Neither "family" nor "corporate" farming: Australian tomato growers as farm family entrepreneurs', *Journal of Rural Studies*, **23**, 75–87.

Pritchard, W. and P. McManus (eds) (2000), *Land of Discontent: The Dynamics of Change in Rural and Regional Australia*, Sydney, NSW: University of New South Wales.

Sayer, A. (1992), *Method in Social Science: A Realist Approach* (2nd edn), London: Routledge.

Schwartz, H. (1989), *In the Dominions of Debt: Historical Perspectives on Dependent Development*, Ithaca, NY: Cornell University Press.

Stutz, F. and B. Warf (2005), *The World Economy: Resources, Location, Trade, and Development* (4th edn), Upper Saddle River, NJ: Pearson Prentice Hall.

Thrift, N. and A. Leyshon (1994), 'A phantom state? The detraditionalization of money, the international financial system and international financial centres', *Political Geography*, **13**, 299–327.

Tickell, A. and J. Peck (1992), 'Accumulation, regulation and the geographies of post-Fordism: missing links in regulationist research', *Progress in Human Geography*, **16**, 190–218.

Watts, M. and D. Goodman (1997), 'Agrarian questions – global appetite, local metabolism: nature, culture, and industry in *fin-de-siècle* agro-food systems', in D. Goodman and M. Watts (eds), *Globalising Food: Agrarian Questions and Global Restructuring*, London: Routledge, pp. 1–31.

Whatmore, S. (2002), 'From farming to agribusiness: global agri-food networks', in R. Johnston, P. Taylor and M. Watts (eds), *Geographies of Global Change: Remapping the World*, Oxford: Blackwell Publishing, pp. 57–67.

Whatmore, S. and L. Thorne (1997), 'Nourishing networks: alternative geographies of food', in D. Goodman and M. Watts (eds), *Globalising Food: Agrarian Questions and Global Restructuring*, London: Routledge, pp. 287–301.

Wonder, B. (1995) *Australia's Approach to Agricultural Reform*, Department of Primary Industries, Canberra, accessed at www.dpie.gov.au/dpie/agriculture/agricultural_reform.html.

Woods, M. (2007), 'Engaging the global countryside: globalization, hybridity and the reconstitution of rural place', *Progress in Human Geography*, **31**, 1–23.

3. Market efficiency, agriculture and prosperity in rural Australia

Bill Pritchard and Matthew Tonts

INTRODUCTION

Several years ago, in December 2004, 21 Canberra-based diplomats representing countries of the European Union (EU) visited the rural city of Orange, in central-west New South Wales (NSW), with the intent to: 'alter some of the negative perceptions in regional Australia about the EU and what are widely seen as its protectionist agricultural policies' (Banham 2004, p. 4). Naturally enough, media accounts of the visit painted a diversity of views amongst local residents regarding this initiative. Some residents perceived it as an opportunity to build business linkages, while at the other extreme, the *Sydney Morning Herald* reported one as complaining that the EU was: '"so incredibly uncompetitive" in its agricultural policies that it was "quite galling" to have the ambassadors visit Orange' (Banham 2004, p. 4).

The visit to Orange by the EU diplomats holds no significance in itself. It gained fleeting media attention only and did not lead to any lasting announcements. But for the purposes of this chapter, it represents a poignant vignette of how the debate over agriculture's regional economic contributions has been constructed over the years. The dominant politico-economic discourse on these issues in Australia is rooted in neoliberal economic theory. It asserts that the market efficiency of agriculture provides a powerful engine for economic growth in the regional economies of non-metropolitan Australia, but this capacity is undermined by the extensive 'distortions' of global agricultural markets because of state interventions of various kinds. Correspondingly, so goes this argument, regional development in non-metropolitan Australia is best advanced through policies that give space to the efficiency-enhancing prospects offered by market freedoms. At the international level, these arguments suggest that efforts by Australian diplomats to reduce the 'distortions' in international agricultural markets become the magic elixir for regional Australia. All would be well if only the Europeans (and Americans and Japanese) would embrace liberal agricultural and food policies. At the domestic level, the arguments suggest that governments need do little more than to promote the market efficiency of agriculture. If agriculture is efficient, then agricultural regions will capture economic benefits when (eventually) the actions of Australian trade diplomats bear fruit. Consistent with these sentiments, leading Australian agricultural economists have suggested that the best 'regional policy' for agricultural-based areas of Australia is not to have any regional policy at all (Freebairn 2003; cf. Pritchard 2005a).

Certainly there is considerable truth in the proposition that improved prospects for the agricultural sector would generate positive spillover benefits to the local economies in which farms are situated. The market efficiency of agriculture provides the economic bedrock for many rural regions in Australia. Internationally competitive agricultural sectors would certainly benefit from efficiency-enhancing policies and more liberal agricultural and food policies being adopted by competitor countries and in destination markets. But does reliance on market efficiency alone provide the optimal policy framework to secure the economic, social and environmental interests of Australia's agricultural regions? For the sustenance of these regions, is it sufficient that Australian state and federal governments simply depend on market forces? And what if in the name of market efficiency some people and communities lose out – should governments ameliorate the hard edge of the market reform agenda? Is it more appropriate that governments entertain more sceptical policy gazes towards the spatial ramifications of market efficiency?

The purpose of this chapter is to examine these questions critically. Although agriculture generates considerable prosperity for many rural regions, we ask whether the connection between agricultural efficiency and socio-economic well-being in regional Australia is as strong as it is often assumed to be. Centrally, we observe that much of the direction of change under contemporary economic policies is serving to restructure and, in many cases, weaken the economic role played by the farm sector in regional economies. To our minds, these issues have received insufficient attention within policy debates over recent years. In the next section of this chapter, we sketch out some of the major political and economic drivers of change in regional Australia. Then, we point to four core components of recent change; first, the role of liberalisation and globalisation in changing the nature of agricultural competition; second, the restructuring of selling markets for agricultural produce, with particular attention to the role of contract farming; third, farm consolidation and concentration, and fourth, the changing environmental dynamics in which farming takes place. The chapter concludes with some observations about the future shape of the farm–region relationship.

AUSTRALIAN DEBATES ON REGIONS, AGRICULTURE AND EFFICIENCY

Market efficiency became the organising set of principles for Australian agriculture in the 1980s on account of the wider ideological embrace of neoliberalism within Australian governments. The spread of these arguments into the field of agricultural policy can be dated from the coming of power of the Hawke government in 1983, when 'old guard' National Party interests were removed from the primary industries and trade portfolios. This provided an opening for 'new' neoliberal ideas to flourish (Jones 1994; Pritchard 2005b). The tangible policy implications of this shift were evidenced in the Australian government's advocacy of multilateral free trade in agriculture via the Cairns Group initiative of 1987, and the comprehensive programme of domestic agricultural deregulation that culminated with the National Competition Policy agreements of 1995.

The shift towards these principles was wrapped in a discursive justification of 'self-reliance'. The overriding mantra within policy pronouncements was that farmers and agricultural regions had to become more productive and find 'their own answers' to the challenges of a more competitive economic climate. This perspective is consistent with the 'individualisation' ethic of neoliberalism; that individuals should to take charge of their circumstances rather than seek assistance via what is disparagingly labelled 'the nanny state' (Larner 2003; Peck and Tickell 2002). Within farmer politics, the National Farmers' Federation's 1993 strategy document *New Horizons* (NFF, 1993) officially pronounced this seachange in Australian agrarian politics. Both sides of politics assumed and asserted that the resourcefulness, energy and acumen of the farm sector would enable agricultural-based regions to 'pull through' the traumas of economic restructuring, thus generating viable and prosperous futures. In the words of the former National Party leader Ian Sinclair:

> The theory behind trade liberalisation, globalisation and the new economy may be well understood and even accepted; but adapting to change remains difficult. For country Australia the pressures are more intense than in the cities because of the progressive decline in rural incomes from traditional farming sources, aggravated by selling on open markets where price has no relationship to the cost of production. (Sinclair 2001, p. 94)

Yet:

> Regional renewal does not mean recreating the industries of 30 or 50 years ago in their former image. It means applying today's technology and finding new opportunities enjoying comparative advantage. (Sinclair 2001, p. 102)

Consistent with this approach, governments by and large have intervened only marginally in terms of providing income support to distressed
farmers. Exceptions are notable. In the dairy and sugar industries, governments consented to reform packages to minimise adverse political
consequences of industry restructuring, with an eye to upcoming electoral
prospects (the federal elections of 2001 and 2004, respectively, for dairy
and sugar). More generally, the Rural Adjustment Scheme (renamed
Agriculture – Advancing Australia in 1996) was initially premised on
providing a policy framework that would help farmers adjust to change,
but as documented by Gray and Lawrence (2001, p. 61) and Higgins and
Lockie (2001), this rapidly evolved into a scheme for facilitating farmer
exit, when conditions were unfavourable. Yet other areas of government
activity sent contradictory messages with regards to farm restructuring.
In drought policy, the principle of 'Exceptional Circumstances' (EC) has
provided a basis for governments to spread income support to farmers,
without ostensibly departing from free-market principles. Yet by 2010,
even this set of policies had come under serious challenge. At the 2010
Australian Bureau of Agriculture and Resource Economics (ABARE)
Outlook Conference, the Federal Minister for Agriculture, Tony Burke,
bemoaned that the provision of such funding might perpetuate adverse
social and economic impacts as barely viable farms 'hung on':

> instead of helping them get out [of farming] we gave them just enough money to
> hold them in that precise situation. They then had seven years on the property
> where its not making money, where they're staying just afloat, and only just
> afloat. And at the end of it, either because they lose their EC declaration or
> because they reach the maximum of the half a million dollar payment they get
> told, now you've got to make the hard decision that you probably could have
> made seven years earlier. I am not surprised at a whole lot of mental health
> challenges that we have in this portfolio. I am not surprised at the number of
> times when I go into a town people talk about the latest act of self-harm that
> very frequently it was somebody who was getting very significant amounts of
> Government support. And I think we need to be brave enough to acknowledge
> that just because we are giving people money does not mean that we are doing
> them a favour. We need some really strong transitional mechanisms as we move
> to the new drought policy. (Burke 2010, not paginated)

Mainstream agricultural economists in Australia, in general, have not
taken a great interest in such spatial and equity dimensions of policy,
but instead have suggested that the efficiency principles of the 'invisible
hand' would address such concerns over time (Pritchard 2005a, footnote
1). Hence, economists have generally supported the official government
line of the need for 'self-reliance'. Of key interest to this chapter, however,
social scientists of other hues have interpreted events quite differently.

Although a range of views exists, these researchers have tended to pinpoint contradictions in the market-efficiency paradigm and document an array of social, economic and environmentally uneven outcomes arising from its implementation. This scepticism is expressed most obviously in the titles of two prominent books published by researchers from these fields. *Land of Discontent* (Pritchard and McManus 2000) was an edited collection that sought to bring into focus and to debate the claims by rural Australians that they were being disadvantaged, compared to their city cousins, as a result of contemporary government policies. More explicitly, the subtitle of Gray and Lawrence's (2001) *A Future for Regional Australia: Escaping Global Misfortune* attached the concept of globalisation to misfortune, thus reversing the causality generally assumed in mainstream economic discourse.

THE UTOPIAN IMAGINARY OF GLOBALISED AGRICULTURE

The standard approach of neoliberal analysis is to calibrate a given situation against a perfectly efficient alternative in which resources are allocated to their (economically) optimal use and markets are in equilibrium. Applied to the case at hand, Australian agricultural and trade economists have argued that there are substantial potential benefits available to Australian agriculture, if and when these conditions are met at a global level. Practically, this has resulted in much research within Australian agricultural economics since the late 1980s being aimed at developing successively more technically sophisticated iterations of the quantum of benefits the Australian economy might receive from 'globally efficient' agricultural markets; in other words, markets liberalised from economic interventions by governments.

Agri-food researchers[1] in other disciplinary fields comprehend the political impact and efficacy of the neoliberal approach – it manifests a utopian future as a measurable 'reality' (Pritchard, 2005c) – but question its practical utility. From these perspectives, the imaginary end-point of agri-food globalisation (entirely free flows of trade and capital in these sectors) is understood to provide a misleading basis from which to seek to secure the futures of agricultural regions. To measure contemporary economic conditions against the supposed end-point of globalisation is to assume into existence a set of political relations about food, agriculture and the environment that have never been met in human history (McMichael 2000), and are unlikely to emerge in simple form any time soon. Instead, the future trajectory of global economic liberalisation of food and agriculture is far from certain. As argued by agri-food researchers, the time- and space-compressing properties of globalisation are rooted in political decisions that have complex reactions and unintended consequences (Le Heron 2005). As concrete examples, globalisation tendencies in agri-food sectors are challenged by 'nature biting back' via biophysical reactions to industrialised agriculture (bovine spongiform encephalopathy – BSE, avian influenza, and so on), and new consumer-based articulations of the politics of food (the organic and 'local food' movements, for example). As such, the neoliberal propensity to argue that regional futures will be secured by globalisation ignores the complex realities of global agri-food restructuring in favour of a reading of change that is overdetermined by a particular set of theoretical preferences.

THE TANGIBLE EFFECTS OF LIBERALISATION AND GLOBALISATION

The extent to which Australian rural regions would benefit from further global trade liberalisation depends on their mix of products, and the ways in which their output is connected into world markets. Understanding these spatial and sectoral outcomes requires an appreciation of the way in which neoliberal reforms have affected various segments of the agricultural supply chain. During much of the twentieth century, Australian governments intervened at almost every point in the supply chain. For example: farm inputs were often produced by firms protected by tariffs; agricultural development banks and various industry adjustment schemes provided cheap credit to farmers; tax breaks reduced the costs of farm inputs and capital expenditure; government agencies offered farm advice and were active in improving farming systems; vast networks of public transport infrastructure enabled the subsidised mass movement of farm inputs and outputs; and statutory authorities controlled the marketing of most commodities on international and domestic markets. This strategy not only helped to protect agriculture, but also contributed substantially to broader regional economic and social development through employment, infrastructure provision and service delivery. The changing economic conditions and political ideals of the 1970s and 1980s, however, saw this system of intervention become regarded as trade-restrictive, excessively expensive and economically inefficient (Cockfield 1993).

Regulatory changes to the agricultural sector since the 1980s have resulted in government intervention being replaced by growing levels of private sector involvement at all levels of supply chains. Indeed, almost all of those activities undertaken by government are now in the hands of the private firms and corporations. Major changes include:

- the privatisation of agricultural development banks;
- the privatisation of government-owned transport services;
- the transfer of research and development functions to private firms;
- the deregulation of statutory marketing authorities;
- a reduction in import restrictions;
- a reduction in both direct and indirect subsidies for primary producers.

Part of the rhetoric in favour of deregulation was that it would increase competition and choice, thereby reducing costs and increasing profits to farmers. While this may have been the case in some sectors and regions, there is considerable evidence to suggest that the outcome has been an increasing concentration of economic power amongst larger corporations (see Fold and Pritchard 2005; ActionAid International 2005). Agri-food corporations have, in effect, colonised the space vacated by state institutions and regulations. As a result, farmers have found themselves dealing directly with large firms and corporations, particularly in the marketing and processing segments of the commodity chain. However, the relationship between buyer and seller is not straightforward. Rather than agri-food corporations being involved in a single segment of the commodity chain, the trend has been one of vertical coordination (see McMichael and Lawrence 2001). This involves single corporations owning and/or controlling multiple segments of the supply chain, including farm inputs, transport and logistics, processing and marketing. Thus, farmers are often now enmeshed in a complex web of connections with different parts of the same corporation.

The significance of these economic changes should not be underestimated. No longer are farmers shielded from the sharp end of agribusiness by state marketing authorities and a regulatory framework that was designed to foster economic stability. This means that negotiations on the quality of commodities, prices received, delivery times and even farm management systems form part of the negotiation between farmer and firm or corporation. Clearly, given the difference in economic scale and power, farmers are potentially in a vulnerable economic position. At the same time, however, proponents of the liberalisation of the agrarian economy argue that farmers now have freedom of choice with regard to whom they sell their commodities, and can adapt their farm business to emerging market conditions. As pointed out later in this chapter, this tends to overlook a range of economic and social realities facing certain agricultural regions and individual farm businesses.

While vertical coordination has been an important economic phenomenon, it is also fundamentally geographical in nature. Not surprisingly, firms have tended to concentrate their activities in those regions that have the potential to maximise capital accumulation. The outcome has often been increasing regional specialisation in agricultural production. For example, in the Riverland region of South Australia, the economic influence of major wineries has seen a reduction in the production of fruit, and an increase in the area of land devoted to growing wine grapes (Tonts et al. 2003). Similarly in the cattle industry, the growing popularity of beef grown in feedlots, particularly in the Japanese market, has seen this type of production locate in areas dominated by grains, such as the Darling Downs in Queensland and the Riverina region of NSW. By co-locating with grain producers, feedlots can easily access large volumes of feed, particularly sorghum, barley, wheat and oats (Clark et al. 1992). Increasingly, grain producers in these regions are selling their produce to feedlots under contracts, rather than in more traditional grain markets. Buttel (2003) suggests that this trend towards regional specialisation is not restricted to subnational regions, but is gradually extending to global farm regions as processing and marketing firms source their products from around the world in order to maximise profitability in an uneven world market.

The impact of global sourcing has the potential to impact directly on Australian agricultural regions, particularly under conditions of free trade. In 2005, for example, Tasmanian fruit and vegetable growers launched a national awareness campaign highlighting the possibility of lost local sales from import competition. Growers claimed that the major supermarkets and food service chains were replacing Australian-grown with imported fruit and vegetable products. Tasmanian potato growers were at the forefront of this campaign, because of their dependence on two processing firms (Simplot and McCains) who, in turn, are heavily reliant on contracted sales to the large food service firms, such as McDonald's and KFC. Although these dependencies have existed since the 1980s (Miller 1996; Tonts et al. 2003), the vulnerabilities of this situation only became evident in 2005.

Clearly, heightened import competition from Southeast Asia, China and South America have major implications for Australian agriculture. As McMichael (2003) has documented, there is an increasing level of activity by agri-food corporations in key production regions. The combined effects of the low cost of on-farm production, cheap labour, favourable tax regimes and liberal environmental regulations mean that these developing regions potentially have a competitive advantage over developed regions in terms of both production and processing. When coupled with the footloose nature of global capital, this means that Australian regions are likely to face growing competition from developing regions.

CONTRACT FARMING AND THE REGIONS

In the new era of liberalisation and globalisation, farmers tend to be inserted within agri-food supply chains more directly. Traditional open-market mechanisms such as auctions are giving way to vertically coordinated supply chain structures. Central to these processes is contract farming. It is through contracts that the links between corporations and farmers are formalised and, in many respects, they are reshaping regional patterns of agriculture (Burch and Rickson 2001; Tonts et al. 2003; Lawrence 2005). As the following discussion illuminates, the emergence of contract farming regimes brings with it a set of transformative effects for the ways that farms interconnect with regional economies, including vulnerabilities of various kinds.

Contracts vary considerably from sector to sector, company to company, and region to region. However, most involve an agreement that a farmer will supply a processor with a particular quantity and quality of commodity at a specified time for a previously agreed price. The contracting company often provides the farmer with some inputs and/or technical advice. Contract farming is well established in the beef, fruit, vegetable, viticulture, chicken meat and hop industries. In the early 1990s, for example, it was estimated that around 80 per cent of hops, 85 per cent of chickens and nearly 100 per cent of peas were grown under contract (Burch et al. 1992; Miller 1996). It is also becoming increasingly common in the grains, hay, rice and cotton industries.

Contract farming is not a new phenomenon in Australia (see Lawrence 1987; Burch et al. 1992; Miller 1996). Early research by social scientists on this phenomenon tended to emphasise the potential problems associated with contract farming, particularly the issue of farm 'subsumption' (see Lockie 1997). At the heart of this is a concern that, under contracting arrangements, farmers may cede control of the key farm management decisions to contracting firms. These include decisions about farming methods, land use and inputs. Indeed, a study of farmers conducted by Tonts et al. (2003) suggested that one of the main concerns of landowners was that, under certain contracts, they might become little more than labourers on their own properties. By contrast, some contracting firms argued that by specifying how farms should be managed they are able to control quality and maintain stability of supply. In the wine industry, for example, Fraser (2003) suggests that wineries use a number of strategies to influence farmer behaviour:

- A winery can monitor grower effort. This is usually done by visiting the vineyard and discussing issues such as sharing information about vineyard management, crop development and harvesting.

- A winery can exert more direct influence over the vineyard by specifying input use, such as the form of rootstock used or the choice of irrigation technology. The obvious outcome here is that as the winery takes more control of production, the grower has less responsibility for the final quality of the grapes.
- A winery can measure the quality of the grapes supplied.

Similar strategies are used in the potato sector. The following are a number of extracts of clauses from a contract established between a processing firm and a grower in Tasmania:

1. The grower will plant at the time specified herein with seed purchased with company approval from the seed grower to produce the following quantity, area and variety of potatoes from the specified area only . . .
2. The grower will grow the crop of potatoes on land approved by a representative of the Company and free from weeds or other foreign plants and where considered necessary by the Company and will spray the crop for weed, fungus and pest control.
3. The company may at any time prior to or during harvest submit samples of the grower's crop to an independent laboratory for chemical residue analysis.
4. The grower will permit the Company representative to inspect the land and potatoes at any reasonable time.
5. The grower will comply with directions given by the representative of the Company as to the time and manner of cultivating, sowing, weeding, spraying, irrigating, harvesting and delivery of the crops. (Tonts et al. 2003, p. 30)

While contracts generally specify the nature of the production process and the outputs of farming, they are also used to specify the inputs into agriculture. Often this is linked to contracting firms' attempts to maintain quality and uniformity in the product. However, in the case of some of the larger vertically integrated agribusiness firms it is also a mechanism to ensure that their own products are used in the production process. For example, delivery contracts for some grains specify that certain brands of fertiliser and herbicide must be used. This not only ensures a degree of standardisation in the production process but also helps to maximise profits for the firm producing the specified chemicals. Indeed, in some cases particular plant breeds can only be treated using particular herbicides and insecticides, thereby ensuring that farmers have no alternatives but to use a particular product (see Burch and Rickson 2001).

Not all farmers regard this as a disadvantage, and many see contracts as providing access to technology that might otherwise not be available. In Tasmania's potato industry, for example, farmers have access to discounted seed bred by the processing companies, as well as free agronomic advice. According to the processing companies, rather than reducing farmer control of the property, this advice is designed to improve overall yield. Providing seed stock and agronomic advice is not restricted to the potato sector, and is a key feature of the horticulture, viticulture and cotton sectors. While it is less common in the beef and dairy sectors, there are cases where farmers are provided with advice on some matters, particularly in relation to farm management and planning (Tonts et al. 2003).

While some farmers regard access to new technologies and farm services as an important benefit of contract farming, there is some evidence to suggest that access to these resources can very easily lead to a 'technological dependence' that erodes farmer autonomy (Gray and Lawrence 2001). Some types of contracts carry the risk of a loss of farmer autonomy and create a dependent relationship between farmer and corporation. It is, however, important to stress that not all contracts lead to a direct intrusion by corporations into on-farm management decisions. While there has been a rise in external penetration in terms of dependence on technology, marketing and even institutional finance, farmers often still exert a controlling influence over a range of key decision-making (Tonts et al. 2003).

The tendency to highlight the negative elements of contract farming needs to be weighed up against what many farmers see as the benefits. Recent research suggests that farmers often see contracts as providing a degree of financial stability and certainty (Tonts et al. 2003). This is particularly important in sectors where large price fluctuations are common, such as vegetable, livestock and grain sectors. Contracts were also important when negotiating finance for infrastructure or land purchases. Other benefits can include:

- The role of contracts in providing a stable cash flow.
- The ability to forward-plan activities, particularly major purchases, as a result of the regular income associated with having a contract.
- The benefit of having a contract as a form of security when applying for credit from a financial institution.

The Impacts of Collapsed Contracting Firms

In terms of regional development, this financial security has the potential to provide wider economic stability. However, there are also some very clear examples of where this type of dependence can undermine the viability of both local and regional economies. Indeed, over the past few years there have been a number of cases where the collapse of a firm upon which numerous farmers are dependent has had negative impacts on localities and/or regions. The demise of Normans Wines in the Riverland of South Australia in 2001 is a case in point. Normans Wines was a major producer of wine in South Australia and owned two wineries, one at Monash (near Berri) in the South Australian Riverland and one at Clarendon. The Monash winery processed around 22 000 tonnes of grapes annually and had contracts with 120 growers. Increasing competition in the wine industry contributed to falling profits (the company recorded a $10 million loss for the 1999/2000 financial year) and increasing debts, which were estimated to be around $20 million in 2000.

In June 2001, Normans informed growers that it could not meet contracted payments. It offered most growers 20 per cent of their contracted payments and claimed that the funds owed would be paid 'in due course'. This raised widespread community concern, with 90 of the contracted growers holding a meeting in Berri to discuss the problems associated with the winery. The local newspaper, the *Murray Pioneer*, even questioned the point of having contracts, asking: 'is the supply contract for future vintages worth the paper it is written on?' (6 June 2001, p. 3). The newspaper pointed out that a failure by growers to meet the terms of contracts generally results in some sort of penalty, but when a company fails to meet the terms then farmers generally have to accept the outcome. Normans went into receivership in August 2001, with growers still owed amounts of between $20 000 and $400 000. Collectively, growers were owned a total of $11 million. Despite having contracts with Normans these growers were regarded as unsecured creditors. As a result, proceeds from the sale of the winery (or its assets) would go first to secured creditors, such as the ANZ Bank, which was owed A$34 million.

The collapse of contracting firms is not uncommon. In the Riverland region alone three major firms went out of business in the five years to 2003. All of these left dependent growers in a difficult financial position. In many respects this highlights the dangers associated with a shift towards a more liberal trading environment in agriculture. While the assumption underlying the liberalisation agenda is that there will be relatively high levels of competition in the agri-food industry, the reality is that in most regions a small number of firms tend to dominate a sector. As such, these firms not only have the potential to exert considerable influence over the nature of production, but also have major financial impacts if they are unable to honour contracts with farmers. This problem is particularly acute in areas where there is no alternative buyer for the commodity produced, as in the case of the Normans Wines collapse. The fallout from such collapses is not restricted to individual farm businesses, but can have a much wider impact on local and regional economies. The loss of local income, and the concomitant reduction in spending, has the potential to reduce business viability, employment opportunities and economic confidence in the future of affected localities and regions.

Many of these kinds of complaints were aired in a Senate Inquiry into the wine industry, held in 2005. The final report of the inquiry held:

> During the inquiry the committee received evidence of exploitative business relations between winegrape growers and winemakers, as winemakers take advantage of their stronger bargaining power in the present oversupply of grapes . . . They give a clear picture of the grievances of growers. Those grievances go beyond matters of price. The committee also notes comments made by grower organisations to the effect that many growers hesitate to complain for fear that it will count against them in future dealings with wineries. Growers emphasised that their complaints about the way business is done are quite distinct from their regret that prices are currently low. While some of the issues impacting on grape growers are cyclical or caused by outside influences and may or may not be overcome through changing conditions over time, the root cause of much of the current crisis is not cyclic but rather, unsatisfactory terms and conditions by which grapes are sold, prices are set and payments are made. (Senate Rural and Regional Affairs and Transport References Committee 2005, p. 29)

Price-making Powers of Buyers

One of the most widely reported trends in the literature on contract farming is the extent to which large buyers can exert price-setting influences over sellers (Welsh 1997). This tends to happen in regions where processing and other upstream industries are concentrated (usually as part of a monopoly, duopoly or oligopoly). Over recent years, a number of notable examples of price manipulation have emerged. Pritchard (1999) discusses how an imbalance of power between wineries and contract growers in the Murrumbidgee translates into pricing disputes based on issues of quality. In South Australian wine growing regions, for example, it is apparent that a number of wineries are using very stringent quality standards as a means of minimising prices paid to grape growers. In the case of winemaker BRL Hardy in the Riverland region, all of its 1600 contracted growers are required to meet very stringent quality standards. These include standards for colour, chemical balance, food safety and so on. Growers not meeting these standards may be paid lower prices or even have their produce rejected. According to many growers, the imposed standards are almost impossible to meet, and were being used simply as a means of reducing prices (Tonts et al. 2003). While BRL Hardy clearly had a right to impose quality standards, it is also apparent that farmers were in a largely powerless position.

These issues of power are also evident in other sectors and regions. In the case of the potato sector in Tasmania, the financial dependence of growers on one of two processing firms, multinational corporations McCain Foods and Simplot, meant that there was little option but to accept the prices on offer. In 2001, a number of farmers under contract to McCain Foods began to agitate for a A$30 per tonne increase in the contract price for potatoes. Similar pressure was placed on Simplot. Both companies initially refused the increase, claiming that potato growers were paid more in Australia than in the United States and New Zealand. In response to the inaction by the multinationals, around 500 farmers blockaded McCain's Smithton factory in August 2001. The most common banners at the blockade summed up the extent of farmer anger: 'Ah McCain, you've done us again', and simply, 'Simplot sucks'. The blockade was followed by a series of meetings at which farmers agreed to continue their push for higher prices.

Following considerable negotiation and widespread national media attention, McCain Food's agreed to pay an extra A$22 a tonne in 2001 and a further A$9 a tonne in 2002. Growers under contract to Simplot later accepted an increase of A$36 per tonne (they had earlier declined an increase of A$30 per tonne over three years). However, it was pointed out by some farmers that, if they were to keep pace with the rate of inflation over the past decade, then an increase of A$60 per tonne would have been appropriate. For its part, McCain suggested that such an increase was not possible due to international competition in the frozen French fries industry. Importantly, the benefits were not restricted to growers in Tasmania, with McCain and Simplot increasing potato prices across Australia following threats of further blockades and disturbances elsewhere in the country. By 2005, as discussed above, growers faced the serious threat of wholesale loss of sales from these companies, as end users threatened to replace Tasmanian product with imports.

The issue of price manipulation by contracting firms has significant implications at the regional level. The prices received for commodities by farmers generally have a direct impact on local and regional economies. Quite obviously, if farm profits are eroded by low commodity prices, the outcome is often lower levels of spending and economic activity in the towns and regional centres that support agriculture. Not only does this reduce employment opportunities, but it can also contribute to out-migration and further population decline (Stayner 2005). However, it is important to stress that these problems are not restricted to those areas dominated by contract farming. As Hugo (2005) has demonstrated, many agricultural regions in Australia are experiencing economic hardship, falling populations and service withdrawal. Nevertheless, it is clear that contract farming, which has emerged largely in the wake of agricultural deregulation and liberalisation, poses particular risks to regional areas. In other parts of the world, such as the United States and Canada, contract farming is often directly implicated in the economic and social hardship faced in rural areas, largely because of the considerable power wielded by large corporations that control much of the agri-food chain (Rodefeld 1978; Winson 1996; McCannell 1988; Lobao 1990; Hoppe et al. 2001). The emerging evidence would suggest that similar risks exist for Australian agricultural regions.

Contract Individualisation

Important legal differences exist between the American contract farming situation, and that present in Australia. In the US, farmers are specifically entitled to bargain collectively with buyers (processing firms or retailers) through legislative exemptions from antitrust provisions. These exemptions were first established with the Clayton Act of 1914 and further enshrined with the Capper–Volstead Act of 1922. Under this Act, farmers organised as a 'cooperative' (effectively defined as a non-profit organisation representing more than half of an industry's output where voting rights are more or less 'one member, one vote') were shielded from antitrust prosecution so long as their actions were not predatory (Pritchard and Burch 2003 pp. 149–51). Although US farmer organisations decry limitations to these rights, the operation of Capper–Volstead acknowledges the economic reality that farmers tend to be in an inferior position when negotiating with larger buyers, and that collectivised rights are essential to repair this disadvantage.

Australia has never had an equivalent piece of legislation to Capper–Volstead but through the course of the twentieth century state and federal governments enacted many legislative rights to farmers on an industry-by-industry basis. From 1995, however, these were wound back in the name of National Competition Policy. Consequently, it is now mostly the case in Australian agriculture that contract farming arrangements are understood as no more than a common-law contract between two parties. Under these circumstances, any group of farmers seeking to negotiate collectively with a processing firm or retailer over the terms of the contract potentially breaches the collusive conduct provisions of Australia's Trade Practices Act. Comparable to the debate on individual workplace agreements, these transformations were undertaken with the objective of encouraging individualisation with assumed benefits to productivity. However, in a study of how contract farming regimes have evolved over this period, Pritchard and Burch (2003, pp. 101–26) conclude that the enforced shift to individualisation had no apparent benefits to industry productivity, but tangibly lessened the economic status of contracted farmers.

THE REGIONAL IMPACTS OF FEWER BUT LARGER PRODUCERS

Changes in the nature of agricultural regulation and the supply chain have been accompanied by a much broader set of economic trends in agriculture. One of the most significant of these has been the gradual exit of farmers from the industry. Since the 1960s, the total number of farms in Australia has nearly halved, falling from 201 000 to a little over 100 000 by the mid-2000s. This trend has been particularly evident in Australia's mixed crop and livestock heartland. In the Western Australian grain belt (Figure 3.1), for example, the number of farms fell from 6278 to 5774 between 1993 and 2006; a decrease of some 8 per cent (Australian Bureau of Statistics 1994, 2008). During the same period, the average size of farms increased from 2272 hectares to 2550 hectares; an increase of 12.2 per cent.

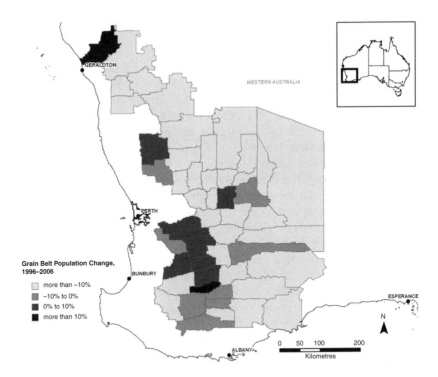

Source: Map compiled by authors using data from Australian Bureau of Statistics (2007).

Figure 3.1   Population change in the Western Australian grain belt, 1996–2006

While the reasons for these changes are complex, the pressure for farmers to increase economies of scale has played an important role. In effect, smaller less efficient farmers have made way for larger operators. This has been driven by, *inter alia*, an ongoing cost–price squeeze, volatile market conditions, fluctuating exchange rates and changing lifestyle preferences.

Much of the available evidence suggests that, in those areas experiencing farm amalgamation and expansion, families leaving the industries also tend to leave their communities, often relocating to urban or coastal areas. Accompanying this has been the reduction in demand for farm labour, largely as a result of the adoption of new technologies and as a result, further population drift away from agricultural regions. Here, the experience of the Western Australian (WA) grain belt is again instructive. Between 1996 and 2006, most local government areas experienced population decline (Figure 3.1), with the most significant contraction occurring in those areas with the highest level of dependence on agriculture for both employment and economic activity (Davies and Tonts 2010).

As Hugo (2005) points out, this link between agricultural restructuring and demographic change has had significant implications for social and economic structures in rural Australia. One of the most obvious trends has been a reduction in local and regional employment opportunities, spending and service provision (Stayner 2005). Between 1996 and 2006, for example, the number of people employed in the WA grain belt's agricultural sector decreased from 13 749 to 11 324 (−18.9 per cent), while the wider labour force fell from 32 749 to 29 528 (−9.8 per cent). Perhaps not surprisingly, some of the most striking impacts have occurred in the agricultural services sector. Herbert and Pritchard (2004), for example, provide evidence of the dramatic contraction and centralisation of the tractor dealership network in New South Wales, pointing to the combined impacts of falling farm numbers, economic uncertainty and the impacts of drought. Similar rationalisation has occurred in other businesses, such as fuel supplies, transport services, livestock saleyards and financial services (Stayner 2005).

While the changes in traditional agricultural sectors are contributing to a degree of economic and social upheaval, it is important to stress that these trends are not spatially or sectorally uniform. In a number of regions, the emergence of new, specialised forms of agriculture have been particularly important in contributing to vibrant economies and population growth. Many of these new, high-value niche agricultural industries are located in scenic inland and coastal areas (Tonts and Greive 2002; Bunker and Houston 2003; Costello 2007). Indeed, although the total number of farms in Australia is steadily falling, there has been relatively strong growth in the number of farms under 100 hectares. In the WA grain belt, for example, an increase in the number of smaller holdings has been accompanied by rising populations and economic expansion, particularly in those areas within 90 minutes or so drive of Perth (Figure 3.1) (Davies and Tonts 2010). The investment in these industries appears to be linked not simply to traditional notions of agricultural production, but to a more complex view of rurality. Such businesses are often associated with lifestyle choices on the part of the owners to relocate from urban areas to rural areas (Costello 2007). Furthermore, there is an increasing tendency for these businesses to be engaged in a wider range of activities than farming, including tourism, recreation, environmental services and craft-based industries (Davies and Tonts 2010). There are strong resonances here with recent literature describing the emergence of a multifunctional countryside, based on a complex mosaic of economic activities and socio-cultural aspirations for rural environments (Argent 2002; Smailes 2002).

It is also apparent that wider processes of agricultural restructuring have, in effect, created the space in which many of these newer industries operate. In Western Australia, for example, much of the growth of small-scale farming has occurred in the southwest of the state. Until recently, wool and dairy farming dominated the economy of the region. The economic difficulties experienced by farmers in these industries during the 1990s contributed to an increased number of properties being offered for sale. The rising demand for land in the region by 'sea-changers' saw a transfer of land to people with a different set of expectations and sensibilities to those of sheep and dairy farmers. The outcome has been the emergence of a more diverse set of land uses and, often, more vibrant and resilient local and regional economies.

TRADE-OFFS BETWEEN PRODUCTION AND THE ENVIRONMENT

The broad economic and social changes affecting agriculture have had important implications for the environment. Australia's agriculture has traditionally emphasised the importance of economic productivity ahead of environmental protection. The very establishment of agricultural systems in Australia required the removal of large areas of native vegetation and radical alterations to land and water systems (Tonts 2002; Davidson 2005). In a number of Australia's agricultural regions less than 5 per cent of the original vegetation cover remains. Removal of the original land cover has also had other serious consequences, including secondary soil and water salinisation and its associated problems of groundwater acidification, waterlogging and increased flood risk. According to recent estimates, 1.8 million hectares of agricultural land in the southwest of

Western Australia are now affected by secondary soil salinity (Pasqual 2010). A further 4.4 million hectares are 'at risk', expected to double in extent by 2050. The proportion of affected agricultural land could reach 30 per cent (currently about 12 per cent) over the next 50–100 years (Pasqual 2010) with annual production losses of A\$300 million to A\$400 million (in present-day terms), reflected as an estimated A\$3 billion to A\$4 billion loss to the capital value of farmland (State Salinity Council 2000).

While secondary salinity is a major concern, numerous other land degradation problems are affecting agricultural regions. They include: soil acidification (an even greater threat to production than soil salinity in terms of area affected); soil structure decline and water repellency; wind and water erosion; the spread of agricultural pests (including weeds) and diseases; and accumulation or mobilisation of agricultural chemicals in the atmosphere, soils and water bodies (Conacher and Conacher 2000). This problem has wider consequences as it not only removes productive land from agriculture but also impacts adversely on remnant vegetation, surface and groundwater quality, rural and regional infrastructure and social systems (Conacher et al. 2004). There is also a financial and physical burden imposed on communities in taking remedial action.

One of the issues facing farmers is how to remediate land at a time when there are serious financial stresses in agriculture. While the rehabilitation of land might increase levels of productivity, investing in this necessarily diverts resources from elsewhere in the farm operation. At a time when farmers are being forced to invest in more land, larger and more sophisticated machinery, and biotechnologies to remain viable, land rehabilitation is inevitably not the highest priority for the allocation scarce capital. In many respects, these pressures on the environment have been exacerbated under a liberalised agricultural economy as the pressure to increase production intensifies (Broderick 2005).

Despite this, there have been extensive efforts at regional and local levels to respond to these problems. Local community organisations, such as Landcare groups, have devoted considerable time and energy to tackling environmental problems in agriculture. There has also been considerable investment by commonwealth and state governments in land rehabilitation. Increasingly the message for farmers is that, unless there is a shift towards more sustainable farming practices, then it will be difficult to maintain productivity and remain economically viable (Conacher and Conacher 2000).

There is evidence to suggest that this message does have currency amongst some farmers. In a number of parts of Australia, for example, farmers have been experimenting with new products that have the potential not only to generate income, but also to tackle land degradation, such as sandalwood and oil mallee plantations, organic foods and aquaculture (see, for example, Barton 2001; Tonts and Selwood 2003; Bell 2005). Part of this shift has been linked to the need for greater income diversification in the face of deteriorating returns from traditional commodities. Thus, the economic challenges facing farmers do have the potential to contribute to sustainable solutions. However, it is important to stress that these cases are relatively rare, and the overwhelming direction of Australian agriculture is towards increasing levels of production per hectare, usually through the greater application of chemicals and biotechnologies.

Perhaps a more likely scenario for a more sustainable agriculture in a liberalised economy is the role of consumer demand. Increasing demand for 'clean and green' foods and other agricultural products may help in developing an agriculture that is less environmentally destructive. It is clear that a growing number of supermarkets and food producers are attempting to highlight their green credentials, and in so doing may pressure farmers to adopt practices that are ecologically sound. Indeed, it is here that contract farming appears to have contributed to a number of changes. In a number of industries, notably horticulture and beef production, consumer demand for environmentally friendly products has resulted in environmental clauses being incorporated into the contracts between farmers and firms involved in marketing and processing commodities. These generally require producers to engage in a range of practices that conform to certain environmental standards, and can specify, for example, levels of chemical use, husbandry techniques for animals and even land use management (Tonts et al. 2003). While this is certainly a positive move, it does not necessarily help farmers to overcome the fundamental economic barriers facing those farmers intent on altering their farming systems. Ultimately, in a neoliberal policy environment, it will be up to individual farmers to take responsibility for ensuring the sustainability (in economic and environmental terms) of their farm business. Whether this is an appropriate response given the scale of environmental problems in rural Australia remains open to question.

CONCLUSION

A recent report published by Land and Water Australia has argued:

> The agricultural sector's economic importance, performance and ability to adjust are taken as a given. However it is in these arenas that myths and fixation are most evident. These myths need to be dispelled so that more insightful approaches to developing rural policies might evolve. (Gleeson and Piper 2002, p. 101)

This chapter has sought to synthesise and elaborate upon the background to why many social scientists in Australia remain doubtful of neoliberal arguments that the market efficiency paradigm will secure the future well-being for agricultural-based regions. Being competitive in national and world markets is obviously important for the economic viability of Australian agriculture. However, the process by which Australian agriculture achieves international competitiveness impacts unevenly on the regions in which these activities take place. Australian policy-makers have tended to disavow such concerns for the sake of national benefits. The point of this chapter is to present an alternative policy vision; to suggest that the pursuit of agricultural efficiency has blinkered governments from some of the potentially adverse associated implications. It is timely that the regional and distributional implications associated with Australia's pursuit of market-efficient agriculture be given greater attention by governments. All too often, policies for 'rural Australia' are conflated too simplistically with policies for efficient agriculture. The regional economies of rural Australia no longer ride on the sheep's back to the extent that they once did. Policy discourses and practices should catch up with this reality.

NOTE

1. 'Agri-food studies' is a multidisciplinary research area inhabited mainly by geographers, rural sociologists, political scientists and so on. Its scholarly communities are grounded in the Research Committee 40 (Food and Agriculture) of the International Sociological Association, and in Australia, in the Australasian Agri-food Research Network. An overview of this research field is provided by Buttel (2001).

REFERENCES

ActionAid International (2005), *Power Hungry: Six Reasons to Regulate Global Food Corporations*, Johannesburg, South Africa: Action Aid International.

Argent, N. (2002), 'From pillar to post: in search of the post-productivist countryside in Australia', *Australian Geographer*, 33(1), 97–114.

Australian Bureau of Statistics (ABS) (1994), *Agricultural Statistics: Selected Small Area Data, Western Australia, Season 1992/93*, Canberra: Commonwealth of Australia.

Australian Bureau of Statistics (ABS) (2007), *Time Series Community Profiles, 1996–2006*, Canberra: Commonwealth of Australia.

Australian Bureau of Statistics (ABS) (2008), *Agricultural Commodities: Small Area Data, Australia, 2005–06*, Canberra: Commonwealth of Australia.

Banham, C. (2004), 'Don't remind them of their farm policies – old Europeans have the juice for Orange sceptics', *Sydney Morning Herald*, 6 December, p. 4.

Barton, A. (2001), *Western Oil Mallee Project*, Perth WA: Murdoch University.

Bell, S. (2005), 'Constructing sustainable rural landscapes: oil mallees and the Western Australian wheatbelt', *Geographical Research*, **43**, 194–208.

Broderick, K. (2005), Sustainability and rivers: a case study of communities in the Collie Catchment, Western Australia, unpublished PhD thesis, School of Earth and Geographical Sciences, University of Western Australia.

Bunker, R. and P. Houston (2003), 'Prospects for the rural–urban fringe in Australia: observations from a brief history of the landscapes around Sydney and Adelaide', *Australian Geographical Studies*, **41**(3), 303–323.

Burch, D. and R. Rickson (2001), 'Industrialised agriculture: agribusiness, input-dependency and vertical integration', in S. Lockie and L. Bourke (eds), *Rurality Bites: The Social and Environmental Transformation of Rural Australia*, Sydney, NSW: Pluto Press, pp. 165–177.

Burch, D., R. Rickson and H. Annels (1992), 'Agribusiness in Australia: rural restructuring, social change and environmental impacts', in K. Walker (ed.), *Australian Environmental Policy*, Sydney, NSW: University of New South Wales Press, pp. 19–40.

Burke, T. (2010), opening address, Australian Bureau of Agricultural and Resource Economics, Canberra, accessed at: maff.gov.au/transcripts/transcripts/2010/march/tony_burke_-_abare_outlook_opening_address,_canberra.

Buttel, F.H. (2001), 'Some reflections on late twentieth century agrarian political economy', *Sociologia Ruralis*, **41**(2), 165–81.

Buttel, F.H. (2003), 'Continuities and disjunctures in the transformation of the US agro-food system', in D. Brown and L. Swanson (eds), *Challenges for Rural America in the Twenty-First Century*, Philadelphia, PA: Pennsylvania State University Press, pp. 177–89.

Clark, J., M. Lembit and S. Warr (1992), *A Regional Model of Australian Beef Supply*, Canberra: Australian Bureau of Agriculture and Resource Economics.

Cockfield, G. (1993), 'The vision rational: rural policy in the 1990s', in A. Hede and S. Prasser (eds), *Policy Making in Volatile Times*, Sydney, NSW: Hale and Iremonger, pp. 239–53.

Conacher, A. and J. Conacher (2000), *Environmental Planning and Management in Australia*, Oxford: Oxford University Press.

Conacher, A., M. Tonts and J. Conacher (2004), 'Education and land-use planning for agricultural development in Western Australia', *Land Degradation and Development*, **15**(2), 299–310.

Costello, L. (2007), 'Going bush: the implications of urban–rural migration', *Geographical Research*, **45**, 85–94.

Davidson, G. (2005), 'Rural sustainability in historical perspective', in C. Cocklin and J. Dibdin (eds), *Sustainability and Change in Rural Australia*, Sydney, NSW: University of New South Wales Press, pp. 38–55.

Davies, A. and M. Tonts (2010), 'Economic diversity and regional socioeconomic performance: an empirical analysis of the Western Australian grain belt', *Geographical Research*, **48**, 223–34.

Fold, N. and B. Pritchard (eds) (2005), *Cross-Continental Food Chains*, London: Routledge.

Fraser, I. (2003), 'The role of contracts in wine grape supply coordination: an overview', *Agribusiness Review*, **11**, accessed at: www.agrifood.info/review/2003/Fraser.html.

Freebairn, J. (2003), 'Economic policy for rural and regional Australia', *Australian Journal of Agricultural and Resource Economics*, **47**(3), 389–414.

Gleeson, T. and K. Piper (2002), 'Institutional reform in rural Australia: defining and allocating property rights', in C. Mobbs and K. Moore (eds), *Property: Rights and Responsibilities*, Canberra: Land and Water Australia, pp. 99–118.

Gray, I. and G. Lawrence (2001), *A Future for Regional Australia: Escaping Global Misfortune*, Cambridge: Cambridge University Press.

Herbert, B. and W. Pritchard (2004), 'The changing geographies of power and control in rural service provision: rural restructuring within the Australian tractor dealership system', *Australian Geographical Studies*, **42**(1), 18–33.

Higgins, V. and S. Lockie (2001), 'Getting big or getting out: government policy, self-reliance and farm adjustment', in S. Lockie and L. Bourke (eds), *Rurality Bites: The Social and Environmental Transformation of Rural Australia*, Sydney, NSW: Pluto Press, pp. 178–90.

Hoppe, R., J. Johnson, J. Perry, P. Korb, J. Sommer, J. Ryan, R. Green, R. Durst and J. Monke (2001), *Structural and Financial Characteristics of US farms: 2001 Family Farm Report*, Washington, DC: United States Department of Agriculture.

Hugo, G. (2005), 'The state of rural populations', in C. Cocklin, and J. Dibdin (eds), *Sustainability and Change in Rural Australia*, Sydney, NSW: University of New South Wales Press, pp. 56–79.

Jones, E. (1994), 'Bureaucratic politics and economic policy: the evolution of trade policy in the 1970s and 1980s', University of Sydney Department of Economics working papers in economics 212.

Larner, W. (2003), 'Neoliberalism?' *Environment and Planning D: Society and Space*, **21**, 509–512.

Lawrence, G. (1987), *Capitalism and the Countryside: The Rural Crisis in Australia*, Sydney, NSW: Pluto Press.

Lawrence, G. (2005), 'Globalization, agricultural production systems and rural restructuring', in C. Cocklin and J. Dibdin (eds), *Sustainability and Change in Rural Australia*, Sydney, NSW: University of New South Wales Press, pp. 104–20.

Le Heron, R. (2005), 'Re-constituting New Zealand's agri-food chains for international competition', in N. Fold and B. Pritchard (eds), *Cross-Continental Food Chains*, London: Routledge, pp. 52–65.

Lobao, L. (1990), *Locality and Inequality: Farm and Industry Structure and Socioeconomic Conditions*, Albany, NY: State University of New York Press.

Lockie, S. (1997), 'Is subsumption still relevant? The question of control in Australian broadacre agriculture', *Rural Society*, **7**(3–4), 27–36.

MacCannell, D. (1988), 'Industrial agriculture and rural community degradation', in L. Swanson (ed.), *Agriculture and Community Change in the United States*, Boulder, CO: Westview Press, pp. 15–75.

McMichael, P. (2000), 'The power of food', *Agriculture and Human Values*, **17**(1), 21–33.

McMichael, P. (2003), 'The impact of global economic practices on American farming', in D. Brown and L. Swanson (eds), *Challenges for Rural America in the Twenty-First Century*, Philadelphia, PA: Pennsylvania State University Press, pp. 375–84.

McMichael, P. and G. Lawrence (2001), 'Globalising agriculture: structures of constraint for Australian farming', in S. Lockie and L. Bourke (eds), *Rurality Bites: The Social and Environmental Transformation of Rural Australia*, Sydney, NSW: Pluto Press, pp. 153–64.

Miller, L. (1996), 'Contract farming under globally-oriented and locally emergent agribusiness in Tasmania', in D. Burch, R. Rickson and G. Lawrence (eds), *Globalization and Agri-Food Restructuring: Perspectives from the Australasia Region*, Aldershot: Avebury, pp. 203–18.

National Farmers' Federation (NFF) (1993), *New Horizons: A Strategy for Australia's Agrifood Industries*, Canberra: National Farmers' Federation.

Pasqual, G. (2010), 'Bridging the science–policy interface: reflections and lessons from a study of natural resource management policy-making in Australia', unpublished PhD thesis, Crawley: School of Earth and Environment, University of Western Australia.

Peck, J. and A. Tickell (2002), 'Neoliberalizing space', *Antipode* **34**(3), 380–404.

Pritchard, B. (1999), 'The regulation of grower–processor relations: a case study from the Australian wine industry', *Sociologia Ruralis*, **39**(2), 186–201.

Pritchard, B. (2005a), 'Unpacking the neoliberal approach to regional policy: a close reading of John Freebairn's *Economic Policy for Rural and Regional Australia*', *Geographical Research*, **43**(1), 103–12.

Pritchard, B. (2005b), 'Implementing and maintaining neoliberal agriculture in Australia. Part I: Constructing neoliberalism as a vision for agricultural policy', *International Journal of the Sociology of Agriculture and Food*, **13**(1), 1–12.

Pritchard, B. (2005c), 'Implementing and maintaining neoliberal agriculture in Australia. Part II: strategies for securing neoliberalism', *International Journal of the Sociology of Agriculture and Food*, **13**(2), 1–14.

Pritchard, W. and D. Burch (2003), *Agri-food Globalisation in Perspective: Restructuring in the Global Tomato Processing Industry*, Adlershot: Ashgate.

Pritchard, B. and P. McManus (eds) (2000), *Land of Discontent: The Dynamics of Change in Rural and Regional Australia*, Sydney, NSW: UNSW Press.

Rodefeld, R.D. (1978), 'Trends in US farm organizational structure and type', in R.D. Rodefeld, J. Flora, D. Voth, I. Fujimoto and J. Converse (eds), *Change in Rural America*, St Louis, MO: CV Mosby, pp. 158–77.

Senate Rural and Regional Affairs and Transport References Committee (2005), *Inquiry into the Operation of the Winegrapes Industry*, Canberra: Parliament of Australia.

Sinclair, I. (2001), 'Globalisation and regional renewal: compatible or mutually exclusive?', *Australian Journal of Social Issues*, **36**(2), 93–103.

Smailes, P. (2002), 'From rural dilution to multifunctional countryside: some pointers to the future from South Australia', *Australian Geographer*, **33**(1), 79–95.

State Salinity Council (2000), *Natural Resource Management in Western Australia: The Salinity Strategy*, Perth, WA: Government of Western Australia.

Stayner, R. (2005), 'The economics of rural communities', in C. Cocklin and J. Dibdin (eds), *Sustainability and Change in Rural Australia*, Sydney, NSW: University of New South Wales Press, pp. 104–20.

Tonts, M. (2002), 'State policy and the yeoman ideal: agricultural development in Western Australia, 1890–1914', *Landscape Research*, **27**(1), 103–15.

Tonts, M. and S. Greive (2002), 'Commodification and creative destruction in the Australian rural landscape', *Australian Geographical Studies*, **40**(1), 58–70.

Tonts, M., D. Halpin, J. Collins and A. Black (2003), *Rural Communities and Changing Farm Business Structures: An Assessment of the Socio-Economic Impacts*, Canberra: Rural Industries Research and Development Corporation.

Tonts, M. and J. Selwood (2003), 'Niche markets, regional diversification and the reinvention of Australia's sandalwood industry', *Tijdschrift voor Economische en Sociale Geografie*, **94**(5), 564–75.

Welsh, R. (1997), 'Vertical coordination, producer response, and the locus of control over agricultural production decisions', *Rural Sociology*, **62**(4), 491–507.

Winson, A. (1996), 'In search of the part-time capitalist farmer: labour use and farm structure in central Canada', *Canadian Review of Sociology and Anthropology*, **33**(1), 89–110.

4. Globalisation, agriculture and development: New Zealand's path to prosperity?

Kenneth E. Jackson

INTRODUCTION

Agriculture has always been seen by many as the key feature of the New Zealand economy, and sometimes as the key to the essential nature and being of the society. To the degree that overemphasis of agriculture's importance has been evident, it has been more due to the desire to portray New Zealand as a settler society, based on an agricultural and rural dominance, than to any social reality. The picture is, of course, more complex, with relatively sparse settlement and extensive farming systems characteristic of most rural areas, and a general disconnect between these landscapes and wider urban and national economic realities.

It is true that underlying dictates of comparative advantage appear to have favoured primary production for much of New Zealand's development, with attempts at protection and diversification into manufacturing and import substitution being as fashionable (and as unsuccessful) as they generally proved to be elsewhere. By the 1980s a return to open market dominance had occurred, accompanied by a rise in indicators such as the share of export income generated by the primary sector, and movements within the primary sector towards products offering a higher rate of return. Amongst the significant outcomes of this process were that the wool sector moved downwards in relative importance, whilst the dairy sector moved very strongly upwards.

Much of the relative movement reflects a growing interaction with the global market and a shift towards high technology, as well as a concern for the quality and assurance of the supply of products. Agricultural marketing has altered significantly in the recent past with the rise of the processing giant Fonterra to a dominant position in the dairy sector and a general shift towards a corporate model of integrated production, processing and distribution.

This chapter portrays a particular view of the historic path to the recent dairy payouts bonanza of the present day, reviewing and analysing New Zealand's engagement with global agricultural markets, ideas, capital and labour mobility. It moves in sequence from an exposition of the 'supposed' historical dependency upon agricultural exports and trade in general, through agriculture as the 'backbone' of the nation, and on to the dramatic changes since the mid-1980s that have been inherently driven by the forces of globalisation operating on ideas concerning methods and practices, as well as through markets and financial structures.

This chapter is divided into four main sections. The first examines Leamer's Indices of Openness, building on previous work by the author and briefly considering the indices over time. The second section considers the degree of openness of the New Zealand economy. Together these two sections set out to demonstrate something of the extent and nature of the 'supposed' dominant nature of the agricultural–trade nexus. The question of agriculture as the backbone of the country and its economic development is also considered, as a way of suggesting that, in terms of path-dependency, New Zealand is overly reliant on exports of primary products and agriculture specifically, and also that high trade levels are more myth than reality. It is additionally noted that in a world of services trade, diasporas and their networks, Leamer's indices may not fully cover the possibilities for the source of dynamic impacts.

The third section attempts a decomposition of export totals to demonstrate the extent of agricultural dominance in New Zealand and movements within agriculture. The story follows the path from the primacy of wool, and the introduction of substantial meat and dairy sectors after the introduction of refrigeration, through to the more recent, post-1980s, removal of wool from the major player list, following the opening up of the economy and deregulation. The description is important in that it reflects a desire to move in line with the dictates of more markets and reap the 'benefits' of openness, globalisation, gains from trade and comparative advantage.

In the fourth main section, some of the question of changing input requirements and systems, the changing nature of stock and station agents, production systems and suppliers are all considered, in the light of a fluid and more market-orientated approach.

At various points there are reflections on the current challenges and opportunities arising from the present agreements at both the global and the regional level, including the World Trade Organization (WTO), and the Uruguay Round. This includes questions concerning single-desk selling and environmental challenges such as carbon footprints, 'food miles', food security, phyto-sanitary and other thinly disguised non-tariff barriers to trade. Additionally, investment agreements, capital movement and service trade in agricultural services and supply, including extension services and genetic crop research, are examined.

The chapter concludes by reviewing the importance of agriculture to New Zealand development in this new globalising age with its highly integrated factor and product markets, as well as macro impacts of innovations and shocks from the historical introduction of refrigeration, through to the impact of British entry into the European Union (EU), the post-1984 world of deregulation, and the industry switch to dairy products and diversification into horticulture and viticulture, not to mention aquaculture. All of these factors exhibit their own particular global supply chain impacts. While agriculture in New Zealand remains largely pastoral in nature, it is far more complex and capital-intensive than it was, even as recently as the mid-1980s and is certainly more globally integrated. The question remains, however: is it capable of being a sustainable driver of growth into the future? Growth rates above the Organisation for Economic Co-operation and Development (OECD) average of 3.1 per cent per annum to early 2008, according to Statistics NZ figures, are a notable recent development and are significantly above the previous year's 1.7 per cent growth to March 2007 (Jackson 2007, p. 853); but can they be sustained? The very long-run growth rates of 1.6 per cent for 1900 to 1999 (Greasley and Oxley 2000) might suggest otherwise, while the Ministry of Economic Development indicators for 2007 suggest that they have been maintained in recent years (MED 2007).

MEASURES OF OPENNESS AND PROBLEMS IN APPLYING THEM

Trade is a significant part of the process of opening economies to the outside world and enhancing their productivity and growth, as well as allowing them to reap the direct benefits of gains from trade. However, trade measures can be enhanced or negated by a range of institutional factors. Also important are the role of the exchange rate, barriers to trade and international investment, and the movement of people. Trade liberalisation has generally been found to assist growth practically, both directly and by encouraging investment (see Levine and Renelt 1992), and is best seen as part of a process towards greater integration, both globally and regionally. If, as some writers suggest, this is enough to ensure rapid growth, then all is well, but if the route leads to a place on Krugman's (1991, 1998) new economic geography's periphery, with a dependence on agriculture and services, then all may not be well in the long run.

Other outcomes are seen as possible, as can be judged from the writing of Litchfield et al. (2003), amongst others.

In the best of all possible theoretical worlds, openness can be viewed as readily assessed, desirable and achievable. To assume that this can be transferred to the analysis of a historical case, with social and political concerns and all the other everyday forces, which are all difficult to measure, constitutes the height of misguided optimism. Practical issues, including what measures exist and their accuracy, have to be considered, as well as policy aims and interventions and their impacts.

There is no one measure of openness that has so far been accepted as all but a universal standard. In a pure world with perfect information, the degree of integration of an individual economy with the global economy can be accurately measured. Measures of deviation of actual trade growth from predicted pure trade growth along the lines of Leamer's Openness Index (Leamer 1988) are unlikely to be of much practical use with deficient historical data, where even the actual measure is best prefaced with 'once upon a time'. However, some use may be made of the trade–income ratios approach to indicate general levels of protection and openness, at least in a historical context, but they are somewhat more deficient for the current situation. Increasing migration and other newer aspects of openness, including communications, networks and the spread of ideas, have all grown significantly in recent years, rendering Leamer's indices little more than a starting point.

Historically, the examination of exchange rates would be important in this case. Although New Zealand appears to have had a high level of convertibility through its fixed link to sterling, it was not entirely free of distortions emanating from the particular operations of the commercial banking sector. Even with the floating exchange rate from the mid-1980s there are still considerable fluctuations in the rate, with frequent interventions by the Reserve Bank. Open, but not entirely hands-off.

There are some conceptual difficulties with measuring openness. For example, the commonly used trade intensity ratios can be affected by the size of the country involved, as much as by national differences in trade policy stance (Pritchett 1996, p. 309). New Zealand, as a small, open economy, would normally be expected to demonstrate a high trade intensity ratio, but many of the potential problems related to comparing its degree of openness with that of other countries of larger size are not an issue here because the comparison is not between countries, it is over time rather than space. Given the conceptual problems, some of the analysis is by necessity qualitative as well as quantitative.

In the empirical studies undertaken for rapidly growing countries in the 1990s, there are several common variables that were brought into consideration. Most of these are concerned with levels of import penetration of consumer goods, where the greater the penetration the greater the degree of openness. Consumer, or finished, goods are likely to be the ones most protected and therefore a better target to use in assessing indicators of openness. Historically the New Zealand case reveals greater effectiveness of protection through reductions in duty on intermediate goods at times, reflecting less openness. Now the push is concentrated on real openness and liberalisation in expectation of reciprocity with respect to liberalised access for agricultural exports on the part of trading partners.

Several variables are typically used in current studies, starting with the more general and moving to the more specific. These variables relate to trade intensity ratios, movements in the real exchange rate, the ratio of imports to gross domestic product (GDP), and of consumer imports to total imports, the existence of any premium in the black market, the ratio of non-food consumer imports to total non-food imports, of consumer imports to consumption, and of non-food consumer imports to consumption. Trade intensity ratios tend to dominate. Data problems often ensure that investigation of much more than this is rarely possible.

OPENNESS AND THE NEW ZEALAND ECONOMY

J.B. Condliffe (1959) described New Zealand as exhibiting the highest level of trade per capita of any economy in the world in the 1950s. This would suggest a high degree of openness, but the contradictions are abundant. The early 1950s was a time of both exchange regulation and restriction, as well as physical trade restriction. Whilst New Zealand has experienced fluctuating degrees of openness over time, available indicators suggest that the underlying trend since the late nineteenth century has been downward. From such a high trade per capita position New Zealand declined in ranking when compared to other countries, many of whom were, in the 1950s, still disadvantaged by the disruptions visited on them during the interwar, wartime and immediate post-war eras. Growth has also been slow over the long run and since agriculture was an important source of income for much of the time, the Singer–Prebisch thesis, Krugman's new geography and Thirlwall's Law (Thirlwall 2003, pp. 277–82) suggest that caution be exercised in pursuing this route. Since the mid-1980s the pursuit of comparative advantage and market rules have not apparently paid heed to the perils that might exist.

Agriculture has remained important as an export contributor, although declining relatively over the long run, but its composition has altered and it has been greatly affected by technological change and development in production and processing, as well as in terms of the type, quality and nature of its inputs. If the perils seen by Thirlwall and others are not sufficient warning of danger, then the Grossman and Helpman (1991) endogenous growth approach, with its talk of innovation driving growth and its linkage to industrial output, may do so.

In the earlier period, before the Second World War, it is possible to argue that there are three possibilities when trying to characterise the degree of openness of the New Zealand economy: open, shut or sheltered. A truly open economy was never that likely, at least in the free trade sense. The brief attempt at removal of all duties on imports was as long ago as 1844–45 (Isles 1986, p. 195). The mid-1980s also met stumbling blocks, some of which can be seen later in this chapter. The very short-lived early attempt to encourage activity through free trade in New Zealand foundered on the lack of any viable alternative source of revenue for government. The current one stumbles on market access, food miles, sanitary provisions and a myriad of new protective devices.

Effectively, revenue may have been the chief aim in the government's mind in the 1840s, but protective effects and less openness were inevitable, if incidental, outcomes of the approach, which did not pass unnoticed either by politicians or by rent-seeking local interests. Agricultural interests also long continued to proclaim the injurious effects on them of protection of local production of inputs and services to the farming sector. Trade barriers in the form of tariffs and import restrictions became important parts of agricultural policy and, in a broader sense, to rural development.

It is important to note that the free trade ideals expounded in Britain in the second half of the nineteenth century did not exist in the New Zealand case (Hawke 1985, p. 112). Protection, intended or unintended, was present and faced no legacy of free trade orthodoxy to overcome. The New Zealand Industrial Association had developed a strong protective leaning, requiring its new members to support tariff adjustment so as to favour locally produced manufactured products over imported ones by 1886 (Linge 1959, p. 158). It was aided by pressure from the New Zealand Protection Association, bringing the protection point home to politicians as a balance to the complaints from the primary sector, which argued that they suffered from protection as a result of having to pay higher prices for their inputs than they otherwise might have done. For example, they argued that they in fact suffered from competitively supplying their export products to monopsonistic cartels of international meat companies. A continuing complaint through to the present, although one perhaps forgotten in the rush to float the former dairy co-operative Fonterra.

Through the First World War and into the interwar period such protectionism appears to have gathered strength, although the value of tariffs relative to import prices fell between 1900 and 1920 from 20 per cent to 13 per cent. Duties on foreign products were raised during the war with extra imposts on imports from 'enemy' countries. Moves to counter dumping (Australian roofing products) and to protect against 'unfair' competition (devaluation and low wage costs), on the part of Japan, appear in 1919 (Isles 1986, p. 198). Sheltering, in the sense of secure British markets through the commandeer process for bulk purchase of some food products during the war, meant that there was a move to 90 per cent or more reliance on one export market. New Zealand was trading, but not globally integrating. The switch to a free market approach is a very recent one, by such standards. Concern with growth drivers was sunk under other objectives and goals.

However one views the post-mid-1980s move to openness and liberalisation, along with an unhealthy growth in reliance, on primary exports, it is a stance which is radically out of kilter with much of the path along which New Zealand had developed in the past. Generally it can be postulated that the New Zealand commercial policy stance is characterised in time as broken into the following phases. First, from the early days of European settlement through to the early 1850s, when the early preference for Empire products disappears and a settled period of looking to customs duties, primarily for revenue, appears. Second, from the 1850s, the primary reliance on duties for revenue purposes runs through to the early twentieth century. This second period sees strong links to Britain, but is essentially a relatively open one. The third period starts with the renewal of an Empire preference scheme, developed in a 'protective surcharge' manner at the beginning of the century. It sees an attempt to differentiate New Zealand from not only New South Wales, but also the other Australasian colonies in the eyes of the British. The wartime period through to the early 1920s extended the sheltered reliance on Britain as a major market, through the imperial commandeer and guaranteed markets for food products. A fourth period from the early 1920s through to the early 1950s saw a period of relative closure with some degree of sheltering. The more open approach of the recent past starts only from the early 1950s, but in rather hesitant fashion, until the impossibility of relying on British markets and sheltering as being effective is finally made apparent with British entry into Europe. A liberalising approach is then seen, gathering pace through the 1970s and more particularly the 1980s, giving a fifth period which can be described as more open, allied to liberal free market approaches. The potential for growth through this 'allocatively efficient' approach does not, however, seem to pay off fully.

Trade to income ratios seem to suggest that New Zealand has fought a long and slow decline in trade intensities (Table 4.1). 'Imports to income' is the figure that most policy operators have sought to influence. Export

Table 4.1   Trade to income ratios 1870–2000

Year	Exports to income (%)
1870	40.29
1880	24.44
1890	30.55
1900	31.81
1910	30.50
1920	26.68
1930	28.63
1940	37.08
1950	30.50
1960	20.70
1970	18.70
1980	25.00
1990	22.00
2000	32.00

Sources: 1870–1940 author's calculations from data contained in Bloomfield (1984), Hawke (1975, 1985) and Lineham (1968). 1950–70 taken directly from Carey and Smith (1981, p. 548). 1980–2000 estimates taken from Briggs (2003, p. 60).

promotion is a somewhat more nebulous operation and usually it is the level and total value of imports that have been affected in periods of less openness. A structural tendency to import, and consequent high propensity to import, has been said to have prevailed into the modern era.

New Zealand, however, proves not to be as open as conventional wisdom suggests. Simkin's 'high trader time' of the early 1950s saw an export to GDP ratio of just over 30 per cent, and nearly 33 per cent for imports. Twenty years later these numbers had declined to under 20 per cent in each case (Carey and Smith 1981, p. 548) causing the heretical comment that maybe New Zealand was not as great a trader as conventional wisdom would like to suggest. Exports to national income below the 30 per cent level was not something new by the 1980s; what was new, was their being below the 20 per cent level. Not that this downward trend has consistently continued. As at 2000, the export to GDP ratio was approximately 32 per cent (Briggs 2003, p. 60).

At the early stage, the typical trade to income ratios are far higher than for the 1970s, but for a small open economy with some abundant natural resource endowments to exploit, this is not surprising; indeed they look low on average, with the positive influence of gold discoveries still traceable in the 1870s and the impact of refrigeration showing through at the turn of the century. Trends are not strong, and 30 per cent seems about the consistent norm right through the present. Agriculture figures highly as a contributor, whether in an open or a restricted period of policy stance. In the early years of the new millennium it has frequently been argued that the exchange rate is the problem for exporters, rather than trade policy as such.

Real exchange rates in the period through to the late 1990s have been analysed by Dalziel and Lattimore (1999, p. 123). They base their research on a different approach, more suited to the changes in export direction and other changes occurring at this time, including the composition of exports and the composition within export groups such as agriculture. The period from the beginning of the 1970s saw the demise of attempts at fixed exchange rates or pegging to the pound sterling. Such fixed exchange rate mechanisms effectively ceased from 1972–73. Various floating regimes have been operated from that date. From the mid-1980s, when floating was introduced, the real rates were somewhat more stable than the nominal ones.

The implications and importance of the exchange rate shifts lie in their indication of levels of protection, and therefore the degree of openness present in the economy at any point in time. The real rate is a more effective indicator of levels of competitiveness and protection than the nominal one. A similar method of evaluation, using the difference in wage costs as a deflator, was employed by Lloyd (1984), to assess the impact of the New Zealand Australia Free Trade Agreement (NZAFTA) trade policy arrangements between 1966 and 1982. Significantly, that study found the impact of bilateral real exchange rate movements to be far greater than that produced by the weak and permissive trade agreement itself. Even with stronger trade agreements than that one, the impact of exchange rate changes is still a significant factor to bear in mind.

In summary, since 1960 the movements in real exchange rates (Dalziell and Lattimore 1999, p. 123) show major breaks associated with the discrete regime changes of the late 1960s, early 1970s and mid-1980s. The free float and more open regime of the recent past is reflected in much greater year-to-year fluctuation, with the trends far from uniform. Growth in dairy receipts in recent years has been so pronounced as to wash out any apparent disadvantage to producers from high exchange rates.

DECOMPOSITION

If New Zealand is very open, but trade intensity has not dramatically increased, the opportunities for agriculture to be a dynamic driver of growth must be looked for in terms of particular strengths. The role of agriculture in economic development is usually analysed in terms of a structural shift, either from primary to secondary and tertiary in the guise of Clark (1940) and others, or from the low-productivity labour-intensive agricultural and rural sector to higher-productivity, usually urban, manufacturing and service sectors, in the guise of W. Arthur Lewis (1954) and the dual sector approach. Agriculture is variously seen as the provider of food and labour to the non-agricultural sector. Any improved efficiency and resultant growth in the agricultural sector leads to faster structural transformation. The World Bank devoted its *World Development Report* for 2008 to agriculture and its role in development, including poverty reduction. This is a return to a longstanding debate in the literature on development economics. In New Zealand, agriculture has always been a significant element in the economy, but a changing one in terms of both overall contribution and in its structure and make-up.

Conventional patterns of structural change do not always explain what is occurring or, even more importantly, why. A description of how the agricultural sector has altered in the recent past cannot of itself explain the dynamics behind the changes, or the outcomes and impacts of those changes. The more market approach of the mid-1980s onwards can be seen as the driving force behind some of this, but whether this has significantly contributed to overall growth is less than clear. The New Zealand economy is a robust (or dogged) animal that does not seem to produce rapid changes in its growth path. Briggs's account of growth periods ranges from a high of 4.4 per cent average between 1934 and 1966, and a low of 1.4 per cent between 1914 and 1934 (Briggs 2003, p. 37).

Structural change and economic growth may be causally interrelated, although the direction of the causal relationship is questionable. Certainly any increase in economic growth leads to a faster structural change, as noted by Syrquin (1988), but does structural change lead to faster economic growth? Structural changes, not just economic but in social institutions, culture, politics and beliefs, may be a necessary but not sufficient condition for economic growth (Kuznets 1971, p. 248). Structural change that assists in better resource allocation, or allocative efficiency, can however contribute positively to growth (Syrquin 1988, p. 258).

Did the Roger Douglas revolution and more market approach lead to faster rates of growth from the mid-1980s onwards? There was certainly a structural change within the economy and within the agricultural sector at this time. It would appear that changes made were in line with Syrquin and others' suggestions, to the extent that they were in line with greater alignment with market principles. External trade was sought in the areas that were accessible. The General Agreement on Tariffs and The General Agreement on Tariffs and Trade (GATT) and the 1994 Uruguay Round affected trade in an export-oriented and comparative advantage fashion, so that agriculture went against a long-term trend to become a slightly greater part of the whole of export receipts by 2000. Recently, concern has been expressed that trade shares are falling away, with the switch from concentrating on global WTO-type agreements to regional or bilateral ones. New Zealand's keenness not to be locked out of the Association of South East Asian Nations (ASEAN) plus 1, 2, 3 or 6, is symptomatic of this concern in the post-Uruguay Round world.

ASEAN represents the greatest growth in export receipts by region, with a 16 per cent change between 2004 and 2006 estimates, more than double the next best, the Pacific Islands (Statistics NZ 2006, Table 3.04), which are of very limited size in terms of their market. If the WTO is really going nowhere fast for agricultural products, then the regional and bilateral agreements are key and the Asian market is the predominant target.

Within agriculture itself, wool has lost out and dairy production has soared since the late 1980s. New Zealand no longer rides on the sheep's back, if it ever did so. From the 20 sheep per person ratio of the mid-1980s, the country has moved to 12 sheep per person. Externally the change is even more pronounced, with wool exports moving from representing 30 per cent of total exports at its peak, down to a level of just half that of sheep meat exports by 2000. Wool receipts are now fifth on the commodity list rather than the predominant source that they were historically. Dairying now produces approximately one-sixth of all export receipts. Does this accommodation of market forces assist with growth and development? In the short run the answer may be yes, but the longer-run dynamics of comparative advantage may require a different outcome to the short-run static finding. Expansion in meat and dairy export receipts has been large, forming over 30 per cent of total receipts in 2005.

Continuing dependence on agricultural exports is fine if the items are not basic commodities. Wool has suffered from a modern version of the Singer–Prebisch thesis (see Singer 1950; Prebisch 1950) that primary commodity prices tend to suffer long-run declines in their terms of trade as against manufactured products and services. Meat and dairy products are more likely to face difficulties associated with environmental concerns, including food miles campaigns and methane emissions as well as food safety issues. The latter may be largely only new versions of a protectionist tune, but the effect is negative nonetheless.

SUPPLIES, INPUTS AND PROCESSING

Dairying has also been successful in seeing consolidation into some large units of processing, essentially remaining in New Zealand hands with the rise of the global giant Fonterra. Globalco was formed in 2001 out of the legacy of the interwar establishment and the development of a series of marketing mechanisms, such as the Dairy Board, along with other boards for each of New Zealand's major export products, with significant government support and involvement. These mechanisms tried to combat the falling demand and prices experienced once the war was over. The Imperial Government ceased its 1915 imposed wartime requisition of farm produce for export in 1920 for all but butter, which was requisitioned until 1921.

The 1920s were times of depressed commodity prices and reduced trading activity. In recent times this is the story for wool, but not the other commodities. Employment protection and dealing with persistent balance-of-payments problems were the avowed aim of the policy stance through to the 1950s when objectives altered somewhat in character, but there remained a relatively protectionist and British-focused approach.

It was not until the 1970s that there was a move towards a more universal stance. Preferences to Britain and the Commonwealth were reduced or incorporated into the Generalised System of Preferences. By July 1978 the results of a tariff review investigation were implemented, further globalising the stance with some moves made towards a more open regime (Smith and Miller 1981, p. 449). It was the period after the mid-1980s, however, that saw the more radical steps taken towards reducing tariffs and the final elimination of quantitative controls. If the recent past can be described as a fully open one from both the tariff policy stance perspective and that of relatively unrestricted capital flows, the same cannot be said of the movement of people, which is reflective of a somewhat less open attitude. The attempts to open up special registration schemes for horticultural workers from five Pacific Islands through the Department of Labour is really an acknowledgement of the difficulties of finding labour at rates of pay below those prevailing for other jobs in an era of near full employment.

Other institutional forms have had to adapt to the more open era. The stock and station agents' role has altered, with financing coming from a range of sources in a more competitive and sophisticated structure. This process commenced in the 1970s, and gathered momentum during the 1980s (Ville 2000, p. 18). Financing and supply of inputs, however, is a servicing facilitator rather than an independent driver of growth. Its expansion was that of a dependent rather than an independent force.

Efficiency in the input and servicing areas, as well as processing, was certainly improved by the post-1980s liberalisation; not without some social cost, but also with some rationalisation and economic benefit.

CONSEQUENCES AND CONCLUSIONS

The qualitative assessment of the trade policy stance, and its affect on agriculture and exports generally, is characteristic of an early period of protected economic activity. From 1850 to 1900 approximately, New Zealand trade was characterised as dominated by the government seeking tariff revenue rather than acting in an avowedly protectionist manner, although becoming more explicitly protectionist towards the end of the century.

For whatever reasons, including protection, the period through to the early to mid-1970s saw trade intensity fall to historically low levels. Agriculture remained a dominant, although declining, force. It was conservative in its nature and changing only slowly, not likely to be a dynamic source of growth and innovation.

The major period of global interest here may well be the questioning of what happened in the interwar period. The global typology provided by Summers (1999, p. 5) suggests that 1914–50 saw a literal disintegration of the world economy. Conventional wisdom and traditional qualitative assessment of this period for the New Zealand case suggests a similar outcome, but the trade intensity measures suggest more, not less integration. Perhaps the farming sector was not that lacking in dynamism after all.

Pritchett's (1996) findings state that whilst it is generally held that a country's trade policy stance can determine economic performance, what it is that does the trick is less obvious and less often questioned. The New Zealand case study is very incomplete at this point in time and needs more work, but it is clear that New Zealand is not the trading power that the conventional wisdom suggests and there are some particular discrepancies in our thinking. However over-reliance on the primary sector and agriculture, in particular through export growth, appears to be a risky business within a world that appears to be closing in, at least into large regional blocks, rather than pursuing the global openness that New Zealand has appeared to favour since the mid-1980s. Some of the economic theorising also suggests caution about expecting too much from even a technologically driven agriculture and other primary-based activities. A continuation of historically low growth rates seems the likeliest outcome.

REFERENCES

Bloomfield, G.T. (1984), *New Zealand: A Handbook of Historical Statistics*, Boston, MA: G.K. Hall & Co.
Briggs, Phil (2003), *Looking at the Numbers*, Wellington: NZIER.
Carey, D.A. and A.A. Smith (1981), 'The external dependence of the New Zealand

economy', in R.S. Deane, P.W.E. Nicholl and M.J. Walsh (eds), *External Economic Structure and Policy: An Analysis of New Zealand's Balance of Payments*, Wellington: Reserve Bank of New Zealand, pp. 47–65.

Clark, C. (1940), *The Conditions of Economic Progress*, London: Macmillan.

Condliffe, J.B. (1959), *New Zealand in the Making: A Study of Social and Economic Development* (2nd revised edn), London: George Allen & Unwin Ltd.

Dalziel, P. and R. Lattimore (1999), *The New Zealand Macroeconomy: A Briefing on the Reforms*, Oxford: Oxford University Press.

Greasley, D. and L. Oxley (2000), 'Outside the club: New Zealand's economic growth, 1870–1993', *International Review of Applied Economics*, **14**, 173–92.

Hawke, G.R. (1975), 'Income estimation from monetary data: further exploration', *Review of Income and Wealth*, **21**, 301–7.

Hawke, G.R. (1985), *The Making of New Zealand*, Cambridge: Cambridge University Press.

Isles, J. (1986), 'Trade and protection', in B. Fraser (ed.), *The New Zealand Book of Events*, Auckland: Reed Methuen, pp. 194–203.

Jackson, K. (2007), 'The New Zealand economy', in Lynn Daniel (ed.), *Regional Surveys of the World: The Far East and Australasia* (38th edn), London: Routledge, pp. 852–8.

Krugman, P. (1991), *Geography and Trade*, Cambridge, MA: MIT Press.

Krugman, P. (1998), 'The role of geography in development', in B. Pleskovic and J. Stiglitz (eds), *Annual World Bank Conference on Development Economics 1998*, Washington, DC: World Bank, pp. 89–1070.

Kuznets, S. (1971), *Economic Growth of Nations: Total Output and Production Structure*, Harvard, MA: Harvard University Press.

Leamer, E. (1988), 'Measures of openness', in R. Baldwin (ed.), *Trade Policy Issues and Empirical Analysis*, London: National Bureau of Economic Research, pp. 147–200.

Lewis, W.A. (1954), 'Economic development with unlimited supplies of labour', *Manchester School of Economics and Social Studies*, **22**, 139–91.

Lineham, B.T. (1968), 'New Zealand's gross domestic product, 1918–38', *New Zealand Economic Papers*, **2**, 15–26.

Linge, G.J.R. (1959), 'The geography of manufacturing in New Zealand', University of Auckland unpublished PhD thesis.

Litchfield, Julie, Neil McCulloch and L. Alan Winters. (2003), 'Agricultural trade liberalization and poverty dynamics in three developing countries', *American Journal of Agricultural Economics*, **85**, 1285–91.

Lloyd, P. (1984), 'New Zealand, CER and the Pacific', *New Zealand Economic Papers*, **18**, 1–12.

Ministry of Economic Development (MED) (2007) *Economic Development Indicators 2007: A Summary*, accessed at: www.med.govt.nz/indicators.

Prebisch, R. (1950), *The Economic Development of Latin America and Its Principal Problems*, New York: United Nations.

Pritchett, L. (1996), 'Measuring outward orientation in LDCs: can it be done?', *Journal of Development Economics*, **49**(2), 307–35.

Singer, H.W. (1950). 'US foreign investment in underdeveloped areas: the distribution of gains between investing and borrowing countries', *American Economic Review, Papers and Proceedings*, **40**, 473–85.

Statistics New Zealand (2006), *External Trade Statistics, December 2006*, Wellington: Statistics New Zealand.

Summers, L.H. (1999), Distinguished lecture on economics in government 'Reflections on Managing Global Integration', *Journal of Economic Perspectives*, **13**(2), 3–18.

Syrquin, M. (1988), 'Patterns of structural change', in H. Chenery and A. Srinivasan (eds), *Handbook of Development Economics*, Volume 1, Amsterdam: Elsevier, pp. 275–331.

Thirlwall, A.P. (2003), *Growth and Development* (7th edn), New York: Palgrave Macmillan.

Ville, Simon, P. (2000), *The Rural Entrepreneurs*, Cambridge: Cambridge University Press.

World Bank (2008), *World Development Report 2008*, Washington, DC: World Bank.

5. Agriculture and economic development in India and China: an overview

M.A.B. Siddique

INTRODUCTION

India and China are among the fastest-growing economies in the world. Although both countries exemplify economic accomplishment, their individual experiences have been vastly different. Since the late 1980s, India and China have been successful in achieving a turnaround in economic conditions, reaching annual gross domestic product (GDP) growth in excess of 10 per cent, and have withstood trying times in Asia (WDI online). The two countries are major players in the global economy, accounting for a large proportion of the world's population and producing 17.6 per cent of global GDP. China and India are both likely to continue to exhibit strong growth, alongside features typical of developing countries: a significant proportion of the population in both countries lives below the poverty line (US$1 per day), and rural areas are still reliant on agriculture. Agriculture can determine the pace of industrialisation and development in other sectors of the economy.

This chapter is a modest attempt to assess the role of agriculture in promoting economic development in India and China. These two economies have been selected on the basis of their significant importance to the global economy and due to the substantial role that agriculture has played in promoting development in these countries. Agriculture in India and China is assessed in the next two sections, which look at the historical growth patterns of the respective countries, followed by an examination of the significance of agriculture to their economies. The two country-specific sections then address the major agricultural reforms that have been implemented, both in their domestic economies as well as internationally, before addressing the problems faced by the agricultural sector in the respective countries. The sections conclude with an assessment of the performance of the agricultural sectors in India and China, respectively. A fourth section concludes the chapter.

INDIA

Although India is now renowned for its expertise in manufacturing and service provision, like China its agriculture continues to be one of the more prominent sectors in its economy. It accounts for a large share of India's GDP and a significant proportion of its exports. However, in recent years Indian agriculture has hit a dead end, with stagnation of technology and problems in marketing produce, among other things. As such, Indian agriculture may be hindering economic progress. This is in contrast to the initial spurts of growth, post-independence and economic liberalization, when much of the growth was due to expansion in the agricultural and primary sectors. This chapter attempts to provide an overview of the development of Indian agriculture, post-independence, and to assess economic reforms that have attempted to globalise Indian agriculture.

The Historical Growth Pattern of the Indian Economy

Post-1947, the Indian economy was characterised by low per capita income, little infrastructure and low productivity. Initial steps to improve the economy were taken by centralising the means of production, with pervasive planning methodology. However, progress remained below potential and this was recognised by the government in the late 1980s. The Indian economy was liberalised in the early 1990s under Finance Minister Manmohan Singh.

The recent success of the Indian economy has been observed by the global economy and India has achieved extraordinary rates of growth. There has been an upward trend in growth since 2000; however, it has been volatile at best. Economic growth was at an all-time low in 1979, possibly as a consequence of the war of 1971 with Pakistan and the oil shocks of 1973–74. Evidently, as Figure 5.1 illustrates, economic growth has been less volatile since the economic and financial reforms of the early 1990s.

The Indian economy is extremely diversified, encompassing agriculture, low-scale as well as high-tech manufacturing and provision of services. Although the large majority of the Indian population still relies on agriculture and allied industries, such as fisheries, as a source of livelihood, the services industry is growing and becoming an increasingly integral part of the Indian economy. An important consequence of the financial reforms of the 1990s was that India found its niche in service providing,

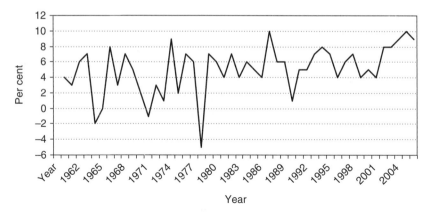

Source: World Bank (2007).

Figure 5.1 GDP growth rate, India, 1962–2004

particularly in the information technology (IT) sector, quite unlike other Asian countries such as China and Vietnam, which have found their niche in manufactures.

The prospects for the Indian economy are strong for future growth and development. With rising demand for the provision of Indian services, the Indian economy is booming with record levels of growth. However, at the same time, Indian agriculture remains relatively stagnant.

Agriculture and Economic Growth

Composition

India's most important crops are rice, wheat, sugarcane and cotton (WTO 2007, p. 100). India is also a large producer of oilseeds such as groundnut, mustard and sunflower. Cash crops cultivated in India include the afore-mentioned sugarcane and cotton, as well as jute and onions (Giriappa and Vivekananda 1984, p. 14). Additionally, India is the largest producer of tea and dairy products, and is the second-largest producer of fruit and vegetables (WTO 2007, p. 101).

The northern states of Punjab and Haryana are among the higher-performing states in India, in terms of output growth (Alagh and Bhalla 1979, p. 25). Data from 2004 indicate that 32.03 per cent of Haryana's GDP was contributed by agricultural produce, while 39.8 per cent of Punjab's GDP constituted agriculture(IFFCO 2004). The following is a summary of the main crops, described above, that are produced by India and the regions in which they are cultivated:

- Food grains: the primary food grains produced in India are rice, wheat and maize. Uttar Pradesh excels in growing wheat and pulses. Punjab is a large producer of rice and wheat. Uttar Pradesh, West Bengal and Punjab account for 43.23 per cent of the country's total food grain production (IFFCO 2004).
- Oil seeds: India produces groundnut, mustard, sunflower and soy beans; which are used in oil production. Rajasthan produces mustard and rape seed, while Madhya Pradesh and Maharashtra cultivate soy beans. Collectively Madhya Pradesh, Maharashtra and Rajasthan contribute 47.01 per cent of India's total oil seed produce (IFFCO 2004).
- Cash crops: cash crops cultivated in India include jute, sugarcane, cotton, potato and onions. Uttar Pradesh is the main producer of sugarcane and potatoes, while Maharashtra and Gujarat produce cotton and West Bengal produces jute. Together, Maharashtra, Gujarat and Karnataka account for 56.69 per cent of India's cash crop produce (IFFCO 2004).

The higher living standards in India are causing a change in the structure of demand for food. Per capita consumption of cereals has decreased, while that of meat and dairy has increased (WTO 2007, p. 101). This will likely lead to a change in production in the period 2010–20. The food processing sector has also been taking off recently and is set to expand further in the future. In general, the composition of agriculture in India has changed only slightly over the past 50 years. Most importantly, the production of wheat (by weight) has increased while that of coarse grain has fallen (see Figure 5.2). This may also be attributed to the improvement in living standards in India.

Contribution of agriculture to GDP

Agriculture's value-added as a percentage of GDP has declined over the years. It remained high until the mid-1970s, and began to decline from around 1978 (Figure 5.3). This is in line with India's economic development; that is, as the economy grows, agriculture's share of output contracts with respect to other sectors. Although the contribution of agriculture to GDP has fallen steadily over the years, it still contributes 18 per cent of India's value-added as a proportion of GDP. Despite India's high rate of growth in the industrial and service sector, agriculture continued to be the main source of livelihood for over 60 per cent of the Indian labour force in 1995 (Kumar 2005).

Since 1960, India's economy has shifted away from agriculture and towards the tertiary sector. In 1960, GDP was made up of agriculture (46

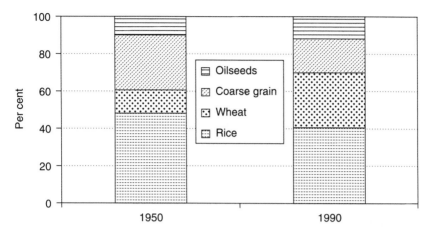

Source: World Bank (2007).

Figure 5.2   Composition of agriculture in India by weight

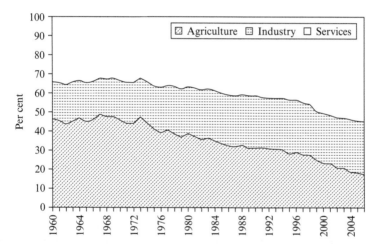

Source: World Bank (2007).

Figure 5.3   Composition of economy (value-added, % of GDP), India, 1960–2004

per cent), industry (20 per cent) and services (34 per cent). By 2005, the contribution of agriculture to GDP had fallen to 17 per cent while that of services had increased to 55 per cent. Industry became slightly more important too.

In 2003, 60 per cent of employment was in agriculture, while 12 per cent was in industry and 28 per cent in services (World Bank 2009). Yet in 2003, agriculture accounted for only 21 per cent of GDP, implying that labour productivity in agriculture is a third of that in other sectors.

Contribution of agriculture to foreign exchange

India's trade import and export policies are designed to aid in achieving self-sufficiency in food, while the flow of trade is also monitored to stabilise prices. India achieved self-sufficiency in agriculture in the early years of its development. Subsequently it has been a net exporter of agricultural commodities, with agricultural exports outweighing agricultural imports. The 2001/02 survey reports that in 2000, India's agricultural imports were only US$1.8 billion, as compared to agricultural exports of more than US$6 billion. Imports stagnated in the early 1990s, and have since grown at a slower rate than exports. This outcome is most likely a reflection of the government's aim to promote exports while restricting imports. However, Indian agricultural exports have slowed in recent years. This has been partly contributed to by distorted domestic prices of products such as rice, wheat, tea, coffee and so on. Indian agricultural exports have also stagnated due to a shortage of infrastructure specific to agriculture.

Indian agricultural exports can be divided into three broad categories: (1) raw products; (2) semi-raw products; and (3) ready-to-eat products (Ministry of Finance 2001 p. 168). Agricultural exports account for 13 per cent to 18 per cent of total exports (Ministry of Finance 2001, p. 168). Cereals (mostly basmati and non-basmati rice) are the most prominent Indian agricultural exports. In 2005/06, rice and marine products represented the largest share of exports, with 19.2 per cent and 15.8 per cent respectively. Tea, coffee, cashews and oil meals are other major agricultural exports (Ministry of Finance 2006, p. 68).

In recent years edible oils have been the single largest agricultural import commodity, accounting for 56.1 per cent of total agricultural imports in 2005/06. Other major imports include raw cashew nuts (from the USA) and pulses, each of which account for over 10 per cent. These are mainly imported to supplement domestic supply. Raw cashew nuts are imported for processing and re-exporting as domestic cashew supply is not sufficient to meet the processing capacity. Sugar and cereals, which account for a small share of imports, have experienced a decline in recent years (Ministry of Finance 2006, p. 169).

It has generally been the policy that import duties should be low for essential products where domestic production cannot meet demand. This is reflected in the case of pulses, which have zero import duty. In 2000/2001 import tariffs were increased for many agricultural and allied imports, such as rice, wheat, millet and apples. This was in response to fears of large-scale dumping of such products in the Indian market as a result of import liberalisation. The Ministry of Commerce and Industry states that India's priority lies in safeguarding the interests of Indian farmers by providing appropriate levels of tariff protection on agricultural imports while taking into account food security and livelihood concerns and increased access of Indian agricultural exports. However, contrary to concerns, agricultural imports have continuously contracted.

Overall, Indian tariffs fell from 32 per cent in 2002 to 16 per cent in 2007 (WTO 2007, p. 38). Meanwhile the tariff on agricultural products (HS01-24) increased slightly from 41.7 per cent to 42.7 per cent (WTO 2007, p. 39). Most tariff percentages are in the high 30s, but there are some exceptions, such as the tariff on beverages, spirits and vinegar (HS22) at over 120 per cent. There is also a substantial difference between applied and bound tariff rates on many goods. This leaves the Indian government scope to adjust tariffs from year to year, creating uncertainty in the market, especially among farmers. Indian policies have generally promoted exports of agricultural products. Recently, policy has focused on making exports more competitive by trying to strengthen research and development (R&D). On rare occasions, however, the government intervenes to reduce exports of food if it feels this may be needed domestically. In spite of this, exports have fallen relative to total trade (see Figure 5.4). Meanwhile, food imports have remained at around 5 per cent of total imports since 1988. The relative decline in exports reflects India's rise as a manufacturer.

Reforms

Preplanning period

During the early stages of British rule there was no state policy that aimed at improving the utilisation of natural resources. Land tenures, irrigation schemes and so on were motivated by revenue considerations (Sarma 1981, p. 11). Subsequent to the recommendations of the Royal Commission on Agriculture, 1928, steps were taken to undertake agricultural research and education, but action on recommendations was not taken due to financial constraints (Sarma 1981, p. 11). After the fall of Burma in the Second World War, the government launched a Grow More Food Campaign, to meet demand that was previously fulfilled by Burmese imports. This was done through diversion of land from cash crops to food, intensive cultivation, fertilisers and irrigation.

In 1946 the first agricultural plan was issued as the Statement of Agricultural and Food Policy in India. It was aimed at increasing food grain production, stimulating raw material production, securing fair

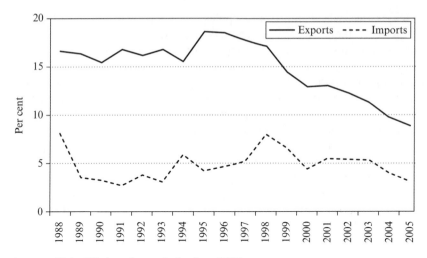

Source: United Nations Comtrade database (2007).

Figure 5.4   Trade in food as a proportion of total trade, India, 1988–2005

wages for agricultural labour and distributing food fairly. The implementation of this plan receded into the background in the face of Partition and Independence in 1947 (Sarma 1981, p. 12).

Agricultural policy 1950–70

When India gained independence in 1947, the task at hand for policy-makers was to assess economic resources and productive capacity on hand. The main economic activity, agriculture, was stagnant, characterised by primitive technology and a feudal land system. As a result total output and productivity were low, and poverty was widespread (Prasad 2006, p. vii). There were very few educational institutions, little industry, low national savings, minimal capital and the prospect of a grim future. Prime Minister Nehru faced the daunting task of using agriculture to stimulate India out of poverty, while aiming for rapid growth and industrialisation through the development of basic industries such as steel and machinery. Kaushik (1997, p. 71) refers to this as the two-sector model, where agriculture, as one sector, will maintain growth at a steady pace while industry, as the second sector, will be instrumental in development and industrialisation.

The solution was found in economic planning, and the First Five Year Plan was developed for the period 1951 to 1956. It was acknowledged that agriculture was the main occupation for roughly 70 per cent of the population, yet it suffered from low productivity. The First Five Year Plan (Planning Commission, Government of India 1951) recommended equal investment in agriculture as well as industry. The government was to provide loans, seeds and irrigation to farmers at subsidised rates. Agriculture was given top priority. The plan placed emphasis on the diversion of agriculture and recognised that without having high productivity of food and raw materials it would be impossible to achieve higher levels of investment (Sarma 1981, p. 12).

Subsequently, agriculture was not given paramount importance in the Second Five Year Plan (1956–61) since the targets for food grain production had been met by the first plan. The Second Five Year Plan stated that during the first year it was of crucial importance that the agricultural programmes must succeed, for no other consideration had equal significance for the stability of the economy as a whole. The second plan focused on strengthening the interdependence between agricultural and industrial development. It took a long-term view of growth, in order to ensure balanced development of agriculture as well as industry. Priority was given to heavy industry over agriculture.

The Third Five Year Plan (1961–66) took a comprehensive approach to developing agricultural infrastructure and reconstruction of the rural economy. Financial support was provided at an adequate scale, and programmes including irrigation networks and soil conservation were undertaken. During this period, Indian farmers faced adverse weather conditions and a severe drought. Nineteen million tons of cereal were imported to prevent widespread starvation, and it became clear to the government that food self-sufficiency had to be achieved as early as possible.

Agricultural policy 1970–90
The Fourth Plan and plans thereafter evolved from the successes and failures of the 1960s (Kaushik 1997, p. 75). In the agricultural sector, focus shifted from increasing food grain output through more land cultivation, to increasing productivity through expansion of irrigation and use of fertilisers and hybrid seeds.

The Fourth Five Year Plan stated its first objective as sustaining an increase in agricultural production of 5 per cent (Planning Commission, Government of India 1969). The plan recognised that the pace of development in the agricultural sector was limiting the rate of growth of industry and the economy as a whole. The second objective was to enable as large a section of the rural population as possible to participate in the development process and share its benefits. The strategy for achieving higher agricultural growth was centred on intensive agriculture; that is, expansion of irrigation facilities, as well as fertiliser supply, plant protection material, farm machinery and credit. Measures were also taken to improve the marketing of agricultural output and increase the intensity of cultivation.

Subsequent to the success of the Fourth Five Year Plan and the Green Revolution, the Fifth and the Sixth Five Year Plans focused on consolidating the gains that had already been achieved. In addition to this, the Fifth Plan stated the goal of making agricultural growth not just an instrument of maintaining an effective national food security system, but also a source of income growth and employment generation in rural areas (Planning Commission, Government of India 1974). The Ninth Plan defines food security as adequate availability of basic food items, particularly food grains, in the country as a whole; and also the availability of adequate purchasing power to meet food requirements at the household level (Planning Commission, Government of India 1997). These plans were successful in increasing agricultural output; however the large increases remained confined to areas that were well endowed with infrastructure such as irrigation, electricity and roads. The Seventh Plan stated that although these areas accounted for less than 15 per cent of the area under cultivation, they contributed up to 56 per cent of the increase in food grain production (Planning Commission, Government of India 1985).

Eradication of imbalances of distribution associated with previous plans was an objective of the Seventh Five Year Plan (Planning Commission, Government of India 1985). This was to be achieved through the development of small and marginal farmers. Special programmes were designed to provide assistance in irrigation and provide various inputs. The programmes were supplemented by measures to increase their access to credit facilities.

Policies regarding availability of infrastructure and technology were successful to a large extent. Much of the increase in the usage of tractors and fertilisers occurred in the 1970s, during the Green Revolution, and continued in the decades to come. The Eighth Five Year Plan acknowledged that over this period agriculture made important strides and was able to meet the growing demand for food.

Policy reforms 1991 onwards
The 1990s saw India take an aggressive approach to opening up to the outside world. This had important implications for the agricultural sector due to the liberalisation of trade policy. P.V. Narsimha Rao became party leader after the assassination of Rajiv Gandhi. Rao accepted that India had matured as a country (Kaushik 1997, p. 78). It now had an economy that needed less supervision and planning. Economic liberalisation and opening up to the world was deemed to be essential to achieve a higher rate of growth and development. Soon after coming to power, Finance Minister Dr Manmohan Singh announced financial liberalisation which led to significant reductions in tariffs and import quotas.

The Eighth Five Year Plan was aimed at consolidating the gains that

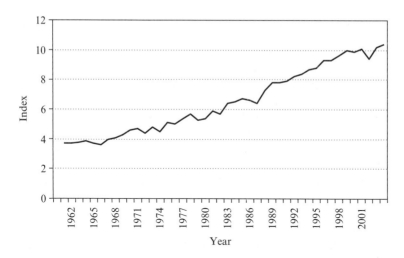

Source: TISS (2005).

Figure 5.5   Crop production index (1999–2001 = 100), India, 1962–2001

were made over the years (Planning Commission, Government of India 1992, s. 1.11.1). This included sustaining the improvements made in productivity and production to meet the demands of an increasing population, increasing agricultural exports and increasing the income of farmers. Special emphasis was placed on the cultivation of specific crops such as rice and oilseeds. Plantation crops were also given greater importance, due to their export value.

The Ninth Five Year Plan acknowledged the growth of Indian agriculture, from the stagnant agricultural system that was inherited from the British in 1947, to a system of high productivity and production due to the use of modern technology (Planning Commission, Government of India 1997). For example, agriculture had grown at a rate of 2.7 per cent per annum after Independence, which was much higher than the 0.3 per cent pre-Independence. In the period 1962–2001, for example, crop production increased steadily (Figure 5.5), and made a significant contribution to agricultural output. The Ninth Plan focused on ensuring food security. This could be achieved through doubling food production and distributing food to those below the poverty line.

Many have been critical of the government's reform of agriculture. Firstly, some suggest that the government went too far in neglecting agriculture in favour of industry. Further, public investment in infrastructure has fallen dramatically since the 1980s. Unfortunately, much of this infrastructure is subject to the free-rider problem, such as roads and water management systems (Ahluwalia 2002, p. 77). A further problem is that property rights are poorly defined for tenant farmers; thus there is little incentive for farmers to improve their land (WTO 2007, p. 101). It has also been suggested that the subsidisation of fertilizers and irrigation has led to waterlogging and degradation of the land (WTO 2007, p. 100).

The Uruguay Round was the first forum to discuss agricultural trade. This resulted in the Agreement on Agriculture. Prior to this, trade negotiation excluded agricultural trade. World Trade Organization (WTO) members entered into the Doha Round in 2001, agreeing to meet three requirements, the first of which was the elimination of export subsidies which distort trade. The second was substantially to reduce domestic subsidies which distort trade and the third was to provide improvements in market access by lowering tariffs and reducing quota restrictions. At the moment there are two primary groups of countries: a group that is protectionist towards domestic agriculture, including countries such as Norway, Japan and Korea; and a second group, which consists of agriculture-exporting countries. This group is in favour of liberalising agricultural trade and reducing distortion caused by protection.

The Indian Ministry of Commerce and Industry states that India has been building coalitions with other WTO members which are pursuing similar objectives. India organised a meeting in 2003 of 'like-minded developing countries' (Ministry of Commerce and Industry, Government of India 2003) to discuss issues of common interest, such as food security, rural development and livelihood concerns. In 2001 India presented a list of proposals to the Committee on Agriculture, which highlighted that the main issue of the negotiations was to phase out distortions and provide food and livelihood security in rural sectors.

The Indian Ministry of Finance has acknowledged that following the removal of quantitative restrictions on imports according to the Agreement on Agriculture, one of the major challenges faced by Indian agriculture is to raise the level of productivity and quality standards to internationally competitive levels. However, despite the challenges, the liberalisation of world agricultural trade has also opened new avenues of growth for the Indian economy.

In 2007, the Indian Ministry of Commerce and Industry stated that it was disappointed with a WTO draft paper on agriculture because it took into account the concerns of developed countries, whereas the issues of developing countries were left unaddressed. India continues to feel that any outcome of the Doha Round that does not address the issues faced by farmers in less developed countries (LDCs) may risk the failure of negotiations (Ministry of Commerce and Industry 2007). It is imperative for the

Indian government to form concrete plans to increase the competitiveness of Indian agriculture in world trade. This can be done through negotiating a reduction in support given to agriculture in developed countries, while simultaneously maintaining domestic support to increase competitiveness. However, one of the points that the policy-makers must keep in mind, while formulating policies to develop agriculture, is to undertake measures to support small and marginal farmers as well.

Problems Faced by the Indian Agricultural Sector

Increasing debt of Indian farmers

In terms of obtaining finance, the Indian agricultural sector is greatly dis-advantaged relative to other sectors such as industry. Farmers are often left in the hands of money lenders who charge exorbitant rates of interest on their lending. Borrowing costs must be reduced, but the urban-based banks are reluctant to venture into rural credit.

Farm and non-farm productive purposes account for only 37 per cent of total debts, while unproductive purposes accounted for the remaining 63 per cent (Agrawal 1964). A considerable amount of the borrowings for productive purposes may in fact be used in unproductive purposes. Thus a high proportion of debt in Indian agriculture is used to fund current consumption and does not enhance repayment capacity. Furthermore, a given amount of debt bears heavily on Indian farmers due to high interest rates.

The major cause for farmer suicides is indebtedness (TISS 2005, p. 17), and indebtedness is the product of bad credit policy that has been followed for a long period of time. Tata Institute of Social Sciences (TISS) reports that: 'the indebtedness results from a mismatch in the cost of production and the support price and the market price that the cultivators are receiving at the end of every cropping cycle' (TISS 2005, p. 35). Farmers who borrow money so that they may feed their families are getting stuck in a vicious cycle.

Problems in marketing produce

Marketing is the last stage in the production process. If the marketing system is inefficient, it denies farmers a reasonable return for their effort, and they may be less inclined to produce more (Prasad 2006, p. 15). Traditionally, farmers have been price takers. There are several reasons for this: (1) because weak finance force farmers to sell their produce promptly after harvest; (2) supply is elastic; and (3) the farmer has to sell at the going price even if he finds it too low. Farmers require warehouses that can be used to store the crop. This will give them greater flexibility regarding the timing of the sale, and may enable them to realise a higher price. The Indian government, however, has been slow to recognise this growing need of farmers, and the required investment has not been made.

Small landholdings
As a result of population growth, there has been increased pressure on cultivated land, resulting in fragmentation and overcrowding on land-holdings. Consequently, it has become increasingly difficult to use modern machinery and technology. Additionally, there are several quarrels and litigations among farmers (Prasad 2006, p. 15).

Archaic methods of cultivation
As mentioned above, various attempts have been made to modernise cultivation techniques in India. However they have remained largely inadequate, as Indian farmers continue to depend on the often untimely monsoon, and use primitive technology; 63 per cent of arable land is still rain fed, with the slow pace of irrigation development constraining agri-cultural productivity (Passi 1998). The lack of good-quality seeds is also to blame for agricultural backwardness in India. This problem has been corrected to a large extent through the provision of high yielding variety (HYV) seeds during the Green Revolution (Agrawal 1964). Furthermore, modern farm machinery is limited, as is the use of fertilisers.

Instability in agricultural output
Although growth in the rate of food grain output has improved dramati-cally over the decades, the growth performance has not been consistent. Instability in agricultural output has in fact increased since the Green Revolution. The poor, particularly those belonging to drought-prone areas, continue to suffer from fluctuations in employment and income. The main cause for this instability in output is an increase in response of output to water (Hanumantha Rao 1994, p. 24). That is, for a given varia-bility in rainfall or moisture, the instability in output is greater now due to new technology such as fertilisers. The instability is greater for crops such as oilseeds and rice, mainly because there has been an increase in the appli-cation of new seed-fertiliser technology, yet these crops continue to be cultivated in areas that are rain fed, or areas where irrigation is uncertain.

Lack of irrigation facilities and droughts
Despite the efforts of the Indian government, less than a third of cultivated land is serviced by irrigation facilities. Consequently, many Indian farmers still depend on the irregular and uncertain monsoon (Prasad 2006, p. 13). There is a growing indication that the severity of droughts has increased over time (Hanumantha Rao 1994, p. 29). This is due to insufficient

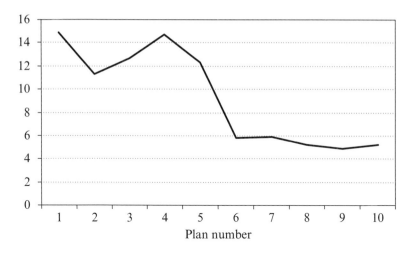

Source: TISS (2005), p. 36.

Figure 5.6   *Percentage of agriculture and allied sector to total outlay, India*

retention of moisture in soil and the subsequent lowering of the water table. In addition, ecological degradation has made droughts more severe.

Fickle monsoons have forced many marginal farmers into cash crop cultivation. Since cash crops require investment in terms of technology, this system is pushing an increasing number of farmers into the debt cycle (TISS 2005).

Government support
The government has remained largely indifferent in its attitute to the plight of the farmers. Many policies have been developed to ease the financial burden, but little has been implemented. There has been a sharp decline in funding for the agricultural sector, even though it continues to employ a large proportion of the Indian population. Funding has fallen in real as well as relative terms, and spending in other sectors of the economy has directed funds away from agriculture, leading to its current situation (TISS 2005) (see Figures 5.6 and 5.7).

The Performance of Indian Agriculture

Agricultural productivity of the four major crop categories has increased since 1950. Productivity of food grains has shown the largest increase, while productivity of pulses has not increased significantly. The main reason for

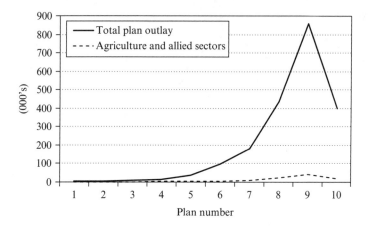

Source: TISS (2005), p. 36.

Figure 5.7   Plan outlay in agricultural and allied sectors, India

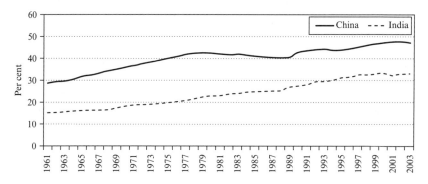

Source: World Bank (2007).

Figure 5.8   Irrigated land (% of crop land), 1961–2003

this observation is the percentage of area under irrigation (see Figure 5.8);
the percentage of food grain cultivated area which is covered by irrigation
facilities has increased from 31.7 per cent in 1950 to 53.6 per cent in 2000.
This has resulted in large increases in productivity. On the other hand the
pulses cultivated area that is covered by irrigation amounted to only 12.5
per cent in 2000. The largest increase in productivity was observed in the
early 1980s, when the effects of the Green Revolution of the 1970s became
evident, mainly due to increased mechanisation, better irrigation, the use
of fertilisers, and the introduction of high-yield wheat and rice varieties

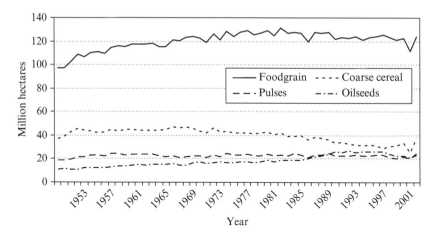

Source: Indian Farmers Fertiliser Cooperative Limited (2004), p. 40.

Figure 5.9   Area under cultivation (million hectares), India, 1953–2001

(WTO 2007, p. 101). Since food grains were the targeted crops in the Green Revolution, the largest increase in productivity is evident in this category.

The use of tractors became popular in the 1970s, and growth in tractors accelerated again in the 1980s. There are more tractors relative to land in India than in China (see next section). However, fertilisers have not taken off in the same way as in China. Fertiliser usage barely increased during the Green Revolution, despite the government's intentions (see Figure 5.9). The area of irrigated cropland has been increasing since the 1970s, though it is still strikingly low at just over 30 per cent.There have been few noteworthy changes in the area under cultivation (see Figure 5.9), yet crop yield has increased (see Figure 5.10) due to an increase in productivity, that is, cropping intensity has increased.

CHINA

China has been the fastest-growing economy in the world since the early 1990s, with an annual GDP growth rate in excess of 10 per cent, increasing GDP per capita and decreasing poverty (Figure 5.11). Although China is renowned for its labour-intensive manufacturing sector and industry, agriculture continues to be a crucial sector in the economy. China is the world's most populous country and has succeeded in feeding over 20 per cent of the world's population with only 7 per cent of the world's arable

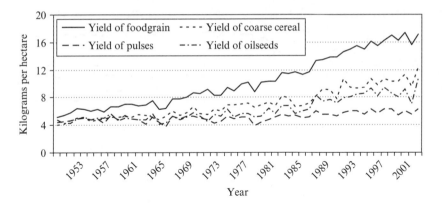

Source: Indian Farmers Fertiliser Cooperative Limited (2004), p. 40.

Figure 5.10   Yield of crops (kilograms/hectare), India, 1953–2001

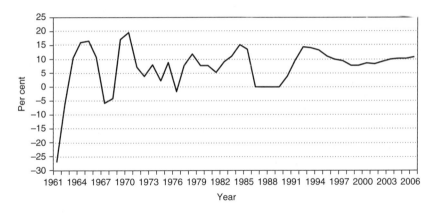

Source: World Bank (2007).

Figure 5.11   GDP growth rate, China, 1961–2006

land. This section provides an overview of the importance of agriculture to the economy of China, with special emphasis on composition of agriculture, agricultural reforms and mechanisation and productivity.

Historical Growth Pattern of the Chinese Economy

When the Communist Party came in to power in 1949, it was faced with widespread poverty, income inequality and productivity unable to keep pace with an increasing population. The government undertook a series of reforms aiming to transform China into a modern and powerful nation, with socialist ideals. Growth was volatile; however good economic policy has ensured that growth has been consistently in excess of 5 per cent for the last decade, withstanding economic and financial turmoil in East Asian countries. While this growth rate may be poised to decline, China has achieved remarkable economic success since the mid-1980s. The Chinese economy has grown at an impressive rate, lifting millions from poverty and raising the living standards of many more.

Despite the size of its population, China has historically had a surprisingly small role to play in the world economy. However, since the 1970s, the Chinese government has taken tangible steps to integrate China with the rest of the world, undertaking a number of reforms aimed at liberalising trade and investment, establishing itself as a key player in the world arena. The structure of the Chinese economy has undergone significant change, with industry and services overtaking agriculture to become bigger employers and contributors to GDP.

Like India, the prospects for the Chinese economy are strong for future growth and development. With consistently high demand for manufactures and services, China is likely to continue to grow steadily, withstanding uncertain economic times in the rest of the world.

Agriculture and Economic Growth

Composition
Grain production is of particular importance to China, as it is by far the largest crop category. Figure 5.12 shows the composition of agriculture in China for selected years, and shows the composition before and after the household system reforms. Products are measured as a proportion of the goods total weight. The changes across time paint an interesting picture of the composition of China's agricultural output. The decline of grain is clear, especially after the introduction of the household responsibility system. In its place, sugarcane, fruit, livestock and aquatic products became much more common. This is in line with the development of the Chinese economy as a whole; however it is not likely that the dominant position of grain cultivation in Chinese agriculture will change in the near future (Guohua and Peel 1991, p. 76).

Chinese custom divides food into two main categories: main food, which includes rice, wheat and maize; and auxiliary food, comprising vegetables, meat, eggs and milk. Rice, wheat and maize are the three main grain crops, and occupied 56.2 per cent of the area sown in 1986 (Guohua and Peel 1991, p. 77). The following provides a summary of the main crops produced:

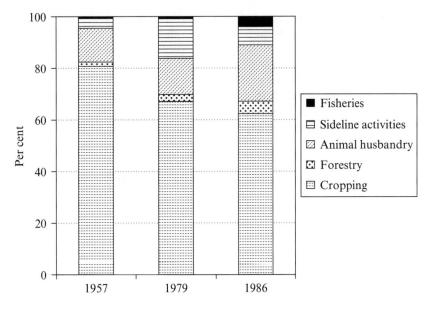

Source: Guohua and Peel (1991), p. 74.

Figure 5.12   Gross output value of agriculture, China

- Food grains: China has the longest history of rice cultivation in
  the world. Rice is the primary crop grown in China, with the total
  planted area of rice in China second only to India and accounting
  for a marked one-third of world production. Wheat is the second-
  largest crop in China. It is the staple for people in Northern China,
  and is mainly cultivated in that region. Maize was introduced to
  China in the sixteenth century, and it is now one of the three main
  crops in the country. Cultivation of maize is concentrated in a belt
  stretching from the Northeast to the Southwest. Other grain crops
  include millet, barley and soya beans (Guohua and Peel 1991, pp.
  83–9).
- Oilseeds: peanut and rape are the main oilseeds cultivated in China.
  In 1986, they accounted for over 80 per cent of oil-bearing crops
  (Guohua and Peel 1991, p. 91)
- Cash crops: cotton is the most important cash crop cultivated in
  China, and is the main raw material for China's large textile industry. Other cash crops include fibre crops, such as jute and hemp,
  sugarcane, tea and tobacco (Guohua and Peel 1991, pp. 90–93).

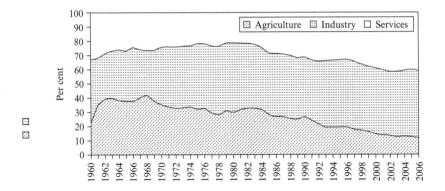

Source: World Bank (2007).

Figure 5.13   *Composition of economy, value-added (% of GDP), China, 1960–2005*

Contribution of agriculture to GDP

Although agriculture has always been regarded as an important part of the Chinese economy, the structure of China's economy has shifted from agriculture to services, while industry has remained important. This is best displayed by Figure 5.13. In 1960, China's GDP was made up of agriculture (22 per cent), industry (45 per cent) and services (33 per cent). In 2005, agriculture fell to 11 per cent of GDP, industry increased slightly to 47 per cent, while the tertiary sector increased to 41 per cent.

Agriculture is closely related to manufacturing and other industries in China. Raw materials used in industry are largely provided by the agricultural sector (see Figure 5.14). Additionally, a large proportion of the Chinese population is employed by agriculture (see Figure 5.15). Although the proportion of the total labour force engaged in agriculture is falling, the actual number is still increasing (Guohua and Peel 1991, p. 187). Agriculture still provides around 45 per cent of employment, despite contributing only 11 per cent to GDP. This anomaly goes some way to display the poor state of labour productivity in agriculture.

Contribution of agriculture to foreign exchange

Agricultural products traditionally play an important role in accumulating foreign exchange. Since the Communist Party took control of China in 1949, after the Chinese Civil War, trade strategy and implementation has been heavily influenced by state ideology (Srinivasan 1994, p. 109). Traditionally, agricultural exports have made up a significant proportion

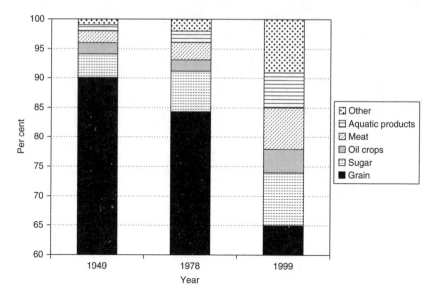

*Figure 5.14   Contribution of major agricultural products (by weights),
China, 1949–1999*

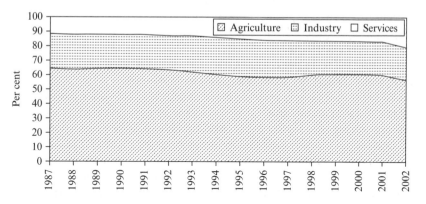

Source: Beijing International (2007).

Figure 5.15   Employment by sector, China, 1987–2002

of China's trade. Exported items include food grains, peanuts, eggs,
poultry, fruit and cotton yarn. Other more traditional items include
herbal medicine and green tea. Although agricultural exports constitute
a considerable proportion of exports, the trend for a number of decades
has been an increase in industrial and mineral exports as a proportion

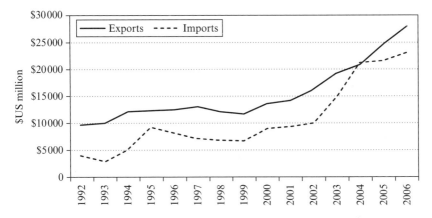

Source: United Nations Comtrade database (2007).

Figure 5.16   Trade in food, China, 1992–2006

of total exports (Guohua and Peel 1991, p. 185). Consequently, agricultural exports are no longer so important for foreign exchange earnings.

China's trade in food was relatively stable up until 2001. After 2001, exports and especially imports increased dramatically (Figure 5.16). This suggests that China's accession to the WTO has strengthened her export ability, while also providing access to international markets. This is in line with China's economic liberalisation process. Meanwhile, the substantial increase in imports goes against China's goal to remain self-sufficient in food. When considering China's recent trade figures, one should keep in mind that many think that China's yuan has been largely undervalued for the last few years. This would effectively widen its trade balance by making exports more competitive and imports less competitive.

Despite these increases, trade in food has decreased relative to total exports. This relationship is shown clearly in Figure 5.17. This reflects the structural changes to China's economy, whereby agricultural production has fallen as a proportion of GDP. Meanwhile, China's manufacturing sector has taken off, becoming the most dominant source of export revenue. Imports of inputs into manufacturing have also become more important in recent years.

China's trade in food is significantly larger than India's, largely due to China pursuing more aggressive open door policies, alongside lower tariffs. Additionally, China has taken substantial steps to establish the competitiveness and quality of its agricultural exports, whereas India has lagged behind in quality control of food exports and has higher tariffs.

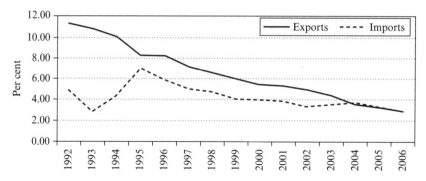

Source: United Nations Comtrade database (2007).

Figure 5.17   Trade in food as a proportion of total trade, China, 1992–2006

Reforms

Agricultural reform in China has been faster and more radical when compared to India. The communist goal of better living for the entire population drove bottom-up change, beginning with agricultural reforms (Gulati and Fan 2007, p. 10). In later years, China placed considerable emphasis on the development of the heavy industry sector; however the pace of industrialisation can be constricted by development in the agricultural sector. The major changes in Chinese agricultural policy can be divided into two phases: the collectivisation period, 1952–78; and the household responsibility system reform period from 1978 onwards (Srinivasan 1994, p. 32).

Pre-reform period
Traditionally, Chinese agriculture has been characterised by small, independent household farms. Typical farms were small and fragmented. At the time of the socialist revolution in the 1940s, close to 40 per cent of the land was owned by landlords, who leased land to peasants at a rent sometimes as high as 50 per cent of the value of the main crop (Srinivasan 1994, p. 33). When the socialists gained control of China in the late 1940s, they initiated reforms aimed at consolidating landholdings. This system became widespread by 1952, and was known as the collectivisation period.

The collectivisation period (1952–78)
As mentioned above, although the Chinese government placed considerable emphasis on the development of heavy industry and industrialisation,

it was acknowledged that agriculture too required resources and investment. However the government, reluctant to divert resources from industrial development, adopted a new agricultural development strategy that it felt would not compete with the industrial sector for inputs (Srinivasan 1994, p. 32). Under the collectivisation reforms, the government confiscated land from landlords and rich peasants, without any compensation, and gave it to poor, landless peasants (Srinivasan 1994, p. 23).

The official approach to collectivisation was cautious initially, with peasant households encouraged to join and form co-operatives on a voluntary basis. Co-operatives ranged from mutual aid teams, in which four to five neighbouring peasant households pooled resources such as tools and animals together, and engaged in labour exchanges; to elementary co-operatives, in which 20 to 30 neighbouring households pooled tools, animals and land under unified management (Srinivasan, 1994, pp. 33–4). The third co-operative was the advanced co-operative, in which all means of production were collectively owned. The most popular co-operative was initially the mutual aid team. In 1957 the number of advanced co-operative farms increased to 753000 from only 500 in 1955, with 119 million member households (Srinivasan 1994, p. 35). Collectivisation was highly successful, with large increases in grain output. The initial success was the basis of greater confidence in the commune system and led to a bolder approach to collectivisation, the people's commune. The people's commune consisted of about 30 collectives, with 150 households each (Srinivasan 1994, p. 35). All resources were shared resources, and peasants were not allowed to work on private land.

The agricultural crisis of 1959–61 ended the commune movement that had experienced great success. Grain output fell alongside the value of agricultural produce, leading to widespread famine. It is estimated that 30 million people died of starvation and malnutrition during this period. Following the crisis, greater emphasis was placed on modern agricultural inputs. Irrigated land was increased, as was the application of chemical fertilisers and use of high-yielding varieties of seeds. Additionally, programmes were established to encourage agricultural research. However, despite the increased agricultural effort, performance in the sector remained poor in the 1960s and 1970s. This prompted further reforms in 1979.

The household responsibility reform period (1978 onwards)   The bleak outlook on Chinese agriculture changed in 1979 when the government created the household responsibility system, as part of the four modernizations campaign. The programme, which only became common in the early 1980s, saw the land divided up and distributed to the production teams, which could lease it under long-term contracts. This strengthened the link between effort and reward. As such, there were greater incentives to become more efficient, produce more and to seek new production opportunities. However, the subdivision of production management to individual households was seen as a violation of socialist principles and initially prohibited.

In 1985, the government sought to resolve the pricing problem further by abolishing the fixed quota system. Any produce not purchased by the government could be sold on the open market. To a limited extent, this allowed demand and supply to help allocate resources between industries. It also helped create incentives for workers and provided price signals to all actors.

The 1990s were troubled by a growing disparity between quota prices and market prices, causing the government constantly to update the quota prices (Saich 2004, p. 250). In 2003, the government abolished this system, paying subsidies directly to farmers and letting them decide what to produce (Saich 2004, p. 250). This was probably inevitable, following China's entry to the WTO.

The state's pricing controls have been eased since 1998. While tobacco is still subject to state pricing, prices on other products are 'guided' by the government. Under this system, the price is usually allowed to fluctuate within a small range (WTO 2006, p. clxxx).

Foreign policy reforms   China's current foreign trade policy is designed to accelerate its opening to the outside world, develop foreign trade and promote sound economic development (WTO 2006, p. liv). However, the policy is still somewhat protective, aiming to safeguard farmers' incomes. China has embraced economic regionalism and free trade in the last few years. In 1991, China joined the Asia-Pacific Economic Cooperation (APEC), an important trading group. China also signed a free trade agreement (FTA) with Chile in 2005 and has agreed to establish FTAs with the Association of South East Asian Nations (ASEAN), Australia and New Zealand. China's commitment to freer trade culminated in the country's entrance to the WTO in late 2001.

China's accession to the WTO has seen major reduction in tariffs across the board (Table 5.1). Applied tariffs on agriculture were 15.3 per cent in 2005, down from 23.1 per cent in 2001. However, tariffs on agriculture are still above the average on all products of 9.7 per cent. Tariffs on grain and dairy products also fell substantially from very high rates in 2001.

Falling protection and changes in domestic and foreign policy have resulted in trade patterns that are more consistent with China's comparative advantage. Exports of bulk commodities such as grains have fallen,

Table 5.1   Applied tarriffs in China, 2001 and 2005

Year	2001 (%)	2005 (%)
Agriculture	23.1	15.3
Grain	51.9	33.9
Oilseeds	32.0	11.1
Sugar	n/a	29.9
Confectionary	n/a	25.4
Dairy products	35.9	12.1

Source: WTO (2006), pp. clxxii–clxxiv.

while those of value-added and more labour-intensive products, such as horticultural and animal products, have risen (Gulati and Fan 2007, p. 287).

Problems Faced by the Chinese Agricultural Sector

Lack of water resources
Like India, China also faces problems in ensuring that irrigation facilities are available to all cultivated areas. Although close to 50 per cent of China's cultivated land is serviced by irrigation systems, the growth of industry and urbanisation has meant that an increasing amount of water is consumed for industrial and domestic purposes (Guohua and Peel 1991, p. 259). A rapid fall in the water table in some regions further aggravates this issue. Moreover, droughts and floods occur regularly in some regions of China, causing great hardship for farmers (Shaohua and Veek 2000, p. 60).

Desertification, soil erosion and loss of cultivated land
Desertification in the arid parts of western China is recognised as a serious problem. Furthermore, fertility and soil quality is decreasing as a result of water and wind erosion (Guohua and Peel 1991, p. 259).

As a result of industrialisation, urbanisation and population growth, large areas of cultivated land have been lost to agriculture (Guohoa and Peel 1991, p. 258). It is reported that on an average over 700 000 hectares of agricultural land was taken over for other activities every year in the 1980s.

Performance of Chinese Agriculture

Agricultural productivity in general has increased in China over the past few decades. China's investment in agriculture was minimal in 1949, but

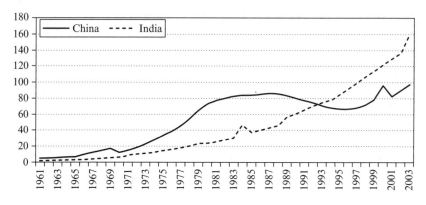

Source: World Bank (2007).

Figure 5.18   Tractors per 100 hectares of arable land, 1961–2003

grew rapidly in the 1950s. The Chinese government gave top priority to irrigation facilities in 1949 (Gulati and Fan 2007, p. 128). Investment in irrigation continued to grow until 1966, establishing an irrigation system that covered 46 per cent of the country's cultivated land by 1986, making China the country with the largest irrigated area in the world according to the United Nations (Guohua and Peel 1991, pp. 144–5). This has led to greater productivity.

Tractors became very popular in China in the 1970s. In 1973 there were roughly 20 tractors per hectare of arable land, increasing to 80 in 1983 (Figure 5.18). The use of tractors increased dramatically in the early 1980s as peasants began to take the initiative to purchase their own capital. Likewise, fertiliser consumption increased dramatically from the late 1980s onwards. The reforms described created incentives for farmers to invest in capital. The private ownership of this capital was an important turning point. In 1982, two-thirds of processing machines for grain, cotton, oil and animal feed were owned by the peasants (Guohua and Peel 1991, p. 165). Furthermore, the peasants also owned a third of the automobiles used in agriculture (Guohua and Peel 1991, p. 168). The use of machinery was limited, however, by the small size of plots.

Chemical fertilisers were not used widely in China until the 1900s; however, Chinese farmers were skilled at using manure. In 1909, ammonium phosphate was introduced in China. Although it led to a considerable increase in productivity, there was scepticism regarding the temporariness of the increase, and fears arose over the possible long-term harm the material caused to soil quality. In addition there was a high monetary cost associated with the use of fertilisers (Guohua and Peel 1991, p.

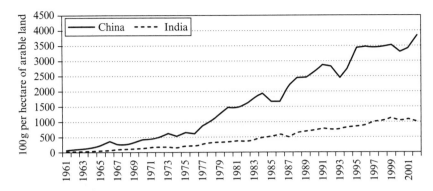

Source: World Bank (2007).

Figure 5.19   Fertiliser consumption (100g per hectare of arable land), 1961–2001

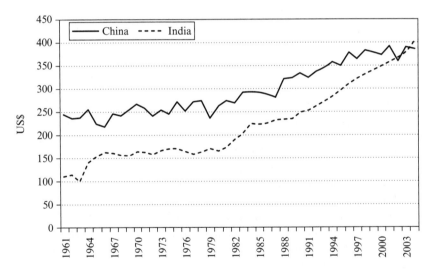

Source: World Bank (2007).

Figure 5.20   Agriculture value added per worker (constant 2000 US$), 1961–2003

151). The country relied heavily on organic manures until the 1950s, after which there was a rapid increase in the use of fertilisers (see Figure 5.19).

Agricultural productivity has increased smoothly (relative to India) over the decades. Figure 5.20 shows that value-added per worker started to increase at a greater rate from about 1980 onwards, just as the household responsibility system came into practice. This productivity may also have been boosted by the higher use of tractors and fertilisers in the early 1980s. The above reforms also saw the total growth in agricultural production become steady and positive, whereas prior to the 1980s growth was volatile and often negative. This is not surprising since the linking of effort to income stimulated enthusiasm for production in the farmers. Productivity in cereal production has also shown a strong positive trend, with the production of cereal per hectare jumping up in the early 1980s. The household responsibility reforms may have helped achieve a more efficient allocation of resources, since farmers had to maximise production subject to the land at their disposal. The new pricing system introduced in 1985 ensured that farmers knew if they were overproducing, and so created incentives for them to alter their behaviour. A paper by Brummer et al. (2005) estimated total fator productivity (TFP) to be 11 per cent in the period 1986–89. They attributed this mainly to technical efficiency. Productivity may also have increased due to the development of township and village enterprises (TVEs). These have seen excess labour absorbed into productive rural, non-agricultural employment.

When compared to India, China's productivity improvements have been more significant. Value-added per worker in India was double that of China's in 1961, but China has recently become more productive. Both nations saw their productivity improve from the early 1980s onwards, yet China's productivity accelerated faster and more consistently. Indian agriculture has also failed to become significantly more productive in terms of the efficient use of land. Cereal yield per hectare doubled in India over 1960–2005; however it increased fivefold in China over the same period (Figure 5.21). The poor productivity performance in India, in comparison to China, can be attributed to the decline in public investment in the 1980s, ill-defined property rights, an abundance of labour and infrastructure bottlenecks. Furthermore, a lower proportion of land is irrigated compared to China, causing output to be heavily dependent on rainfall. This uncertainty discourages farmers to invest in capital.

CONCLUSION

When China and India emerged as new countries in the twentieth century, they were in a similar condition: little industry, high poverty, low productivity. Both countries embarked upon a similar reform method by which they tried to achieve self-sufficiency in food, and focus on the development of the industrial sector. Since the 1950s, both countries have achieved

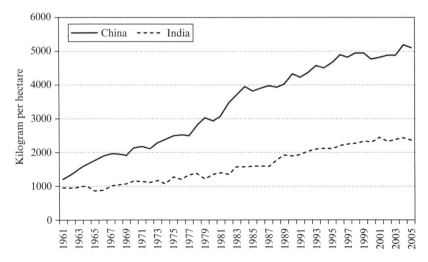

Source: World Bank (2007).

Figure 5.21   Cereal yield (kilograms per hectare), 1961–2003

remarkable success, with China overtaking India in terms of infrastructure and productivity.

Although India and China were essentially agrarian-based, there has been a significant shift away from agriculture to industry and services. This is in line with the economic development of both countries. However, agriculture has continued to remain an important sector of the economy, employing a large proportion of the workforce, and feeding the two most populous countries in the world. Agricultural policy initially focused on self-sufficiency and import substitution, and later on export and globalisation, in tandem with the opening up of the economies. China pursued a more aggressive globalisation policy when compared to India. Overall China has achieved greater success than India due to better infrastructure facilities, greater government investment and better agricultural policies.

REFERENCES

Agrawal, B.L. (1964), 'Comment on "The Burden of Debt in Indian Agriculture"', *Journal of Farm Economics*, **46**, 248–9.
Ahluwalia, M. (2002), 'Economic reforms in India since 1991: has gradualism worked?', *Journal of Economic Perspectives*, **16**, 67–88.
Alagh, Y.K. and G.S. Bhalla (1979), *Performance of Indian Agriculture – a District Wise Study*, New Delhi: Stirling Publishers.

Beijing International (2007), accessed at www.ebeijing.gov.cn/China/Agriculture/t156886.html.

Brummer, B., T. Glauben and L. Wu (2005), 'Policy reform and productivity change in Chinese agriculture: a distance function approach', *Journal of Development Economics*, **81**, 61–79.

Giriappa S. and M. Vivekananda (1984), *Agricultural Growth, Rural Poverty and Environmental Degradation in India*, Delhi: Oxford University Press.

Gulati, A. and S. Fan (2007), *The Dragon and the Elephant: Rural Development and Agricultural Reform Experiences in China and India*, Baltimore, MD: Johns Hopkins University Press.

Guohua, X. and L. Peel (1991), *The Agriculture of China*, New York: Oxford University Press.

Hanumantha Rao, C.H. (1994), *Agricultural Growth, Rural Poverty and Environmental Degradation in India*, Delhi: Oxford University Press.

Indian Farmers Fertiliser Cooperative Limited (IFFCO) (2004), *Agricultural statistics at a glance*, accessed at: http://agricoop.nic.in/Statatglance2004/AtGlance.pdf.

Kaushik, S.K. (1997), 'India's evolving economic model: a perspective on economic and financial reforms', *American Journal of Economics and Sociology*, **56**(1), 69–85.

Kumar, R. (2005), 'Constraints facing Indian agriculture: needs for policy intervention', *Indian Journal of Agriculture Economics*, **60**(1), 49–60.

Ministry of Commerce and Industry, Government of India (2003), *Issues of agriculture in WTO negotiations*, accessed at http://demotemp279.nic.in/PressRelease/pressrelease_detail.asp?id=224.

Ministry of Commerce and Industry, Government of India (2007), *India disappointed with WTO Draft Paper says Kamal Nath sensitivities of developing countries left unaddressed India to work with other developing countries on common response*, accessed at http://commerce.nic.in/PressRelease/pressrelease_detail.asp?id=2024.

Ministry of Finance, Government of India (2001), *Economic Survey 2000–2001*, accessed at http://indiabudget.nic.in/es2000-01/chap820.pdf.

Ministry of Finance, Government of India (2006), *Economic Survey 2005–2006*, accessed at http://indiabudget.nic.in/es2005-06/chapt2006/chap818.pdf.

Passi, S. (1998), 'What is wrong with India agriculture?', *Financial Express*, accessed at http://www.financialexpress.com/fe/daily/19980819/23155144.html.

Planning Commission, Government of India (1951), *First Five Year Plan 1951–1956*, accessed at http://planningcommission.nic.in/plans/planrel/fiveyr/welcome.html.

Planning Commission, Government of India (1969), *First Five Year Plan 1969–1974*, accessed at http://planningcommission.nic.in/plans/planrel/fiveyr/welcome.html.

Planning Commission, Government of India (1974), *First Five Year Plan 1974–1979*, accessed at http://planningcommission.nic.in/plans/planrel/fiveyr/welcome.html.

Planning Commission, Government of India (1985), *First Five Year Plan 1985–1989*, accessed at http://planningcommission.nic.in/plans/planrel/fiveyr/welcome.html.

Planning Commission, Government of India (1992), *First Five Year Plan*

1992–1997, accessed at http://planningcommission.nic.in/plans/planrel/fiveyr/welcome.html.

Planning Commission, Government of India (1997), *First Five Year Plan 1997–2002*, accessed at http://planningcommission.nic.in/plans/planrel/fiveyr/welcome.html.

Prasad, C.S. (2006), *Sixty Years of Indian Agriculture*, New Delhi: New Century Publications.

Saich, T. (2004), *Governance and Politics of China*, New York: Palgrave.

Sarma, J.S. (1981), *Growth and Equity: Policies and Implementation in Indian Agriculture*, Washington, DC: International Food Policy Research Institute.

Shaohua, W. and G. Veek (2000), 'Challenges to family farming in China', *Geographical Review*, **90**, 57–82.

Srinivasan, T.N. (1994). *Agriculture and Trade in China and India: Policies and Performance since 1950*, San Francisco, CA: An International Centre for Economic Growth Publication.

Tata Institute of Social Sciences (TISS) (2005), *Causes of farmer suicides in Maharashtra: an inquiry*, accessed at http://www.tiss.edu/Causes%20of%20Farmer%20Suicides%20in%20Maharashtra.pdf.

United Nations (2007), Comtrade database, accessed at http://comtrade.un.org/db/dqBasicQuery.aspx.

World Bank (2007), *World Development Indicators*, accessed at http://ddp-ext.worldbank.org/ext/DDPQQ/member.do?method=getMembersanduserid=1and queryId=135.

World Trade Organization (WTO) (2006), 'Trade policy review: China', Trade Policy Review Body, Geneva: World Trade Organization.

World Trade Organization (WTO) (2007), 'Trade Policy Review: India', Trade Policy Review Body, Geneva: World Trade Organization.

World Bank (2009), *World Development Indicators*, accessed at http://data.worldbank.org/data-catalog/world-development-indicators.

6. Globalisation, India's evolving food economy and trade prospects for Australia and New Zealand

Srikanta Chatterjee, Allan Rae and Ranjan Ray

INTRODUCTION

Since the early 1990s, the Indian economy has been growing rapidly, both by its own historical standards and relative to many other economies, developed and developing. This has engendered several structural changes both within the economy and in its relationship to the rest of the world. While in many areas these changes are policy-induced – and desirable – some are more like 'side-effects' that need deeper analysis and may call for policies to deal with them. The Indian economy is still largely dependent on agriculture; this dependence is not so much in terms of agriculture's share in the gross domestic product (GDP) – 17 per cent in 2008, and steadily declining, as the share of services increases. In terms of labour employment and absorption, however, agriculture still accounts for around 60 per cent of all employment in the economy (Chatterjee 2008). Agriculture is also significant because of its obvious connection with food security and human nutrition – an issue of national priority since planned economic development began in India in the 1950s.

This chapter has three interrelated aims. First, to examine how India's recent economic reforms have impacted on its agricultural sector, with particular reference to its food production and distribution. Second, how India's economic growth of recent years has impacted on the patterns of food consumption in urban and rural sectors, and how these changes together have impacted on India's trade patterns involving cereal and non-cereal food products. A special focus of this objective is to link these changes to India's trade with Australia and New Zealand, both significant net exporters of food products, to identify the potential growth areas. The third objective of the chapter is to address the wider issue of the impact of India's increasing global integration, via trade and international investment, to its food and nutrition security.

The chapter is organised in the following way: the next section briefly surveys India's economic reform policies since the early 1990s, and notes some of their major outcomes. The third section takes a quick look at India's food grains production and availability, per capita, over time; it then examines the impact of the recent reforms on India's food policy and institutions responsible for implementing these policies. Section 4 considers India's trade policy reforms since the 1990s; section 5 goes on to analyse how India's agricultural trade has evolved over this reform period, with a particular focus on how Australia and New Zealand fit into this evolving trade pattern. Section 6 expands on the Australia–New Zealand focus by linking the observed recent changes in India's food consumption to its imports from these two countries; this enables an assessment of the future trade prospects of the two countries in the Indian market. Section 7 examines the wider issue of India's food and nutrition security along-side its rapid economic growth and increasing integration with the global economy. The chapter ends on the concluding observations of section 8.

RECENT ECONOMIC REFORMS IN INDIA

The Background and a Broad Overview

Three decades of planned economic development until the early 1980s saw the Indian economy achieve an annual average rate of GDP growth of around 3.5 per cent – the so-called 'Hindu rate of growth'. Economic policies pursued in the different areas over this period were conservative and protectionist, with the aim of reducing dependence on external trade – imports in particular – and foreign investment. Indeed, as will be shown below, these policies have helped India emerge, in recent years, from being a net food-importing country to a food-exporting one. A curious aspect of this transformation – also to be noted later – has however been a general decline in food security and nutritional standards of many Indians. Some of the unwanted outcomes of the protectionist policies have, over the years, included: an overvalued exchange rate; proliferation of inefficient, high-cost manufacturing industries; high landed costs of essential imported inputs requiring subsidisation of exports to make them competitive; deterioration in agriculture's terms of trade vis-à-vis industry, and a heavy fiscal burden to sustain the protectionist structure. Although some reform measures were introduced in the 1980s to promote growth and to open up the economy – with moderate success – it was not until the early 1990s, when India faced some serious constraints, that it purposefully made a break from its long-practised policy regime.

As detailed below, it was mainly the high and rising fiscal deficit and the external imbalances that were building up through the 1980s that proved to be the catalyst for the wide-ranging economic reform of the early 1990s. An extensive body of literature (for example Ahluwalia and Little 1998; Bardhan 1984, 2006; Bhagwati 1993; Srinivasan 2003) has critiqued these and other aspects of India's development policies and their outcomes.

Gross fiscal deficits stood at around 10 per cent of GDP by the early 1990s. The costs of servicing the debt kept growing too, and reached over 4 per cent of GDP in 1990–91. Added to this was the steep rise in oil prices in the period leading up to the Gulf Crisis of 1990, and the exchange rate came under intense pressure as the non-resident Indian (NRI) and other offshore investors started withdrawing their investments with the Indian banks and other financial institutions. India's foreign exchange reserves declined to a level that could cover no more than two weeks' imports, and the prospect of India defaulting on short-term foreign debt looked imminent. An Extended Financing Facility of US$4.8 billion was arranged with the International Monetary Fund, and a programme of extensive economic reforms was initiated in 1991. The sum borrowed was soon repaid, but the reforms that radically altered the very ideological basis of economic policy-making in India have continued apace.

The Reform Package and some Broad Macroeconomic Outcomes

Given the background in which the new policy regime was initiated over the period 1991–93, its aims and scope were largely predictable. These were to: address the structural imbalances that contributed to the large and growing fiscal and balance-of-payments deficits; begin a process to liberalise international trade and direct investment, including foreign investment; manage the exchange rate in a manner that helps it to be more responsive to market forces; and take steps to make the rupee convertible – initially for current account transactions. The details of these policies are covered well in the literature (for example Srinivasan 2003; Joshi and Little 1996). Some of the major outcomes of the reforms are noted briefly below.

The growth rate of real GDP from 1992/93 to 1999/2000 was 6.4 per cent, rising slightly to around 6.7 per cent between 2000/2001 and 2003/04, and 8.8 per cent between the second quarter of 2003/04 and the second quarter of 2007/08. In the financial year 2005, India achieved a GDP growth rate of 9.2 per cent, which rose slightly to 9.7 per cent the following year, but fell to 8.7 per cent in 2007. Per capita income growth rose to 3.9 per cent over the decade to 2002, after a decline in 1991/92. It has continued to trend upwards to reach over 7 per cent in the financial year 2006/07 (Government of India 2007b). Remarkably, this acceleration in growth was achieved without increased inflation over nearly a decade to 2004. In the financial year 2005, inflation, as measured by the consumer price index, rose, however, to 4.4 per cent, and in the following three years it accelerated to reach over 8 per cent in July 2008 (*The Economist* 20 September 2008, p. 113), due in some measure to rising prices of food and fuel.

Per capita income in 2008 was around US$2570 at the purchasing power parity exchange rate (World Bank 2008). A large and growing 'middle class' of some 200 million people with the ability to command a more diverse bundle of consumer goods, including food, has emerged (Bijapurkar 2003). The precariously low foreign exchange reserves, which were the main trigger for the radical policy departure in 1991, have turned quite strong, despite the large trade deficits. The increased flow of foreign capital, both direct and portfolio, as well as NRI remittances has pushed the reserves to over US$300 billion in March 2008 (Reserve Bank of India 2008). The fiscal deficits of both central and state governments have also been improving, albeit slowly, and in 2008 stood at 6.3 per cent of GDP, including net lending and subsidies to food, fuel and fertiliser sectors and recurrent Pay Commission awards (OECD 2008). The achievement on the poverty alleviation front – a vital aspect of all development efforts – is somewhat controversial. The most recent estimates of the World Bank, based on the revised poverty line of US$1.25 a day, show that around 42 per cent of India's population are poor (World Bank 2008). One rather curious aspect of these findings is that the rate of poverty decline in India was faster (from 59.8 per cent to 51.3 per cent) over the nine years (1981–90) immediately preceding the major reforms, than over the first 15 years (1990–2005) of the reform which saw the rate decline to 41.6 per cent by 2005. The Indian government estimates, however, put the poverty figures and their decline over time at much lower levels.

AGRICULTURAL AND FARM SECTOR REFORMS AND OUTCOMES

Food Grains Production: a Quick Look

A quick look at the changing pattern of India's food economy over the period since the early 1950s would, at this point, be instructive. Indian planners had an almost obsessive concern to achieve self-sufficiency in food. Given the frequency with which India experienced large-scale food shortages and famines over the period of British rule, this concern is not difficult to understand. Over the period 1950/51 to 2005/06 as a whole, India's population grew at an annual average rate of 2.1 per cent, while the production of food grains grew by 2.5 per cent a year. This led to a steady increase in the per capita availability of food grains and a decline in India's dependence on imported food grains. However, something rather unusual happened over the period since 1990 when India pursued major economic reforms, and achieved a much higher growth rate of GDP. The annual growth of food grains production over the period 1990–2006 fell to 1.2 per cent, against an annual population growth rate of 1.9 per cent, leading to a decline in their per capita availability by some 13 per cent – from a peak of 468 grams a day per head in 1990/91 to 412 grams in 2005/06 (Patnaik 2007).

But, at the same time, India has emerged in more recent years as a net exporter of food grains that have come to account for a large proportion of its agricultural exports, thanks in no small measure to WTO-compatible subsidies paid to exporters. We examine India's agricultural trade issues and policies in greater depth below.

Food and Agricultural Policies and Institutions

The economic reform package of 1991–93 did not contain any specific policies for the agricultural sector, but changes taking place in other sectors of the economy have had several significant effects on Indian agriculture, in respect of both production and consumption. Two main objectives of agricultural policy in India since the early days of planned development have been to increase food production, and improve food availability for the consumers. The overarching aim of these policies, it is useful to remember, was to ensure food security through mainly domestic arrangements. Policies used to achieve these objectives included: (1) the use of minimum support prices (MSPs) via regular and guaranteed procurement of specific food grains; (2) the use of open market operations to maintain seasonal and year-to-year price stability; (3) the maintenance of buffer stocks of food grains; and (4) the use of the public distribution system (PDS) to make food grains available at affordable prices to ensure a degree of food security for poorer people in particular.

The administrative set up to implement these measures consisted mainly of two institutions, namely the Commission on Agricultural Costs and Prices (CACP), which sets the appropriate MSP, and the Food Corporation of India (FCI) which is responsible for procuring the food grains, at prices that are not below the MSP. The minimum support price, revised annually, for fair-to-average quality (FAQ) grains has been used by the government to procure wheat and rice in the surplus areas during harvest either directly from the farmers or from farmers and millers, the latter through a system of levies on the millers (Jha et al. 2007, p. 4). The grains so procured are stored by the FCI for distribution to state governments to ensure adequate supplies through the subsidised PDS. Sufficient buffer stocks are maintained by the FCI to support the PDS, and to permit exporting any surpluses when appropriate.

The economic reforms of the 1990s have resulted in a more open economy that has reduced the protective structure supporting industry. This has helped improve agriculture's domestic terms of trade, thus providing greater incentives for investment in this sector. More importantly, with reduced border controls, the MSPs have, for the first time, started taking international prices into consideration. The more liberal import regime made the generally lower domestic MSPs of food grains face more competition from often cheaper imports. This led to intense lobbying by (big) farmers to increase the MSP to protect domestic farming against cheaper imports. The procurement prices of wheat and rice were raised sharply through the 1990s. While this benefited a small proportion of farmers who received the higher MSPs, it had a seriously detrimental effect on the consumers who faced a sharp rise in the prices of wheat and rice, their staple diet.

One consequence of this rather perverse incentive structure in an economy seeking to become more open had been burgeoning buffer stocks of wheat and rice procured at raised MSPs. At the same time, wholesale and retail prices of wheat and rice in the private markets rose through the 1990s as larger government procurement combined with a stagnant per capita production of these crops started having their impact. All this combined to result in the ominously paradoxical development of a decline in per capita cereal consumption, against the backdrop of India's faster economic growth, as will be analysed below. These developments have been addressed in a number of studies (Chand 2005; Radhakrishna 2005; Landes and Gulati 2004; Ray 2008). In more recent times, however, wheat and rice MSPs have experienced smaller nominal annual increases, and an actual decline in real terms of 14 per cent and 11 per cent in wheat and rice MSPs, respectively, since 2001 (Jha et al. 2007, p. 7). Nevertheless, growth in wheat and rice outputs and government procurements have continued to slow, and trade in food grains has fluctuated rather dramatically in recent years, as will also be noted later. All this has been compounded by the rise and fall of the rupee against most major currencies over the last few years, causing landed costs of imported grains to fluctuate also. The impact of these changes is dealt with later in this chapter.

AGRICULTURAL TRADE POLICY REFORM

A Gradualist Approach to Freeing Up Agriculture

The wide-ranging economic reform policies introduced in 1991 included, in addition to already-noted exchange rate depreciation, and partial convertibility of the rupee for current account transactions, reduction in canalisation (that is, importation via the state monopolies) of exports and imports; selective abolition of import controls; abolition of export control on all but a few selected items; and expansion of the number of items available for easier foreign participation and investment, with less stringent regulation. These initiatives, signalling the change in policy intent, were followed in 1992 by a detailed export–import policy package covering the period up to 1997. The reforms to be implemented in this period included the aim of eliminating restrictive licensing arrangements, and reducing quantitative restrictions (QR) on imports and exports generally, and reducing basic tariffs significantly. With the exception of the items on banned, restricted, and state monopoly lists, all products could be freely imported without needing a licence. The reduction in the weighted average tariff rates was sizeable – from over 72 per cent in 1991–92 to around 25 per cent in 1996–97. Maximum tariff rates, likewise, have been reduced in steps from over 300 per cent to about 40 per cent for most items, with reductions in countervailing duties too.

International Commitments and Agricultural Trade Liberalisation

Agricultural trade barriers, not addressed in the 1991 package, have also come to be gradually reduced in the subsequent trade policy changes. India's agricultural tariffs are *ad valorem*, and the simple average of bound tariffs was 115 per cent in 2004, trade-weighting raises this to 159 per cent. Applied tariffs, however, average 59 per cent, making the binding overhang high (Gopinath and Laborde 2008). The specific changes affecting agricultural items include: curtailment of the regulatory activities of the State Trading Corporation; enhanced market access for many agricultural items through the removal of quotas; easing of tariffs and of licensing arrangements; and allowing private sector participation in the import of food items.

Under the Uruguay Round Agreement on Agriculture (URRA) of 1994, India proceeded to address issues affecting market access, domestic support, export competition, subsidy, and sanitary and phytosanitary standards (SPS) to liberalise agricultural trade. The bound rates of agricultural tariffs came to be set between 0 and 100 per cent for primary products, 150 per cent for processed products, and 300 per cent for edible oils, later reduced to 100 per cent. Having lost the balance-of-payments waiver that permitted trade restrictions, India proceeded to accelerate the removal of QRs. By April 2001, India completed the removal of QRs on agricultural imports, thus making it possible now to import virtually all items subject to the applicable tariffs and to SPS. The average bound tariff for agricultural items in the year 2002/03 was 115 per cent, with a much lower applied tariff rate of 33 per cent. Peak tariffs for non-agricultural imports have been reduced from 30 per cent in 1991 to 12.5 per cent by 2006. To protect the small farmers and small-scale agribusinesses, tariffs on agricultural products had not initially been reduced quite so dramatically, but tariffs on many agricultural products are now set well below the WTO bound rates. For example, applied rates on pulses, wheat and corn are set at 0 per cent (as at January 2008) – against bound rates of 100 per cent for the first two items, and 70 per cent for corn. Likewise, the applied rate for oilseeds is 30 per cent, against its bound rate of 100 per cent. Only in respect of rice is the applied rate the same as the bound one, at 70 per cent (Landes 2008).

New Initiatives to Promote Agricultural Exports

To achieve better export outcomes, Indian trade policies in recent times have included export incentives of different types. Thus, imported inputs required in an exporting activity are liable for a lower import tariff; export restrictions on most products have been removed; and some exports are given subsidies permitted under the WTO rules. Government support for infrastructure and finance is also made available to set up export-oriented agro-processing zones. To assist export promotion, Special Economic Zones (SEZs) are being created where export-oriented production will be permitted under relaxed rules for imports and foreign collaboration

The trade policy announcement covering the period 2004–09 emphasised the need to boost India's export performance, with the aim of doubling the share of global trade to 1.7 per cent by 2009. Reduction in tariff rates and streamlining of procedures to reduce transaction costs would be used to achieve these goals.

In the agricultural areas, new schemes to boost exports of fruit, vegetables, flowers and minor forest products have been announced. Foreign investment of up to 100 per cent will be allowed to set up and develop free trade and warehousing zones (FTWZs) with the aim of making India a 'global trading hub'.

FOOD AND AGRICULTURE IN INDIA'S TOTAL TRADE

Growth in Total Trade and Trade in Agricultural Products

India's international merchandise trade has expanded considerably since the policy reforms of the early 1990s. Between 1990 and 2003, total trade more than tripled, from US$41 billion to US$140 billion (Table 6.1). Imports grew slightly faster than exports over this period, and India's trade deficit increased from US$5.9 billion in 1990 to over US$14 billion by 2003. Between 2003 and 2006, merchandise trade grew at an even faster rate, exports doubling and imports growing by over twice, making the trade deficit widen more than fourfold in three short years.

India's trade in agricultural commodities also grew rapidly over this period, although not quite as fast as total trade. Agricultural trade showed an increasing surplus since 1990, with growth in both exports and imports.

Table 6.1   India's total trade (US$ million)

Year	Exports		Imports		Trade balance	
	Total	Agr and Food* (%)	Total	Agr and Goods (%)	Total	Agr and Food
1990	17940	26.6	23799	4.5	−5859	3685
1991	17900	26.0	19509	3.8	−1610	3909
1992	20711	24.7	24452	5.2	−3741	3826
1993	22237	25.2	23304	4.4	−1067	4569
1994	26330	24.5	28655	7.7	−2325	4255
1995	31699	27.3	36592	5.7	−4893	6547
1996	33469	29.4	39113	5.8	−5644	7587
1997	34794	27.7	41429	6.4	−6636	6985
1998	33207	25.6	42425	9.2	−9218	4616
1999	36672	22.4	49713	8.0	−13042	4257
2000	45250	20.3	51377	5.7	−6128	6264
2001	44306	19.7	51908	7.3	−7602	4957
2002	52471	18.4	61118	6.8	−8647	5510
2003	63035	16.8	77201	6.5	−14166	5570
2004	79834	13.8	108248	5.0	−28414	5629
2005	103404	13.1	149750	3.8	−46346	7803
2006	126126	12.9	185385	3.9	−59259	8943

Note: * Agr and Food = HS01-24 + HS41 + HS51 + HS52.

Source: United Nations, Comtrade database (various issues).

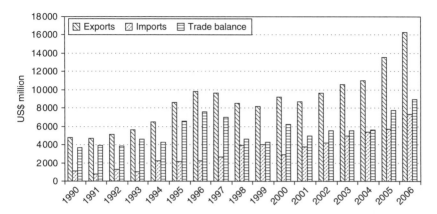

Source: United Nations, Comtrade database (various issues).

Figure 6.1   India's agricultural trade

Total agricultural trade had increased from US$5.8 billion in 1990 to US$15.7 billion in 2003; over the next three years, this upward trend accelerated, and total agricultural trade reached over US$23.4 billion (Table 6.1 and Figure 6.1). Exports of agricultural commodities grew at a slower pace than did total exports, and their share of the latter declined from almost 27 per cent in 1990 to 17 per cent in 2003, and by a further four percentage points by 2006. Agricultural imports, in contrast, grew more rapidly than did total imports and agriculture's share of total imports rose from under 5 per cent to almost 7 per cent over 1990–2003, but declined over the next three years to less than 4 per cent, despite the significant increase in the absolute value of agricultural imports in that period (Table 6.2, Figure 6.1). This of course was the consequence of the very rapid growth in total imports from 2003 to 2006.

Agriculture's trade balance (surplus) had been showing a declining trend since peaking in 1996, reflecting the strong growth in agricultural imports since that time. It improved however over the three years to 2006, despite the continuing increase in the value of agricultural imports (Table 6.1, Figure 6.1). There have however been some rather unexpected developments in regard to India's cereal production, procurement and trade in recent times. These have, potentially at least, serious long-term implications for India's food and nutrition securities. We address these issues below.

Our demand analysis reported below points to increasing consumption shares of dairy products, other animal products, processed foods, and fresh fruits and vegetables as food expenditures rise. To what extent are

Table 6.2   Composition of India's agricultural imports (%)

Year	Animal/ Veg Fats	Hides, Skins	Wool	Cotton	Pulses	Fruit and Nuts	Cereals	Other Processed Foods	Other*	Total
	HS15	HS41	HS51	HS52	HS0713	HS08	HS10	HS9, 16–23		
1990	18.5	9.8	12.2	2.9	27.3	12.2	3.1	9.8	4.2	100
1991	18.6	10.1	12.9	2.3	16.2	19.9	0.6	13.5	5.8	100
1992	8.6	7.2	10.5	8.0	10.2	17.0	23.6	10.5	4.4	100
1993	10.7	10.9	12.9	2.4	18.1	21.6	5.6	12.7	5.1	100
1994	12.7	5.4	6.3	8.3	9.0	14.6	0.1	40.8	2.9	100
1995	36.2	6.3	8.6	8.6	10.1	15.5	0.2	10.1	4.5	100
1996	42.1	5.8	9.0	1.6	11.8	14.3	5.1	7.1	3.3	100
1997	33.8	5.5	7.2	2.5	12.9	13.6	10.0	11.3	3.1	100
1998	51.9	3.8	3.4	3.8	4.9	10.0	7.2	12.1	2.9	100
1999	52.5	3.8	3.1	7.9	2.3	10.4	5.3	10.8	3.9	100
2000	51.5	6.6	3.8	10.1	3.8	13.4	0.3	6.8	3.6	100
2001	42.0	5.8	3.8	12.8	18.6	6.7	0.0	7.2	3.2	100
2002	47.4	4.8	4.7	8.3	14.7	9.4	0.0	7.3	3.4	100
2003	51.2	4.5	4.8	9.6	11.1	9.4	0.0	6.2	3.2	100
2004	45.9	4.9	4.3	8.0	8.0	11.6	0.0	13.9	3.4	100
2005	40.1	5.2	4.6	7.7	11.0	13.8	0.0	13.7	3.7	100
2006	31.0	5.1	3.9	6.4	13.8	11.3	17.7	7.1	3.9	100

Note: * Other includes live animals, meats, dairy, fish etc.

Source: United Nations, Comtrade database (various issues).

these trends observed in India's recent patterns of agricultural imports? This is the issue we examine below.

The Consumption–Import Nexus in Agricultural Trade: a First Look at Australasia as India's Trade Partners

We find that edible oils (HS15) have been India's major agricultural import since the mid-1990s, comprising over 40 per cent of India's total agricultural imports since 1998 (Table 6.2). The major products within this commodity group in 2003 were palm oil (71 per cent of total imports of HS15 – the principal suppliers were Indonesia and Malaysia), and soybean oil (22 per cent of HS15 imports – Argentina and Brazil were the main suppliers). It is worth noting that India reduced the duty on crude edible oil to 15 per cent in August 1998, and in the year 1998–99 edible oil imports registered an increase of 111 per cent over the previous year (from 2.2 to 4.4 million tonnes), making India the largest vegetable oil importer, ahead of China (Jafri 2008). As a share of agricultural imports, the category

HS15 has, however, been on a declining trend since 2003, reaching 31 per cent in 2006. There have been further reductions in the applied tariff rates on a number of items of edible agricultural imports, including edible oils, pulses and maize, in early 2008 (Landes 2008), ostensibly to cushion the impact of rising inflation. How these come to affect imports of these items remains to be seen.

The other major import commodity group has been pulses (lentils, chickpeas, dry peas and so on). Taking edible oils and pulses together, India has emerged during the 1990s as the world's major importer of these commodities. Here too, setting India's applied tariffs well below WTO's bound rates has been a major factor in the observed import surge. Non-food agricultural commodities accounted for around 20 per cent of India's agricultural imports in recent years, with cotton being the major single commodity in this group. Along with edible oils, cotton is one of the few groups shown in Table 6.2 whose share of total agricultural imports has tended to increase since 1990, peaking in 2001. Since then, however, its share has been on a declining trend, reaching 6.4 per cent by 2006. Given the predominance of edible oils in India's recent agricultural trade – which, despite the recent decline in their share, are still the single largest category of agricultural imports – the principal suppliers of those products have also been the major sources for India's agricultural imports.

As indicated by the limited volume of imports, despite increasing consumption, India has managed to remain largely self-sufficient in dairy and other animal products, and in fruit and vegetables, over the 1990s (Figure 6.2). This is in line with India's long-standing policy of minimising trade dependence in respect of foods and some other selected items. Thus, imports of these products make up a very low share of total food imports. Fruit made up 9 per cent and processed foods 6 per cent of total agricultural imports in 2003. These shares had fluctuated around a declining trend until 2001, but have since then been on an upward trend, reaching over 11 per cent by 2006. However, dairy products had only a 0.6 per cent share of total imports in 2003; and for meat and fish, and vegetables other than pulses, the shares were much lower still. These are no higher in the mid- to late 2000s, although imports of these products from Australasia offer a slightly different picture, as we discuss below.

INDIA'S AGRICULTURAL IMPORTS FROM AUSTRALASIA

Since the early 1990s, India's agricultural imports from Australia and New Zealand, both in value and share terms, had shown declining trends.

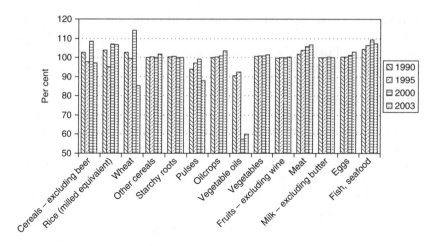

Note: Self-sufficiency = production/domestic supply including net imports.

Source: FAO (various issues).

Figure 6.2   India's self-sufficiency

Combined, both countries contributed 20 per cent (US$260 million) of India's imports in 1992, but just 4 per cent (US$208 million) by 2003 (Table 6.3); perhaps not surprising as India's import growth has been driven by increased demand for, primarily, vegetable oils and pulses. In the three years from 2003 to 2006, however, the total value of imports from Australasia has been on an increasing trend. Their share too had increased – marginally from 2004 to 2005, and then jumping sharply in 2006. This last change has been helped, to some extent, by the increase in India's cereal imports from Australia from under US$1 million dollars, on average in 2000–03, to US$81 million on average in 2003–06. As already indicated, this aspect of India's agricultural trade is addressed later in the chapter. When viewed against the observed proportionate decline in India's agricultural imports overall from 2003 to 2006, the steady improvement in the share of Australasia in this market is particularly impressive. Even if we leave out the impact of cereal imports from Australia in 2006, both countries saw their exports to India trending significantly upwards from 2003 to 2006; Australia gaining a 187 per cent (138 per cent without cereals) increase, and New Zealand 65 per cent in three short years (Table 6.3 and Figure 6.3).

By commodity, the major agricultural imports from Australasia are mainly non-food – wool, cotton, and hides and skins, but also pulses. These four commodities accounted for 90 per cent of India's total

Table 6.3   Australasia's share of India's agricultural imports

Year	Total imports (US$ million)	From: (US$ million)		Australasia's share of total (%)
		Australia	New Zealand	
1990	1083	134	46	16.6
1991	750	64	42	14.1
1992	1283	223	37	20.3
1993	1032	109	43	14.7
1994	2199	119	41	7.3
1995	2099	110	39	7.1
1996	2251	255	46	13.4
1997	2658	455	41	18.7
1998	3890	378	45	10.9
1999	3967	205	49	6.4
2000	2930	138	41	6.1
2001	3780	238	48	7.6
2002	4142	160	47	5.0
2003	4989	168	40	4.2
2004	5377	142	44	3.5
2005	5741	175	50	3.9
2006	7306	483	66	7.5

Source: United Nations, Comtrade database (various issues).

agricultural imports from Australasia on average over 2000–03 (Table 6.4), declining to just over 65 per cent in the next period. This trade has been a fluctuating one, however, with wool exports to India varying between US$88 and US$137 million, and cotton between almost zero and US$54 million, since 1995. Of the food items other than pulses, over recent times, cereals have only been important during the mid-1990s (and again in 2006), when Australia increased its wheat exports in response to India's domestic shortfalls.

Of the foods that have shown an increasing share of Indian household expenditures – fruit, animal products including dairy, and processed foods – imports of these from Australasia totalled US$16.7 million on average, over 2000–03, or just 7.6 per cent, of India's total agricultural imports from Australasia (Table 6.4). The performance of these items improved over the next three years in both absolute and relative terms – reaching US$31.5 million, or nearly 10 per cent of India's total agricultural imports from Australasia. In absolute terms, the three items – fruit, other processed food, and meat and fish – have continued to perform significantly better over the time period covered in Table 6.4. In share terms, two out

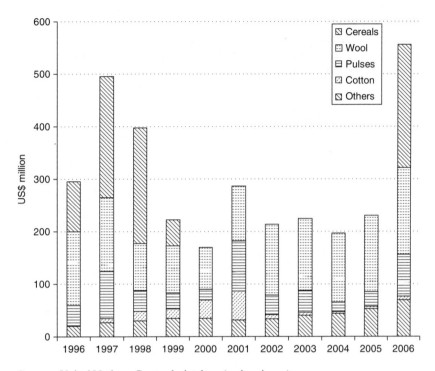

Source: United Nations, Comtrade database (various issues).

Figure 6.3   India's major agricultural and food imports from Australasia

of the three items registered steady improvement, while other processed food had a slight decline in the period 2003–06. Instability in India's annual imports of these foods from Australasia is evident since 1995 – such imports fluctuated between US$0.7 million and US$18 million for dairy, between US$0.03 million and US$16 million for fresh fruit and nuts, between US$1.3 million and US$15 million for processed foods, and between zero and US$0.60 million for meats and fish. These increases are encouraging signs for the prospects of food-exporting Australasia in the fast-growing Indian market, in areas where domestic consumption is likely to keep growing too. Their shares admittedly remain small, indicating perhaps the degree of competition that exporters face in a more open Indian agricultural import market.

Table 6.4 also shows Australasia's performance in the non-food agricultural imports of India. Between 1996–99 and 2004–06, Australasia's share of India's wool imports has fallen from 71 per cent to 53 per cent; from 68 per cent to 19 per cent for cereals; from 23 per cent to 6 per cent in the

Table 6.4 *India's recent agricultural imports from Australasia by commodity*

Commodity	Imports from Australasia (US$ mill)			Australasia's share of India's total imports (%)		
	1996–99 ave.	2000–2003 ave.	2004–06 ave.	1996–99 ave.	2000–2003 ave.	2004–06 ave.
All agriculture	368.6	220.1	319.9	12.3	5.7	5.2
Wool	113.1	109.8	137.4	71.0	66.3	53.0
Cereals	147.9	0.8	81.0	68.0	31.5	18.7
Pulses	51.1	48.8	44.3	22.8	10.4	6.4
Cotton	13.1	27.4	4.2	7.6	7.2	0.9
Hides and skins	12.1	13.5	16.0	8.5	6.4	5.2
Dairy	8.1	6.9	4.7	53.5	50.9	29.0
Fruits and nuts	4.1	6.2	14.4	1.1	1.7	1.9
Other processed food	1.9	3.5	12.0	0.8	2.0	1.8
Meat and fish	0.1	0.1	0.4	0.8	0.8	1.7

Note: a. Dairy = HS0401-0406 + HS2105 + HS3501-3502; Meat and fish = HS02 + HS03; all other commodities defined as in Table 6.2.

Source: United Nations, Comtrade database (various issues).

case of pulses; and from 54 per cent to 29 per cent for dairy products. To the extent that these broad commodity aggregates are differentiated by country of origin, this could reflect changes in India's consumer preferences. But loss of market share could also indicate loss of competitiveness, or India's trade preferences, or increased competition from subsidised exports from elsewhere.

GROWING AFFLUENCE, CHANGING FOOD HABITS AND TRADE PROSPECTS FOR AUSTRALIA AND NEW ZEALAND

Rising Incomes and Changing Food Habits in Rural and Urban India

Since the changing nature of consumer preferences in India has significant implications for its trade patterns, especially in agricultural products, as

indicated above, it is useful to relate the observed changes in food preferences to changes in household incomes, and assess how they might be
influencing Australasia's trade in the Indian market. An extensive and
readily available body of literature records the pattern of changes in
India's food consumption in recent decades (for example, Chatterjee et al.
2006, 2007; Kumar and Mathur 1996; Ray 2008). We use the findings of
some of these studies to focus on our own investigation here.

Empirical work involving the structural shifts in India's consumption
patterns usually make use of the wealth of household level information
contained in the regularly conducted National Sample Surveys (NSS).
These surveys report, amongst other information, the monthly per capita
consumption of the principal food items by rural and urban households,
and also the expenditure shares of the households on the food items. We
use, selectively, the findings of Chatterjee et al. (2006, 2007) and Ray
(2008) to investigate the nature of the changes in India's food consumption patterns over the period 1987/88 to 2001/02, which includes the first
decade of India's recent economic reforms. The datasets used in these
studies are from the 43rd (July 1987 to June 1988), and the 57th (July 2001
to June 2002) rounds of the NSS.

Table 6.5 reports the changes in the monthly per capita consumption
(kg) of the principal food items between 1987/88 (Round 43) and 2001/02
(Round 57) in the rural and urban areas respectively. The following features are worth noting. First, cereals consumption is generally much higher
in the rural areas than in the urban, mainly due to the higher consumption
of rice by the rural household. The reverse is the case for meat, fish and
eggs and fruit and vegetables. Second, there has been a marked decline in
the consumption of all the cereal items over the period 1987/88 to 2001/02,
in both rural and urban areas, with the reduction being particularly sharp
in the smaller cereal items. Third, there has been a switch in preferences
towards non-cereal items such as meat and fish and fruit and vegetables.
The figures reported in Table 6.5 are all-India average values; Ray (2008)
reports these averages for the states, and they reveal a similar picture.

As the lower part of Table 6.5 reports, the food expenditure share is
generally higher in the rural household than in the urban and, in most
cases, this differential increased sharply during the period. In view of
Engel's Law, which postulates an inverse relationship between a household's budget share of food and its aggregate expenditure outlay, the latter
feature suggests a differential income growth between the rural and urban
areas over the 1990s, the latter achieving higher income growth.

While some, such as Rao (2005), have interpreted these movements as
evidence of urbanisation and increased household affluence, others such as
Mehta and Venkatraman (2000) have argued that such changes have been

Table 6.5   All-India mean consumption and expenditure shares

Food items	Urban			Rural		
	1988 (Round 43)	2002 (Round 57)	Change (%)	1988 (Round 43)	2002 (Round 57)	Change (%)
Consumption/capita (kg/30 days)						
Rice	5.65	4.85	−14.2	7.35	6.79	−7.7
Wheat	4.57	4.03	−11.70	4.80	4.05	−15.7
Other cereals	0.83	0.56	−32.5	2.59	1.38	−46.8
Total cereals	11.05	9.44	−14.5	14.74	12.22	−17.2
Pulses	1.06	0.86	−18.8	0.97	0.77	−20.9
Dairy	4.52	5.25	16.2	3.34	3.94	17.9
Edible oils	0.56	0.69	23.6	0.35	0.51	45.4
Meat/Fish/Eggs	2.01	2.49	23.8	0.91	1.50	65.6
Veg/Fruit	11.46	13.44	17.3	6.99	9.48	35.6
Sugar/Spices	1.63	1.46	−10.4	1.53	1.34	−12.7
Share of total food expenditure (%)						
Rice	16.33	14.06	−13.9	24.97	21.32	−14.6
Wheat	9.07	8.70	−4.1	10.99	9.58	−12.8
Other cereals	1.80	1.18	−34.4	5.87	2.83	−51.7
Total Cereals	27.20	23.94	−12.0	41.83	33.73	−19.3
Pulses	6.16	5.66	−8.1	6.48	6.31	−2.6
Dairy	13.23	15.71	18.7	9.87	12.02	21.8
Edible oils	8.65	6.55	−24.4	7.41	6.53	−11.9
Meat/Fish/Eggs	5.37	5.58	4.0	4.27	5.34	25.1
Veg/Fruit	12.29	15.03	22.3	10.32	14.56	41.1
Sugar/Spices	8.12	7.44	−8.4	8.73	8.36	−4.2
Processed food	13.59	13.49	−0.7	8.28	9.31	12.5
Beverages	5.38	6.61	22.8	2.83	3.83	35.5
Share of total expenditure (%)						
All food	66.1	50.0	−24.4	72	60.9	−16.1

Source: Own calculations based on NSS Rounds 43, 57.

involuntary, reflecting the loss in access to common property resources by the rural poor. Whatever the underlying factors causing these changes, these have led to significant declines in calorie consumption, as Chatterjee et al. (2007) and Ray (2008) also report.

These findings imply that, with increasing affluence, Indian consumers' demand for non-cereal food items will keep increasing, and at least a proportion of the increased demand would need to be sourced from imports, and are therefore of interest to food-exporting countries like Australia and New Zealand.

To ascertain how much of these observed changes has been due to changing food habits and preferences, rather than to inflation and changing relative prices between the food constituents, Chatterjee et al. (2006) conducted an econometric investigation into household demand patterns, using the quadratic almost ideal (QAI) demand system. The econometrics of the actual estimation procedure (detailed in Chatterjee et al. 2006) is not of direct relevance to the discussions here, so only the relevant results derived from the estimation are used below to shed light on the trade prospects of Australia and New Zealand in the Indian market, as the Indian economy continues to grow, and its general level of affluence continues to improve.

Expenditure Elasticities and Marginal Household Budget Shares of Food Items

The QAI demand system estimates for elasticities, based on data from NSS rounds 43 and 55 (these two rounds are both 'thick' rounds, that is, based on large samples, and therefore mutually comparable) for 17 major states, show considerable agreement on the main qualitative features of the results amongst these states. The expenditure elasticities for urban households exceed unity for processed foods, meats, fish and eggs, and dairy products, while those for vegetables and fruit, and beverages, are close to unity. The cereals had the lowest elasticities. The conditional elasticity of processed food in 2002 was almost double its 1988 estimate, the result possibly reflecting increased mean incomes over the period. The findings are somewhat similar for rural households, with above-unity elasticities estimated for dairy products, meats, fish and eggs, processed food, wheat and beverages. For this collection of foods, the 2002 elasticities, with the exception of meats, fish and eggs, were greater than their 1988 estimates. As with urban consumption, the lowest elasticities were for traditional cereals, which were also considerably lower than the 1988 estimates.

Marginal expenditure shares for each food item are given by the product of the conditional expenditure elasticity and the expenditure share. The computed results indicate how consumption patterns may continue to evolve in the future as food expenditures rise. For a given increase in food expenditures of urban households in 2002, the largest shares of that increase are estimated to be allocated to dairy products and processed foods, followed in importance by vegetables and fruit, rice, and meats, fish and eggs.

The results are rather similar for rural households, with the largest share of the increase allocated to dairy products, followed by rice and processed foods. For urban households, the marginal expenditure share for processed foods doubled from 1988 to 2002. In rural regions, the marginal shares increased noticeably for dairy, processed foods, fruit and vegetables, and for wheat.

Given that the unequal distribution of income in both rural and urban India has not lessened noticeably through the period of economic reform and faster growth, it is helpful to gain some insight into the demand responses of households at different income levels. Expenditure elasticities for selected items of food were therefore computed by deciles of income from three regionally distant states, with different food habits. The elasticity estimates reveal some common features, despite the regional differences in food consumption. The expenditure elasticities of rice and wheat decline sharply as one moves up the decile groups, with these items displaying mild inferiority at the top decile. This may provide a partial explanation for the observed diversification of food habits away from rice and wheat over the 1990s, since over the reforms period, the higher-decile groups experienced greater income increases than those in the lower deciles. In contrast, the non-cereal items – dairy, and meat, fish and eggs – have high elasticities right across the decile spectrum. This suggests an explanation of the significant increase in their consumption over the 1990s, as alluded to earlier.

How Might Australia and New Zealand Fit into India's Growing Food Market?

These results clearly identify the consumption items that experienced the largest shares of the observed increase in food expenditure, and had the highest expenditure elasticities. These are dairy products, processed foods, meat, fish and eggs, and fruit and vegetables. In all likelihood, as the general level of affluence keeps improving over time, India's food consumption patterns will keep changing along similar lines – a more varied diet, with more non-cereal foods. With an established land use pattern and limited surplus land in India, such increases must be largely met through increased imports of these products. With the complete removal of QR by 2001, tariffs are now the only instrument for restricting imports. A 35 per cent tariff was imposed on items from which QR was removed; this has now been reduced further, as reported earlier. Not unexpectedly, imports of all these items have increased significantly over the period 1990–2006, as Tables 6.3 and 6.4 report. The year 2006 is the most recent year for which information is available; being also five years from the completion of import tariffication, it is likely to reflect better the impact of the removal of QR on the selected imports beyond an initial transition period.

With the opening up of the Indian import sector, import sources have come to expand, and competition has increased. Prior to the reforms, when the demand for these products was more modest and imports of them were subject to QR, the import volumes were small, and the leading import sources shared those volumes in a particular manner. With the growth in imports over time, competition must have become more intense and the search widened for import sources.

The major suppliers in more recent years could also reflect India's trade agreement partners. In particular, the South Asian Preferential Trade Agreement (SAPTA), which commenced in 1995, groups India with six other countries including Nepal, Bangladesh and Pakistan. The latter three countries have come to feature more as India's trade partners in respect of the items in which Australia and New Zealand may have an interest. The relative shares of these countries could be partly driven by preferences given by India and may not reflect underlying comparative advantages. Of all SAPTA members, India has offered the largest number of tariff preferences, even though the majority of these are for non-agricultural products.

The fact that Australia and New Zealand have got what in most cases is no more than a toe-hold in the large and growing Indian market may be considered disappointing. However, as noted earlier, over the latest three years for which information is available, the shares of both countries have improved both in total trade and in respect to the food items for which demand has been growing more rapidly. These are markets that need to be targeted for better results over time. Indeed, Australia has in recent times taken several initiatives, in collaboration with Indian businesses, to increase its food and beverage exports, including fruit, to A$250 million over the period 2001–06 (www.domain-b.com/economy/trade/20060201). As major exporters to the world of dairy products, meat, fish, fruit and vegetables, both Australia and New Zealand have comparative advantages in these areas; they also have an established reputation as exporters of quality processed foods. With a greater focus, the Indian market could yield significant dividends.

SOME EMERGING ISSUES IN INDIA'S FOOD ECONOMY

Production, Procurement and Availability of Food Grains

A decline in India's per capita availability of food grains over the period 1990–2007 has been alluded to above. The reasons for it are rather complex. Let us first acquaint ourselves with a few salient facts about

India's food consumption, availability and production. A few issues and recent developments in regard to India's agricultural trade in a 'globalising world' will then be examined with a view to making an assessment about the future of the food sector of the large and fast-growing, but poor, economy of India.

First, consumption: while the evidence that Indian diets have been becoming more varied is convincing, as detailed above, it is also a fact that the per capita production, availability and consumption of cereals, and with it the intake of calories, have all been either fluctuating or falling over the two decades to 2005, especially since the early 1990s. The *Draft XIth Five Year Plan* document (Government of India 2007a) of the Indian Planning Commission observes:

> the significant point is that, overall, per capita intake of calories and protein has declined consistently over a 20-year period from 1983 to 2004/5 . . . rural calorie consumption per day has fallen from 2221 to 2047, an eight per cent decline. Similarly, the urban calorie consumption fell by three per cent, from 2080 to 2020.

Moving on to the interlinked issues of production, procurement and availability in recent years, the output of rice fell from 88.5 million tonnes in 2003/04 to 83.1 in 2004/05, and then rose to 91.8 million tonnes in 2005/06, but fell again, a little, to 93.4 million tonnes in 2006/07. Wheat output, however, has stagnated at around 70–72 million tonnes over the period 2002/03 to 2005/06, having declined from a peak of 76 million tonnes in 2001/02. In the two years to 2007/08, it has recovered to around 75 million tonnes annually (Government of India 2008).

While domestic availability is sourced mainly from domestic output, it depends also on other sources such as net imports and net changes to public stocks of food grains. India's food policy has always had a strong government involvement in the form of the PDS, as discussed above. The Government of India's (2008) *Economic Survey 2007–08* summarises the objectives of food management in India as follows: 'procurement of food grains from farmers at remunerative prices, distribution of food grains to the consumers particularly the vulnerable sections of the society at affordable prices, and maintenance of food buffers for food security and price stability'.

As observed earlier, the PDS, with a network of nearly half a million fair price shops (FPS), had long been the backbone of India's food safety net and a major instrument in the government's anti-poverty programme. In mid-1997, this universal system was changed to make it a Targeted PDS (TPDS) which introduced the distinction between 'below poverty line' (BPL) and 'above poverty line' (APL) households in setting the quantity and issue price of the subsidised food grain items. This was further tight-ened in December 2000 with the introduction of another food-based welfare scheme, the Antyodaya Anna Yojana (AAY), which made the TPDS even more targeted – in favour of the very poor, that is, the des-titute, who constituted some 10 million out of around 65 million BPL households covered by the TPDS.

The increase in the MSP of wheat and rice through the 1990s, referred to earlier, together with reduced disbursements from the FPS, exacerbated the problem faced by the government's burgeoning grain buffer stocks which peaked at 64.7 million tonnes in June 2002. The following two years saw the stocks ease, with lower quantities procured by the central govern-ment, and larger disbursements, including provisions for drought relief. This led the government to restrict exports of rice and wheat from August 2003.

There was then a sudden reversal in India's net trade in food grains – from being a net exporter of wheat of some 12 million tonnes (with budg-etary subsidies) between 2001/02 and 2004/05, India has, again, become a net importer. With tighter domestic availabilities in 2005/06, the State Trading Corporation was authorised to import 0.5 million tonnes of wheat in that year. This increased to 5.5 million tonnes in 2006/07, as the central government pool of grains was considered inadequate to meet its supply commitments to the TDPS and other welfare schemes. The domes-tic availabilities improved in 2007/08, but a smaller quantity of 1.8 million tonnes of wheat still needed to be imported to ensure adequate supply for the central pool.

The cost of food subsidy – being the difference between the 'economic cost' of wheat and rice and their prices at the FPS and other welfare outlets – has also increased sharply in recent years. This is borne largely by the central government. Several changes have been introduced to some long-standing arrangements in India's food economy which, as already noted, is now more open to international competition. Some of these changes are examined below in the context of a global food scenario facing the Indian economy.

Globalisation, Decentralisation and Global and Domestic Trade in Food Products

The procurement of food grains was 'decentralised' with the introduction of the Decentralised Procurement (DCP) Scheme in 1997. Ten states and a union territory have since then been procuring and storing food grains to distribute them under the TDPS within their jurisdictions. The prices charged at the FPS are the issue prices set by the central government, the difference between these and the economic costs incurred by the states in this operation being passed on to the state governments as subsidy. The results of this scheme have been mixed, some states having procured large quantities, some not so large (Government of India 2008). The overall impact of the procurement system on supply, demand, prices and trade will be small, according to Jha et al. (2007).

In another recent move, with the encouragement of the central government in 2003, most states have amended the Agricultural Produce Marketing Committee (APMC) Act to permit private businesses to procure food grains directly from the farmers, obviously in competition with the governments. Evidence is emerging that private trade has come to procure more wheat than the government for the first time since the FCI was created (http://ww.rupe-india.org/42/failure.html). The Essential Commodities Act that has long required the government to control the storage, movement and prices of essential commodities, including food grains, has also been amended to allow private sector participation in these activities. Critics of these policies argue that the government, by keeping its MSP lower than what the private traders are willing and able to offer, has made it easier for the private sector to purchase wheat from the farmers. An appropriately higher MSP, they point out, would have enabled the government to procure more wheat from the farmers; this would have minimised the import needs and cost the Government less, on the whole (*India Together*, 21 May 2000 http://www.indiatogether. org/2007.may/agr-whimport.htm).

Enter the Multinationals: India as a Food Processing Hub

As has been observed above, India's food economy is no longer as dominated by the public sector institutions and rules as it used to be, for over four decades since the 1950s. Indeed, it would be fair to say that the government has been gradually reducing its involvement, and encouraging and assisting the private sector to play a more active role in all areas of the food economy. Globally, trade involving raw and processed food has always been large. With faster economic growth of some of the more populous countries, including China and India, in recent times, food trade has assumed even greater importance from both demand- and supply-side influences.

As this chapter has recorded, India's food economy has made major strides since its Green Revolution in respect of food grains in the 1970s. India's centuries-old dependence on food grains gradually diminished, and exports started to build up. India's food processing sector, however, has not kept pace with this increased self-reliance experienced by the food economy in general. While China processes around 40 per cent of its agricultural produce, Thailand 30 per cent, Brazil 70 per cent and Malaysia 80 per cent, value addition to agricultural produce in India is only around 20 per cent (SME Rating Agency n.d.).

It is common knowledge that much of this business is dominated, globally, by large multinational corporations (MNCs). For example, 30 companies account for one-third of the world's processed food; five companies control 75 per cent of international grain trade; and six companies manage 75 per cent of the world's pesticide market (*Guardian*, 17 January 2005). The industries processing food, of course, need to acquire the necessary raw materials. They often seek a vertically integrated production system that connects them to the local farmers and the suppliers of other inputs, directly in competition (often unequal), with other purchasers of these goods and services. In the Indian food grains market, as noted above, private sector participation has been steadily increasing. This has seen several foreign-owned MNCs, such as Glencore, Toepfer and Cargill, as well as Indian-owned companies, like the Reliance group, buying wheat directly from the farmers in recent years. This activity has come to coincide with the government having to import wheat for the first time in several years to replenish its buffer stocks to ensure adequate supplies to the food-based welfare programmes. India's (reducing) food security has come to be seen as an issue of concern in consequence of these developments.

The Present and the Future of India's Food Processing Sector

The estimated size of India's food processing industry is US$70 billion; it employs 1.6 million people, its share in world trade is 1.7 per cent and it is India's fifth-largest manufacturing industry (India Brand Equity Foundation 2007). The industry has six key sectors: dairy; fruit and vegetables; meat and poultry; fisheries; packaged foods; and beverages, all with relatively low, but growing, penetration levels in India's household food budgets. India's export of processed food was US$7.9 billion, or 5 per cent of its total exports in 2004/05.

The Reserve Bank of India (2008) records show that foreign direct investment (FDI) flows into the food processing industries have been around $711 million up to March 2004 – a relatively small amount, again, but growing, as indicated by the presence of a large number of MNCs in the Indian market. Among the more high profile foreign companies are Unilever, Cadbury, Nestlé and Pepsi. These companies face competition from strong Indian product brands of companies such as Reliance, Dabur and Haldiram. Another feature of this sector that is also changing fast is the dominance in it of small and medium-sized (unorganised) producers, which account for around 70 per cent of the output (50 per cent in value) of the sector as a whole.

Recognising the potential of the sector, the central government set up a separate ministry, the Ministry of Food Processing Industries, in 1998 to oversee and facilitate the growth of a wide-ranging food processing sector with the participation of both indigenous and foreign participants, in an environment of collaboration. The national aim is to raise the level of food processing from 2 per cent to 10 per cent by 2010, and to 25 per cent by 2025. To this end, generous tax incentives, as well as full repatriation of profits and capital, and an easier approval process for foreign investment, have been put in place. All this would suggest an increasing presence of large processing firms in India's food business.

In addition to processing food, there is also the interest of large multi-national retailers in domestic markets as large as India's to contend with. Retailers such as Tesco, Ahold, Carrefour, Metro and Wal-Mart, for example, already have a presence in many developing economies which they, and other retailers like them, have been seeking to expand and extend. Wal-Mart has been involved in seeking to partner with India's Reliance Industry Ltd (RIL) to build supermarket stores in 784 Indian towns, 1600 farm supply hubs, and move the produce with a 40-plane air cargo fleet (Shiva 2006). If these efforts were to succeed and proliferate, there will be even more intense competition among those at the starting points of India's food supply chain, namely the farmers and growers of farm products.

GROWTH, DEVELOPMENT, HUNGER AND FOOD SECURITY: INDIA'S BURNING QUANDARY

The elaborate discourse of this chapter around India's food economy and some of its selected ramifications provides detailed information on several relevant issues; it also raises some serious questions. One of these questions must be how the changes that are already afoot in India's food sector are going to affect the lives and livelihoods of India's vast population.

While India's faster economic development and its achievements in some other areas have, in recent times, drawn the world's admiring attention, there remain other aspects of its performance that are decidedly less glamorous. For example, India is still home to the largest number of the world's hungry people, with over 200 million people who are food-insecure (Menon et al. 2008). India's score of 23.7 in the Global Hunger Index (GHI) is 66th out of 88 countries. This places India below countries such as Cameroon, Kenya and Sudan, all of which have lower per capita income than India. Estimates of calorie deficiency in the Indian population, as reported in Menon et al. (2008), varies between 20 and 34 per cent, depending on the average calorie requirement figure chosen, and whether average food availability or actual food consumption per head is used in the calculation of the calorie intake. Even the lower figure, used in the GHI calculation, translates into a very large number of people who are regularly undernourished in India. As Ray (2008) points out, the calorie norm, useful as it is, does not of course indicate anything about the considerations of a balanced diet which should be within the rising aspirations of economies experiencing 'development', not just per capita income growth. Perhaps even more alarmingly, the situation in regard to calorie deficiency has been deteriorating over time since the late 1980s, as Ray (2008) has also detailed. The reasons for this deterioration occurring, paradoxically, with India's faster economic growth and increasing integration with the global economy are many and varied; some of these have been explored in this chapter. The solutions to the problem, however, must include easier and more affordable access to basic food items, such as India had in place over many years. The need to achieve this most basic of human needs, freedom from hunger and malnutrition, must be incontrovertible.

REFERENCES

Ahluwalia, M.S. and I.M.D Little (1998), *India's Economic Reforms and Development: Essays for Manmohan Singh*, Oxford: Oxford University Press.
Bardhan, P. (1984), *The Political Economy of Development in India*, Oxford: Blackwell.
Bardhan, P. (2006), 'Awakening giants, feet of clay: a comparative assessment of the rise of China and India', *Journal of South Asian Development*, 1(1), 1–17.
Bhagwati, J. (1993), *India in Transition: Freeing the Economy*, Oxford: Clarendon Press.
Bijapurkar, R. (2003), 'The new improved Indian consumer', *Business World*, accessed at www.businessworldindia.co/Dec0803/coverstory01.asp.
Chand, R. (2005), 'Whither India's food policy? From food security to food deprivation', *Economic and Political Weekly*, **40**, 1055–62.
Chatterjee, S. (2008), *The Anatomy of Recent Growth and Transformation of the Economies of China and India*, Palmerston North, NZ: Massey University.
Chatterjee, S., A.N. Rae and R. Ray (2006), 'Food consumption, trade reforms and trade patterns in contemporary India: how do Australia and New Zealand fit in?', Department of Applied and International Economics discussion paper no. 07.03, Massey University.
Chatterjee, S., A.N. Rae and R. Ray (2007), 'Food consumption and calories intake in contemporary India', *eSocial Sciences*, Mumbai, India, accessed at www.esocialsciences.com/home/index.asp.

Food and Agriculture Organization (FAO) (various issues), *Food Balance Sheets*, Rome: FAO.

Gopinath, M. and D. Laborde, (2008), *Implications for India of the May 2008 Draft Agricultural Modalities*, Geneva: Programme on Agricultural Trade and Sustainable Development, International Food Policy Research Institute.

Government of India (2007a), *Draft XIth Five Year Plan*, New Delhi: Planning Commission.

Government of India (2007b), *Union Budget and Economic Survey, 2006–07*, New Delhi: Ministry of Finance.

Government of India (2008), *Economic Survey 2007–08*, New Delhi: Ministry of Finance.

India Brand Equity Foundation (2007), *Food Processing Report, 2007*, accessed at www.ibef.org/industry/foodindustry.aspx.

Jafri, A. (2008), 'Food crisis exposes failings of India's agricultural reforms', *Mainstream*, **46**(33), 1–7.

Jha, S., P.V. Srinivasan and M. Landes (2007), 'Indian wheat and rice sector policies and the implications for reform', in Economic Research Report No. 41, Washington, DC: US Department of Agriculture.

Joshi, V. and I. Little (1996), *India's Economic Reforms*, Delhi: Oxford University Press.

Kumar, P. and V.C. Mathur (1996), 'Structural changes in the demand for food in India', *Indian Journal of Agricultural Economics*, **51**, 664–73.

Landes, M. (2008), The environment for agriculture and agribusiness investment in India, US Department of Agriculture Economic Research Service, economic information bulletin no. 37, July.

Landes, R. and A. Gulati (2004), 'Farm sector performance and reform agenda', *Economic and Political Weekly*, 7 August, pp. 3611–19.

Mehta, J. and S. Venkatraman (2000), 'Poverty statistics: bermicide's feast', *Economic and Political Weekly*, **35**(27), 2377–81.

Menon, P., A. Deolalikar, and A. Bhaskar (2008), 'The India State of Hunger Index: comparisons hunger across states', advance copy for discussion, 14 October.

Organisation for Economic Co-operation and Development (OECD) (2008), *OECD Outlook: 83 India*, Paris: OECD.

Patnaik, U. (2007), 'Neoliberalism and rural poverty in India', *Economic and Political Weekly*, 28 July, pp. 3132–50.

Radhakrishnan, R. (2005), 'Food and nutrition security for the poor: emerging perspectives and policy issues', *Economic and Political Weekly*, 30 April, pp. 1817–21.

Rao, C.H. (2005), *Agriculture, Food Security, Poverty and Environment: Essays on Post-reform India*, Dehli: Oxford University Press.

Ray, R. (2008), 'Dietary changes, calorie intake and undernourishment: a comparative study of India and Vietnam', *Economic and Political Weekly*, **43**(8), 51–8.

Reserve Bank of India (2008), *Report on Foreign Exchange Reserves*, Mumbai, India: Reserve Bank of India.

Shiva, V. (2006), 'WTO is dead, long live free trade: globalization and its new avatars', Findland, MA: Organic Consumers Association, accessed at http://organicconsumers.org/articles/article_1254.cfm.

SME Rating Agency (n.d.), Rating of Indian Micro, small and medium enterprise, accessed at www.smera.in/home.aspx.

Srinivasan, T.N. (2003), 'Indian economic reform: a stocktaking', SCID working paper, no. 190, October.

United Nations (various issues), Comtrade database, accessed at http://comtrade.un.org/.

World Bank (2008), *World Development Indicators*, Washington, DC: World Bank.

7. Global integration and agricultural productivity in China

Yanrui Wu and Zhao Dingtao

INTRODUCTION

Since the commencement of economic reforms in 1978, China has enjoyed unprecedented economic growth. This growth has boosted China's economic power substantially, with the country now having the world's third-largest economy according to the official exchange rate, or the second-largest if income is measured in purchasing power parity rates.[1] Associated with this growth is China's rapid integration with the world economy. This is reflected in the fact that the country has been one of the largest recipients of foreign direct investment (FDI) and was the world's second-largest exporter in 2007.

This chapter aims to provide an assessment of the impact of global integration on agricultural performance in China, and hence explore the question of whether agricultural growth is sustainable or not. Understanding this question is not only important for China, but it also has implications for the rest of the world, as Chinese agriculture provides food for the largest populace in the world. To answer this question, one has to explore the role of total factor productivity (TFP) in agricultural growth. This is essentially the objective of this chapter. Specifically, this study presents a review of the productivity debate in the context of China and hence new evidence of the contribution of total factor productivity to agricultural growth. The next section of the chapter provides a brief discussion about China's integration with the world. This is followed by a review of productivity studies, particularly studies of agricultural productivity in China. The analytical framework and data issues are then described. Empirical results are reported and analysed next. The final section offers some general conclusions.

CHINA EMBRACING THE WORLD

As a result of the implementation of 'open door' policies in 1978, the Chinese economy has been increasingly integrated with the world economy. This is supported by several popular indicators. For example, China's total value of exports as a share of GDP has been rising steadily for about three decades (Figure 7.1). It was as high as 37 per cent in 2007, in contrast with 11 per cent in the USA and 14 per cent in Japan in 2005 (World Bank 2008). Among the world's large economies, only Germany with an export to GDP ratio of 41 per cent in 2005 is close to being on a par with China. In the meantime, China has also become one of the largest recipients of FDI. In 2006 China's net inflow of FDI of US$78 billion was more than the total combining Brazil (US$19 billion), India (US$17 billion) and Mexico (US$19 billion), the three largest developing economies behind China (World Bank 2008). It is noted that both FDI and exports have increased dramatically since 2001 when China became a WTO member.

During the same period, China's agricultural sector also became more integrated with the rest of the world. FDI and exports from this sector expanded significantly with FDI in agriculture reaching US$924 million in 2007 and exports of food and other edible goods growing from US$12.8 billion in 2001 to US$30.7 billion in the same year (National Bureau of Statistics 2008). In the meantime, China's imports of agricultural goods

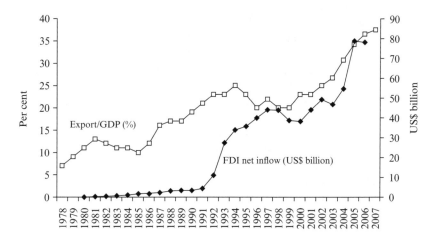

Sources: World Bank (2008) and National Bureau of Statistics (2008).

Figure 7.1   China: export/GDP and FDI net inflow, 1978–2007

have also risen rapidly. For example, the value of imports of food and other edible products increased from about US$5 billion in 2001 to over US$11 billion in 2007 (National Bureau of Statistics 2008). How has integration affected growth in agriculture in general and productivity performance in particular? This is the focus of the rest of the chapter.

PRODUCTIVITY AND GROWTH: A REVIEW

The role of productivity in growth has been controversial and fiercely debated among economists (for a review see Griliches 1994). Research on this topic was particularly boosted by the inquiries into productivity slowdown in the USA in the 1960s and 1970s, especially relative to Japan (see, for example, Baumol 1986; De Long and Bradford 1988; Dowrick and Nguyen 1989; Wolff 1991, 1996). It is argued that the relative productivity slowdown in the USA and European countries may be due to the natural process of convergence as countries with a low level of productivity catch up to those with a high level (Abramovitz 1986; Baumol 1986). Though still unresolved, the debate re-emerged in the 1990s with a focus on the East Asian economies. Krugman (1994) together with Young (1994), and Kim and Lau (1994), raised serious doubts about the role of technological progress in the East Asian growth model and thus the sustainability of growth in those economies. As expected, their views have been questioned by other authors (Kawai 1994; Oshima 1995; Sarel 1995).

The Chinese economy, and the sustainability of its growth, has also been the subject of considerable scrutiny. The role of productivity in growth at the macro as well as the micro level has been investigated intensively, though a consensus has hardly been reached. For more of an overview of research in this area, see Wu (1993, 2008a), Wu and Yang (1999) and Fan and Zhang (2006). Earlier studies of the agricultural sector have focused especially on the impact of rural reforms on agricultural productivity and hence growth (McMillan et al. 1989; Lin 1992; Fan 1991; Zhang and Carter 1997; Fan and Zhang 2002). One common finding in these studies is that economic reforms at the early stage stimulated productivity growth in Chinese agriculture significantly.

However, conclusions with regard to other areas are more controversial. While Borensztein and Ostry (1996) and Hu and Khan (1997) are more positive about the contribution of TFP to China's growth, others only found a minor role played by TFP growth (Woo 1998). At the firm level, authors are more pessimistic partly because of the dominance of the state-owned enterprises (SOEs) in the 1980s and 1990s (Chen et al. 1988; Jefferson et al. 1996; Woo et al. 1994).

Wu (2008a) reviewed over 70 papers and found that the average estimated rate of TFP growth is 3.62 per cent. Twenty-two studies surveyed by Wu (2008a) are related to the agricultural sector and a mean rate of TFP growth of 3.81 per cent can be derived from those studies. There is however substantial variation among the studies. The objective of this chapter is to revisit the debate about the role of productivity in economic growth, using the agricultural sector as the setting. In particular, this study investigates the performance of productivity in Chinese agriculture during the period of rapid global integration. For the first time, capital stock data are estimated for the Chinese agricultural sector. The derived database is then employed to examine the contribution of TFP to growth in the agricultural sector during the period of 1978–2005.

ANALYTICAL FRAMEWORK AND DATA DESCRIPTION

A variety of techniques have been developed to estimate productivity growth. There are advantages and disadvantages associated with each approach. For recent reviews, see Kumbhakar and Lovell (2000), Coelli et al. (2005) and Greene (2008). This study employs a well-developed method which falls into the family of stochastic frontier analysis (SFA) approaches. According to the latter, productivity growth or total factor productivity growth ($T\mathring{F}P$) can be decomposed into two components, namely, technological progress ($T\mathring{P}$) and technical efficiency change ($T\mathring{E}$). That is:

$$T\mathring{F}P = T\mathring{P} + T\mathring{E}$$

The computation of the above decomposition involves the estimation of production functions (see Appendix 7.1 of this chapter for more detailed technical presentation).

To implement the empirical estimation procedure, it is assumed that capital, land and labour are employed to produce one output, that is, value-added. Production occurs among the regions. As a result, regional data of these variables (output, labour, capital stock and land) are required for the empirical exercises. In this study, output represents the value-added and labour is the total employment in the agricultural sector among China's 31 administrative regions. The main challenging task is to estimate capital stock for the Chinese regions. There are some economy-wide estimates of capital stock at the national and regional levels (Wu 2008b; Zhang 2008). The focus of this exercise is hence the construction

Table 7.1   Annual rates of depreciation in the Chinese economy

Region	%	Region	%
Beijing	1.4	Hubei	1.6
Tianjin	1.0	Hunan	1.6
Hebei	1.6	Guangdong	2.3
Shanxi	1.2	Guangxi	2.5
Inner Mongolia	1.6	Hainan	1.6
Liaoning	1.6	Chongqing	1.5
Jilin	1.6	Sichuan	1.5
Heilongjiang	1.6	Guizhou	1.3
Shanghai	0.6	Yunnan	0.8
Jiangsu	2.3	Tibet	0.6
Zhejiang	2.3	Shaanxi	1.8
Anhui	1.6	Gansu	1.8
Fujian	1.6	Qinghai	0.6
Jiangxi	1.6	Ningxia	1.8
Shandong	2.7	Xinjiang	1.9
Henan	1.6	Mean	1.6

Source: Authors' own derivation.

of capital stock data for the agricultural sector that are for the first time obtained in this study. The main breakthrough here is the derivation and use of the rates of depreciation for each region (see Appendix 7.2 of this chapter for details). The latter are reported in Table 7.1. In general, the annual rates of depreciation are very low in the agricultural sector with a national average of 1.6 per cent, which is smaller than the popular rate of 4 per cent employed in the literature. It is also noticed in Table 7.1 that the relatively more developed regions (such as Jiangsu, Zhejiang, Shandong and Guangdong) tend to have high rates of depreciation. This finding is consistent with the trend at the economy-wide level (Wu 2008b).

EMPIRICAL ESTIMATION

To examine productivity performance, the empirical model is estimated using data for the periods of 1978–89 and 1990–2005, respectively. The point of division (in 1990) is determined for three reasons. First, there was a major revision of employment data in 1990 (see Figure 7.2). To ensure consistency, two datasets are constructed with each being internally

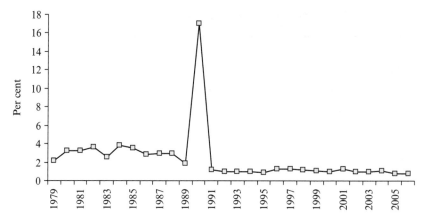

Source: National Bureau of Statistics (various issues).

Figure 7.2   Growth of China's total employment, 1979–2006

consistent. Second, economic reforms and hence growth have accelerated since the early 1990s. Third, the 1990s and onwards represent the period of accelerated economic reforms and liberalisation. Separate estimation of the models may be able to capture the structural changes that occurred between the two periods and hence examine the impact of global integration on productivity performance. The estimation results of fixed-effect models are reported in Appendix 7.3 in this chapter. Most estimated coefficients are statistically significant at the 1 per cent level.

Given the estimation results, technical efficiency scores for the regions can be computed and subsequently the rates of technological progress and efficiency changes are also estimated. Several observations can be made. First, the leaders (the frontier shifters) are identified and illustrated in Figure 7.3. During 1978–2005, Shandong has been the trendsetter for most years. Jiangsu was the best performer in 1982 and 1983, while Hubei was the best in 1978–79, 1981 and 1990. As expected, the leaders are dominantly coastal regions. The latter have also been the front-runners of economic liberalisation in China over the past decades.

Second, the mean TFP growth rates together with the rates of technological progress and efficiency changes are presented in Table 7.2. Since the late 1970s, total factor productivity has achieved considerable growth in Chinese agriculture with an average rate of 3.80 per cent during 1979–2005. It is also found that technological progress was the major contributor to productivity growth, a conclusion supported by others (Wu 2008c; Zheng et al. 2008). Thus the pessimistic view about the East Asian growth

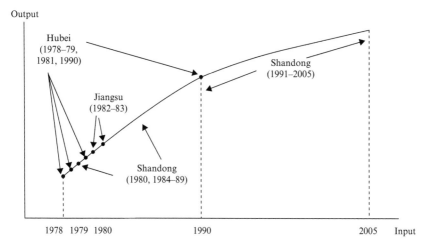

Output

Hubei
(1978–79,
1981, 1990)

Shandong
(1991–2005)

Jiangsu
(1982–83)

Shandong
(1980, 1984–89)

1978 1979 1980   1990   2005   Input

Source: Author's own illustration.

Figure 7.3   Best-practice performers, 1978–2005

Table 7.2   Average annual growth rates (%)

	TE	TP	TFP
1979–89	−0.86	5.75	4.89
1991–2005	0.02	2.98	3.00

Source: Author's own estimates.

model does not hold in the case of the Chinese economy. However China's TFP growth in the agricultural sector has shown a trend of slowdown since the early 1990s.

There is also substantial variation among China's 31 provinces and autonomous administrative regions. However, there is evidence of convergence in terms of TFP performance as demonstrated in Figure 7.4, which shows that the standard deviation of regional TFP growth rates tends to fall over time.

Third, geographically, China can be divided into three regions: the coastal, middle and western regions. The western region includes 12 provinces and autonomous regions that are all covered by the 'western development' programme.[2] Variations among these regions and particularly within the western region can also be examined by analysing the relevant mean rates of growth. In terms of TFP performance, the western

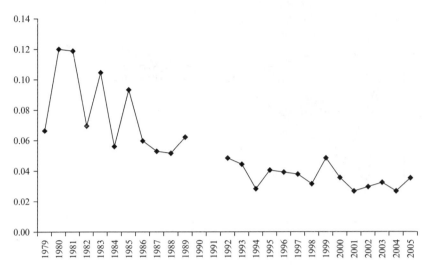

Source: Author's own estimates.

Figure 7.4   Standard deviation of regional TFP growth rates, 1979–2005

Table 7.3   Growth rates (%) of TP, TE and TFP across the regions

Regions	1978–89	1990–2005	2000–05
TP			
Coastal	5.66	3.14	3.27
Middle	5.69	2.74	2.86
Western	5.86	3.02	3.11
TE			
Coastal	−0.46	0.11	0.51
Middle	−1.62	0.16	0.93
Western	−0.63	−0.15	0.49
TFP			
Coastal	5.20	3.25	3.77
Middle	4.07	2.90	3.78
Western	5.24	2.87	3.60

Source: Author's own estimates.

regions lagged behind the coastal regions in the 1990s according to Table 7.3. However, there is evidence of catch-up during the period of 2000–05 that coincided with the implementation of the 'western development' programme. This change has mainly been driven by technological progress.

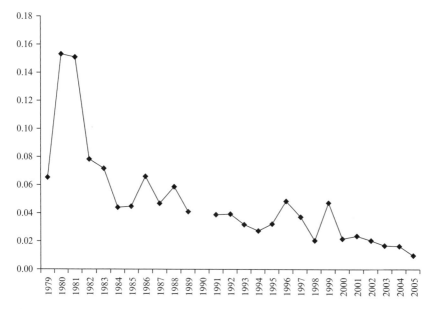

Source: Author's own estimates.

Figure 7.5   *Standard deviation of TFP growth rates in the western regions*

Within the western regions, Chongqing and Sichuan have been found to be the leaders and there is also evidence of convergence (Figure 7.5).[3]

Fourth, agricultural productivity has been very volatile during the process of rapid globalisation (Figure 7.6). There is evidence that agricultural performance has been vulnerable to both external and internal shocks such as the oil price increase in the early 1980s, China's political instability in 1989 and the Asian financial crisis in 1997. The estimation results also show that external and internal shocks mainly affect efficiency performance in the short run.

CONCLUDING REMARKS

The role of productivity in China's economic growth has attracted a lot of attention in academia and hence has been extensively investigated using data at the aggregate, regional and industry levels. This chapter presents detailed estimates of capital stock series for the agricultural sector among China's 31 administrative regions. These estimates are for the first time based on region-specific rates of depreciation. It is found that

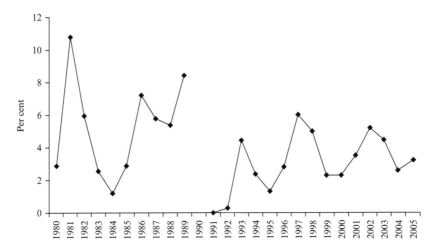

Notes: The numbers are two-year moving average growth rates derived by the author.

Figure 7.6   TFP growth rates in Chinese agriculture, 1980–2005

China's agricultural growth has been driven substantially by productivity improvement, in particular technological progress. This is a good indication of sustainability of growth in the near future. It is also found that there is considerable regional variation in performance. There is, however, evidence of convergence among the regions. Finally, during the process of rapid globalisation, agricultural performance is vulnerable to both external and internal shocks that affect efficiency performance in the short run.

NOTES

1. According to the World Development Indicators (World Bank 2008), China's gross domestic product (GDP) in 2007 was ranked third in the world, behind America and Japan, in terms of constant US dollars; and the second, behind only the USA, in terms of constant international dollars.
2. This classification is slightly different from the traditional, official grouping according to which Guangxi belongs to the coastal region while Inner Mongolia is a middle region.
3. A separate estimation using the western regional data only shows that Chongqing and Sichuan are the leaders among the 12 provinces and autonomous administrative regions. The estimation results are available upon request.

REFERENCES

Abramovitz, M. (1986), 'Catching up, forging ahead, and falling behind', *Journal of Economic History*, **46**, 385–406.

Baumol, W.J. (1986), 'Productivity growth, convergence, and welfare: what the long-run data show', *American Economic Review*, **76**, 1072–85.

Borensztein, E. and J.D. Ostry (1996), 'Accounting for China's growth performance', *American Economic Review (Papers and Proceedings)*, **86**, 225–8.

Chen, K., H.C. Wang, Y.X. Zheng, G.H. Jefferson and T.G. Rawski (1988), 'Productivity change in Chinese industry, 1953–85', *Journal of Comparative Economics*, **12**, 570–91.

Coelli, T., D.S.P. Rao, C.J. O'Donnell and G.E. Battese (2005), *An Introduction to Efficiency and Productivity Analysis* (2nd edn), New York: Springer.

De Long, J.B. and J. Bradford (1988), 'Productivity growth, convergence and welfare: comment', *American Economic Review*, **78**, 1138–54.

Dowrick, S. and Duc-Tho Nguyen (1989), 'OECD comparative economic growth 1950–85: catch-up and convergence', *American Economic Review*, **79**, 1010–30.

Fan, S. (1991), 'Effects of technological change and institutional reform on production growth in Chinese agriculture', *American Journal of Agricultural Economics*, **73**, 266–75.

Fan, S. and X. Zhang (2002), 'Production and productivity growth in Chinese agriculture: new national and regional measures', *Economic Development and Cultural Change*, **50**, 819–38.

Fan, S. and X. Zhang (2006), 'Production and productivity growth in Chinese agriculture: new national and regional measures', in Xiao-Yuan Dong, Shunfeng Song and X. Zhang (eds), *Chinas's Agricultural Development: Challenges and Prospects*, Chinese Economy Series, Aldershot: Ashgate, pp. 129–51.

Greene, W.H. (2008), 'The econometric approach to efficiency analysis', in H.O. Fried, A.K. Lovell and S.S. Schmidt (eds), *The Measurement of Productive Efficiency and Productivity Growth*, New York: Oxford University Press.

Griliches, Z. (1994), 'Productivity, R and D, and the data constraint', *American Economic Review*, **84**(1), 1–23.

Hu, Z.F. and M.S. Khan (1997), 'Why is China growing so fast?', *IMF Staff Papers*, **44**, 103–31.

Jefferson, G.H., T.G. Rawski and Y. Zheng (1996), 'Chinese industrial productivity: trends, measurement issues, and recent developments', *Journal of Comparative Economics*, **23**, 146–80.

Kawai, Hiroki (1994), 'International comparative analysis of economic growth: trade liberalisation and productivity', *Developing Economies*, **17**(4), 373–97.

Kim, J.I. and L. Lau (1994), 'The sources of economic growth in the East Asian newly industrialised countries', *Journal of the Japanese and International Economies*, **8**, 235–71.

Krugman, P. (1994), 'The myth of Asia's miracle', *Foreign Affairs*, **73**, November–December, 62–78.

Kumbhakar, S.C. and C.A.K. Lovell (2000), *Stochastic Frontier Analysis*, Cambridge: Cambridge University Press.

Lin, J.Y. (1992), 'Rural reforms and agricultural growth in China', *American Economic Review*, **82**, 34–51.

McMillan, J., J. Whalley and L. Zhu (1989), 'The impact of China's economic reforms on agricultural productivity growth', *Journal of Political Economy*, **97**, 781–807.

National Bureau of Statistics (2008), *Statistical Yearbook of China 2008*, Beijing: China Statistics Press.

National Bureau of Statistics (various issues), *Statistical Yearbook of China*, Beijing: China Statistics Press.

Oshima, M. (1995), 'Trends in productivity growth in the economic transition of Asia and long-term prospects for the 1990s', *Asian Economic Journal*, **9**(21), 89–111.

Sarel, Michael (1995), 'Growth in East Asia: what we can and what we cannot infer from it', in Palle Andersen, Jacqueline Dwyer and David Gruen (eds), *Productivity and Growth*, Canberra: Reserve Bank of Australia, pp. 237–59.

Wolff, Edward N. (1991), 'Capital formation and productivity convergence over the long term', *American Economic Review*, **81**, 565–79.

Wolff, Edward N. (1996), 'The productivity slowdown: the culprit at last? Follow-up on Hulten and Wolff', *American Economic Review*, **86**, 1239–52.

Woo, W.T. (1998), 'Chinese economic growth: sources and prospects', in M. Fouquin and F. Lemoine (eds), *The Chinese Economy*, Paris: Economica, pp. 17–47.

Woo, W.T., W. Hai, Y. Jin and G. Fan (1994), 'How successful has Chinese enterprise reform been? Pitfalls in opposite biases and focus', *Journal of Comparative Economics*, **18**, 410–37.

World Bank (2008), *World Development Indicators 2008*, accessed at: www.worldbank.org.

Wu, Y. (1993), 'Productive efficiency in Chinese industry: a review', *Asian-Pacific Economic Literature*, **7**(2), 58–66.

Wu, Y. (2008a), 'The blind men and the elephant: productivity estimates for the Chinese economy', paper presented at the 2008 Asia Pacific Productivity Conference, Taipei.

Wu, Y. (2008b), *Productivity, Efficiency and Economic Growth in China*, London: Palgrave Macmillan.

Wu, Y. (2008c), 'The role of productivity in China's growth: new estimates', *Journal of Chinese Economic and Business Studies*, **6**, 141–56.

Wu, Y. and H. Yang, (1999), 'Productivity and growth: a review', in K.P. Kalirajan, and Y.R. Wu (eds), *Productivity and Growth in Chinese Agriculture*, London: Macmillan Press, pp. 29–51.

Young, A. (1994), 'Lessons from the East Asian NICs: a contrarian view', *European Economic Review*, **110**, 641–80.

Zhang, B. and C.A. Carter (1997), 'Reforms, the weather and productivity growth in China's rural sector', *AJAE*, **79**, 1266–77.

Zhang, Jun (2008), 'Estimating China's provincial capital stock (1952–2004) with applications', *Journal of Chinese Economic and Business Studies*, **6**, 177–96.

Zheng, Jinghai, Zheng Wang and Jinchuan Shi (2008), 'Industrial productivity performance in Chinese regions (1987–2002): a decomposition approach', *Journal of Chinese Economic and Business Studies*, **6**, 157–76.

APPENDIX 7.1

Symbolically, assume that the production technology in logarithmic form can be modelled as follows:

$$\ln y_{it} = \alpha_i + \ln f(x_{it}; \beta) + u_{it} \qquad (7A.1)$$

where y_{it} and x_{it} represent outputs and inputs, α is the individual effect, β is a vector of parameters to be estimated and u_{it} is the white noise.

Given equation (7A.1), technical efficiency (*TE*) which is defined as the ratio of the observed output over the best practice output, can be derived using the following procedure:

$$TE_{it} = e^{\hat{\varepsilon}_{it} - \hat{\varepsilon}_t} \qquad (7A.2)$$

where $\hat{\varepsilon}_{it} = \hat{\alpha}_i + \hat{u}_{it}$ and $\hat{\varepsilon}_t = \max(\hat{u}_{it})$.

Furthermore, technological progress ($T\overset{\circ}{P}$) and technical efficiency change ($T\overset{\circ}{E}$) can be estimated using the following equations:

$$T\overset{\circ}{P} = \partial y / \partial t = \partial f / \partial t = f_t \qquad (7A.3)$$

$$T\overset{\circ}{E}_{it} = TE_{it} / TE_{i,t-1} - 1 \qquad (7A.4)$$

APPENDIX 7.2

The derivation of China's regional capital stock in agriculture follows the perpetual inventory method. That is:

$$K_{ti} = (1 - \delta_i)K_{t-1,i} + I_{ti} \qquad (7A.5)$$

where K_{ti} and I_{ti} represent the stock of capital and realized investment at period t for the ith region and δ_i is the rate of depreciation for the ith region. Chinese government has released capital formation data at the sector level for all regions from 1978 onwards. This data series is employed as the realised investment in equation (7A.5). Thus, a capital stock series can be generated using equation (7A.5) if the rate of depreciation and the initial value of capital stock are known. To derive the region-specific rates of depreciation, a simulation process proposed by Wu (2008b) is adopted here. According to this approach, the estimated values of depreciation (using assumed rates of depreciation) converge with the actual value of depreciation reported by the National Bureau of Statistics (various issues).

The derived rates of depreciation are reported in Table 7.1 in the text. To derive the initial value of capital stock, the following formula is employed:

$$K_{0i} = I_{0i}/(g_i + \delta_i) \tag{FA.}$$

where K_{0i} and I_{0i} represent the stock of capital and realised investment in the initial period (say, 1978 for this study) for the ith region and g_i is the average rate of growth in investment or output for the ith region during the initial three years.

APPENDIX 7.3

Table 7.A.1   Estimation results

	1978–89	1990–2005
Time	0.086 (5.40)***	0.058 (8.55)***
LogK	0.096 (1.46)	0.137 (6.55)***
LogL	0.141 (2.06)**	−0.238 (−5.77)***
Time*LogK	−0.004 (−1.77)*	0.003 (2.24)**
Time*LogL	0.005 (1.21)	0.007 (4.23)***
LogLD	0.061 (0.38)	0.592 (7.96)***
Time*LogLD	−0.006 (−1.27)	−0.011 (−4.87)***
Sample size	372	496
Adjusted R^2	0.99	0.99
LM values	1646.77***	3223.37***

Note: *, ** and *** indicate significance at the level of 10 per cent, 5 per cent and 1 per cent.

8. Globalisation and agriculture in the ASEAN region

M.A.B. Siddique

INTRODUCTION

This chapter focuses on agriculture and globalisation in the Association of South East Asian Nations (ASEAN) region from 1984 to 2007. I have opted to omit Brunei and Myanmar, as data relating to the various indicators used in the analysis are not readily available for these two countries for a substantial portion of the period. Singapore is also omitted on the basis of its negligible agricultural sector. Therefore, this study focuses on the following ASEAN countries: Cambodia, Indonesia, Laos, Malaysia, the Philippines, Thailand and Vietnam. The analysis deals with these seven countries in two different groups, namely the ASEAN transition economies[1] (ATEs) and the ASEAN4.[2] These two groups differ in their characteristics: whereas the ATEs have only recently started to slowly embrace market economics, the countries in the ASEAN4 have had capitalistic systems in place for a relatively long time, possibly due to the influence of colonial rule in the earlier half of the century. For example, a political party in Cambodia, one of the ATEs, still adheres to a platform of socialism; and similarly, in Laos, there is still strong socialist rule. At the other end of the spectrum in the ASEAN4 economies, for example in Thailand and Malaysia, capitalism is the dominant form of economic organisation. In this chapter, I also use the term ASEAN7 to refer to all the countries in both groups together.

While there are numerous different definitions of globalisation, the main definition used in this chapter is the one defined by the International Monetary Fund (IMF), where globalisation is a process resulting from human innovation and technological progress, and the increasing integration of economies around the world through trade and financial flows. Another indicator of globalisation, the A.T. Kearney/Foreign Policy Globalisation Index, attempts to track a country's performance in terms of globalisation, given four different classes of indicators. These indicators include the level of economic integration, the levels of personal contact, technological connectivity and political engagement.

The period used in this analysis is 1984 to 2007. This period is chosen because many of the ATEs developed and enacted a more capitalistic stance in their economic policy from 1984 onwards. While it would be ideal to conduct the analysis over a longer time frame, many ASEAN countries have not been updating various key statistics required for such an in-depth analysis. The period under analysis is subdivided into three different periods (1984–95, 1996–2000 and 2001–07) This is done to analyse the effectiveness of the policies within the first period, to isolate the effects of the financial crisis in the second period, and finally to look at the growth of the economies after the recession.

This chapter is divided in to five subsequent sections. In the next section, the chapter explores the levels of openness of the various economies, levels of foreign direct investment (FDI) and the policy initiatives that the respective governments have undertaken to open their economy to the rest of the world. After that, the chapter identifies the state of the agricultural sector in each country with regards to the impact it has on their respective economies. The chapter then identifies the emergence of new technology, its effect on agricultural productivity and its diffusion through the agricultural sector within the two groups in ASEAN. Lastly, the chapter concludes with a general overview of globalisation in the agricultural sectors of these two groups.

ASEAN7 Economic Performance, 1984–2007

Growth in the ASEAN region has been stable in the recent past at high levels. For example, the average growth rate for the nine countries has been 5.93 per cent (including the steep fall in 1998) for the period between 1984 and 2007 (World Bank 2009). This is twice the levels of growth experienced by Organisation for Economic Co-operation and Development (OECD) countries within the same time period (2.77 per cent). In addition, from Table 8.1 it can be observed that the growth rates for the ATEs tend to be higher, compared to the ASEAN4 countries, and that the growth rates for the ASEAN countries as a whole generally outpace the OECD countries.

This growth can be explained using the Solow growth model, which predicts that as developing countries grow and their rates of growth are rapid, they are destined to slow down in the future. Hence, as developing countries move along the Solow growth model, their rate of growth decreases. Such an effect can be observed where the ASEAN4 economies grow at a faster pace than the OECD countries as a whole, and similarly in the years where the ATE economies are growing faster than the ASEAN4. This steep rate of growth could also be due to the rapid accumulation of

Table 8.1 Growth rates of ASEAN countries compared to OECD countries and the world

	Year		
	1984–95	1996–2000	2001–07
ASEAN4	6.24	2.65	5.06
ATEs	5.74	6.83	8.06
OECD	2.69	3.66	2.95
World	3.19	3.33	3.06

Source: World Bank (2009).

capital, as foreigners increase their investments in these countries to earn a higher rate of return. In this case, this flow of capital, also known as FDI, could not only explain the rapid growth rate but it could also signal the increasing levels of openness within the ASEAN economies.

As the two groups in the ASEAN region are well endowed with fertile land and a large population, it is natural that agriculture plays an important role in their economies, regardless of the state of their development. However, it is interesting to look at the rates of development of these countries in the face of globalisation and to see whether globalisation translates into higher growth in the primary mainstay of agriculture. Since they are developing economies, the governments' first priority would be to focus on agriculture, given their comparative advantages and so as to be able to feed their population. Hence, the overview provided in this chapter can be used as a measure of the relative growth in the agriculture sector as well as the effectiveness of the policies employed by the governments in the ASEAN region. Also, it is important from a humanitarian standpoint to see if the region has been able to alleviate poverty and if globalisation has achieved its aim, in the context of agriculture.

GLOBALISATION OF THE ASEAN7 ECONOMIES

Various authors use different indicators to measure globalisation, depending on the availability of data and the purpose of the study. The important point would be to identify the period of commencement of globalisation and apply indicators to measure its progress. Usually the progress of globalisation commences with a major shift in policy measures, undertaken or adopted by the government concerned in order to embrace economic reforms and open up the economy.

Table 8.2   Openness and FDI flows

	1984–95	1996–2000	2001–07
Panel A: Index of Openness (Total trade / GDP)			
Cambodia*	0.78	0.86	1.30
Lao PDR	0.37	0.74	0.74
Vietnam*	0.56	0.99	1.37
ATEs	0.57	0.86	1.14
Malaysia	1.39	2.03	2.00
Philippines	0.60	1.04	0.99
Thailand	0.69	1.02	1.34
Indonesia	0.48	0.68	0.60
ASEAN4	0.79	1.19	1.23
ASEAN7	0.70	1.05	1.19
Panel B: Ratio of FDI to GDP			
Cambodia*	0.05	0.06	0.05
Lao PDR	0.02	0.05	0.03
Vietnam*	0.04	0.07	0.05
ATEs	0.03	0.06	0.04
Malaysia	0.05	0.04	0.03
Philippines	0.01	0.02	0.01
Thailand	0.01	0.04	0.04
Indonesia	0.01	0.01	0.01
ASEAN4	0.02	0.03	0.02
ASEAN7	0.03	0.04	0.03

Note: * For the period of 1984–95, trade data and FDI data for Cambodia are only available for 1995. In addition, the trade data for Vietnam are only available from 1986 for the period, while FDI data are only available from 1985 for the period.

Source: World Bank (2009).

Two important indicators, widely used in the literature to measure the extent of globalisation, are the index of openness and the ratio of FDI to gross domestic product (GDP). In this chapter, we employ these two indicators to measure the progress of globalisation in the selected ASEAN countries (see Table 8.2).

As discussed, many of the reforms in the ATEs were instituted from 1984. For example, although Cambodia had started to adjust its economy to accommodate capitalistic views, it was not until the 1990s that trade reforms were in place. The Royal Government of Cambodia unified exchange rates, abolished non-tariff barriers and implemented the 'Liberal Law on Investment'. In the case of Vietnam, Doi Moi reforms started in 1986 where they abolished the government's monopoly on trade, liberalised retention of foreign exchange, and removed or reduced quotas and tariffs. In Thailand, an ASEAN4 country, trade liberalisation was implemented far earlier, although the majority of the effective reforms came during the mid-1980s where the Ministry of Finance substantially streamlined tax rebate and refund schemes and made changes to the tariff structure. In Laos, the New Economic Mechanism was implemented in 1986 where tariff rates were lowered and quantitative restrictions and licensing requirements were reduced.

Bowles and MacLean (1996) suggest that the changes in the governmental policy regarding FDI were timely, so as to attract capital flows from Japan. This is due to the fact that the Japanese were looking to expand overseas, given the appreciation of the yen due to the Plaza Accord of 1985. In terms of FDI reform, Cambodia provides a liberal investment regime and includes exemptions on investment goods and inputs used to manufacture exports. In 1987, Vietnam implemented the 'open door' policy in a bid to attract FDI. In contrast to Vietnam, Laos allowed the private sector to participate in the divestment of the state-owned enterprises (SOEs).

Given the above examples of policy reforms, from Panel in Table 8.2, the index of openness has unambiguously increased during the period of 1984 to 2007, for all the ASEAN7 countries. The magnitude of the increase, however, varies from country to country. For example, during the period, Malaysia's Index of Openness (IO) increased from 1.0509 to 2.0008, representing an increase of approximately 100 per cent. On the other hand, Indonesia's IO only increased by 0.07, while Laos's IO jumped 1000 per cent to 0.9075. One insight gained from this table is that the increases in the IO for ATEs are much higher than those of the ASEAN4. This could be due to the fact that the ATEs are relatively less open in the beginning of the sample period as compared to the ASEAN4, and hence the potential for growth in openness for the ATEs is much higher.

In Panel B, FDI is scaled by GDP so as to control for the size of the economy. This is important, as a larger economy typically attracts a higher amount of FDI. From Panel B, we can conclude that all of the ASEAN7 countries again have significantly higher FDI inflow in 2007, as compared to 1984. However, there are mixed observations, comparing the FDI inflow in 1996 and 2007, for the ASEAN4 countries. In the case of Indonesia and Malaysia, FDI inflow decreased between 1996 and 2007, whereas for Thailand and the Philippines it increased. As for the ATEs, FDI inflows increased for all of them, except Laos. A possible explanation could be that the ASEAN4 have attracted a large amount of FDI and as more funds entered the region, they sought out relatively newer regions in search of higher returns.

Overall, as the data have shown, the ASEAN4 and the ATE countries have become more globalised in terms of FDI inflow and contribution to world trade, and they have become more interconnected through financial and trade flows. For example, Indonesia had proposed to reduce tariff rates by 13 per cent after the Uruguay Round talks. There have been significant increases (for the ATEs) in their openness and in their FDI inflows. Furthermore, as FDI inflow increases, studies have shown that they increase the level of innovation in the host country (Cheung and Lin 2004). We will now move to focus the discussion on the agricultural sector in the ASEAN countries.

THE AGRICULTURAL INDUSTRY OF THE ASEAN7 COUNTRIES

Developing economies tend to have an initial comparative advantage in the agricultural industry since their labour force is relatively unskilled. Additionally, a focus on domestic agriculture helps feed their often very large populations and has been used as a platform to fuel future growth. For example, it can be used to generate foreign exchange, increase employment, contribute to capital formation and create a market for manufactured goods. Since it is such a crucial primary industry, it is important to see if globalisation has had any impact on it.

Table 8.3 displays the agricultural share of GDP both in absolute terms and in percentage terms. From this analysis several points are particularly noteworthy here. As is evident in Panel A of Table 8.3, during the first period of analysis, the ASEAN7 economies generate a high proportion of their GDP from the agricultural sector (31.03 per cent). However, as time passes and their economies develop, the share of agriculture slowly but surely declines. One may suggest that this is a by-product of rural–urban migration or that the employment of the agricultural sector has decreased as workers migrate toward the industries with a higher skill requirement and better wages. However, in Panel B, it can be observed that as the percentage share of agriculture decreases, the absolute contribution to GDP is increasing at an extraordinary pace. Over the 1984 to 2007 period, the absolute share of agriculture to GDP increased for all ASEAN7 countries by approximately 50 per cent. This highlights that focusing on the

Table 8.3 Agriculture in the ASEAN7 countries

	1984–95	1996–2000	2001–07	% change (1984–2007)
	Panel A: Agriculture share of GDP (%)			
Cambodia*	47.94	44.09	32.82	−31.55
Lao PDR*	58.95	53.14	46.44	−21.22
Vietnam	36.80	25.86	21.76	−40.88
ATEs	47.89	41.03	33.67	−31.21
Malaysia	16.86	9.56	4.427	−73.75
Philippines	22.74	17.87	14.64	−35.63
Thailand	13.39	9.63	10.26	−23.44
Indonesia	20.52	17.21	14.50	−29.33
ASEAN4	18.38	13.57	10.95	−40.54
ASEAN7	31.03	25.34	20.69	−36.54
	Panel B: Agriculture share of GDP (m)			
Cambodia*	1 117.13	1 292.88	1 598.42	43.08
Lao PDR*	559.24	812.69	1 027.45	83.72
Vietnam	5 141.36	7 007.81	8 878.22	72.68
ATEs	2 272.58	3 037.80	3 834.69	66.49
Malaysia	718.66	775.04	911.88	26.89
Philippines	9 813.11	11 374.18	13 951.00	42.17
Thailand	9 141.80	10 413.89	12 474.45	36.46
Indonesia	20 376.54	25 128.62	29 361.41	44.09
ASEAN4	10 012.53	11 922.93	14 174.69	37.40
ASEAN7	6 695.41	8 115.02	9743.26	49.87

Note: * Agricultural data from Lao are not available from 1984 to 1989 and agricultural data are not available for Cambodia from 1984 to 1992. The figures provided in the tables represent the average of the available data of the period.

Source: World Bank (2009).

percentage decreases in agricultural contribution to the growth of the economy may be misleading. Also, this may imply that while agriculture is progressing as an industry, it may be overlooked and hence even neglected by governments since it is perceived to be relatively less important in terms of contribution to growth and wealth. Indeed, as some researchers have highlighted, many governments have focused on developing other industries at the expense of the agricultural sector.

Another observation is that in terms of absolute GDP in Panel A, the ATEs' share of agriculture has decreased marginally less than that of the ASEAN4 countries. This may be due to the fact that the ATEs have not fully industrialised yet, and hence agriculture still plays a relatively more important role in their economies. In Panel B, the ATEs show a larger increase in their agricultural output compared to the ASEAN4 economies. For example, the agricultural sector's contribution to GDP in Laos has increased by about 84 per cent, whereas in Malaysia it has only increased by approximately 27 per cent. While the percentage increase appears impressive, it should be noted that in real terms the results are more modest. In Laos, for example, the increase was US$500 million, compared to an increase of about US$9 billion in Indonesia. Hence, Table 8.3 corroborates that for developing countries the agricultural sector plays an important role that increases both income and wealth for its people who may be less skilled, when compared to citizens in countries that are more developed. Since the ATE countries have most of their population working in the agriculture sector, it is important to improve it, with the support of the government, so that they can improve the living standards of their people.

Increasing productivity is the best step that governments can take to improve the livelihoods of the citizens working in the agricultural sector. Hence, it is important to analyse the productivity of such an important industry and this can be achieved by looking at agricultural employment and cereal yield. This will give an indication of the success of development in the sector. Details are provided in Table 8.4.

As can be observed from Panel A of Table 8.4, there has been an increase of about 17.7 per cent in agricultural employment in the ASEAN7 countries between 1984 to 2005. In regards to productivity, this increase in employment has yielded an approximate 50 per cent increase in agricultural share of GDP (Table 8.3). Furthermore, the cereal yields of the crops have increased about 36 per cent, as shown in Panel B. These numbers point to heightened productivity growth in the ASEAN7 countries as the percentage increase in employment has led to an even greater increase in production. On the other hand, one can argue that while the GDP contribution of agriculture is decreasing rapidly, the labour force could be diverting to another industry with a higher rate of productivity.

Since the ATEs have only recently embraced market economics and hence have relatively young industries, agriculture should be the first step in their process of economic development. Comparing the performance of the ATEs and the ASEAN4 countries highlights the emphasis that both place on the agricultural sector, and from Table 8.4 we can see that in the ATE countries agricultural industry has contributed, to a larger extent,

Table 8.4   Agriculture employment and productivity in terms of cereal yield

	1984–95	1996–2000	2001–05	% change (1984–2005)
Panel A: Agriculture employment (FAO) (millions)				
Cambodia	3.48	4.38	4.89	40.81
Lao PDR	1.58	1.92	2.17	36.91
Vietnam	23.52	27.07	28.75	22.20
ATEs	9.53	11.12	11.94	33.31
Malaysia	2.02	1.88	1.77	−12.49
Philippines	10.96	12.17	12.83	17.09
Thailand	19.76	20.73	20.44	3.45
Indonesia	43.14	48.31	50.04	16.01
ASEAN4	18.97	20.77	21.27	6.02
ASEAN7	10.12	11.33	11.83	17.71
	1984–95	1996–2000	2001–07	% change (1984–2005)
Panel B: Cereal yield*				
Cambodia	1384.85	1881.28	2141.70	54.65
Lao PDR	2250.45	2769.44	3258.80	44.81
Vietnam	3023.32	3869.32	4504.64	48.99
ATEs	2219.54	2840.01	3301.71	49.49
Malaysia	2746.05	3003.22	3260.72	18.74
Philippines	2014.33	2400.14	2852.60	41.62
Thailand	2197.98	2561.10	2816.24	28.13
Indonesia	3701.98	3938.98	4209.62	13.71
ASEAN4	2665.09	2975.86	3284.80	25.55
ASEAN7	2262.36	2760.65	3162.35	40.92

Note: * The definition of 'Cereal yield' by the World Bank is as follows: 'Cereal yield, measured as kilograms per hectare of harvested land, includes wheat, rice, maize, barley, oats, rye, millet, sorghum, buckwheat, and mixed grains. Production data on cereals relate to crops harvested for dry grain only. Cereal crops harvested for hay or harvested green for food, feed, or silage and those used for grazing are excluded.'

Source: World Bank (2009).

to increases in productivity. For example, Cambodia's employment in agriculture has increased 41 per cent, Laos's employment in agriculture has increased 37 per cent and Vietnam's has increased 22 per cent. This is in comparison to a 16 per cent increase for Indonesia, a 12 per cent decline in Malaysia, a 3.5 per cent increase in Thailand and a 17 per cent increase in the Philippines. The cereal yields have also increased for the ATEs at a higher rate as compared to the ASEAN4 countries. Thus, another conclusion that can be drawn from this is that, before this period, the ATEs seem not to have been able to extract the maximum gains from technology. This could be due to the fact that technology had not yet fully spread out within these countries, and its benefits were not experienced by the full population of the labour force in the agricultural sector. During the period of analysis, however, the ATEs would have started the dispersion of technology, and the labour force in the agriculture sector has since benefited with exponential growth and increased yield.

All in all, Tables 8.3 and 8.4 show that agriculture is an important industry in the ASEAN7 countries but that its importance, in terms of contribution to GDP, has declined. Although the share of agriculture to GDP has decreased for the respective countries, it can be seen that most of their productivity in agriculture has increased. To a certain extent, this may lead to governments subsidising industrialisation at the expense of agriculture which may potentially cause imbalances in the economy in terms of resource allocation. Even though industrial production may generate a higher GDP per capita compared to agriculture, the majority of the labour force is not yet educated. As mentioned earlier, the agricultural sector also provides many benefits to the economy as it develops. Hence it may be wise for the ATEs to allocate more resources to the agricultural industries, or perhaps at least to invest as much as is allocated to the other industries they have been developing. While it is important to introduce technology and industrialisation into the economy, the priority should be to improve living standards first. This should be approached through improvements in the agricultural sector, the sector that sustains the highest proportion of the population.

GLOBALISATION AND THE AGRICULTURAL INDUSTRY

As can be seen from the previous section, productivity in the agricultural sector has increased in all ASEAN7 countries, a change which is more significant in the ATEs. This effect could be due to the dispersion of the Green Revolution across the ASEAN7 countries in conjunction with technology improvements, mentioned above.

One of the main arguments of those who promote greater global economic integration is that the dispersion of technology leads to higher gains from productivity in the recipient countries. This also increases their caloric intake and reduces the poverty level (Johnson 2004). As a result of technology transfer, many of the ATEs have benefited from importing Green Revolution technologies. For example, the Cambodian Agricultural Research Institute (CARDI) has instituted reforms central to Cambodia's Green Revolution, using the technologies initially developed by the International Rice Research Institute (IRRI) in the Philippines. This included the increased usage of fertilisers, new rice varieties and improved irrigation. Corroboration between the Cambodian government, the IRRI and the Australian government also saw investment in irrigation, infrastructure and fertilisers. Hence, Cambodia's partnership with the Philippines and Australia portrays increased globalisation through cooperation at a national level and the diffusion of technology.

Another example of the sharing of Green Revolution technologies is seen in Vietnam. In the early 1980s, the Can Tho University developed a new series of modern varieties of rice with good grain quality and a brown plant hopper-resistant gene has been developed by the IRRI. The IRRI also provided other varieties of rice that allowed the Vietnamese farmers to be productive in the monsoonal, high-wind areas of Northern Vietnam (Tran and Kajisa 2006). This inflow of technology could also explain the increased employment and productivity in the agricultural sector evident in Table 8.4.

The decreasing contribution of agriculture to GDP could also be caused by increased productivity lowering prices in general. While this translates to a lower GDP contribution, it does not mean that agriculture is not important, as lower prices help to lower poverty levels in developing countries.

The increased productivity could also be due to subsidies provided by the government. An example would be the case of Malaysia, where the government provides a comprehensive fertiliser subsidy, guaranteed minimum price and a price subsidy scheme. These subsidies create a distortion in the economy and could cause a decrease in the incentive to take up new technologies to increase production. Another effect of such subsidies could be to affect trade through the creation of an artificial price floor.

In terms of connectivity and membership in world bodies, the ASEAN4 countries (Malaysia, Indonesia, Thailand and the Philippines) are members of the Cairns Group, a coalition of 19 agricultural-exporting countries formed in 1986. This group aims to ensure that the mandate set in Doha, will be met by the World Trade Organisation (WTO) membership. This is in addition to being members of ASEAN and the WTO.

The ATEs have made much progress in globalisation. As regards membership of global organisations, Cambodia joined the WTO in 2004, with Vietnam joining in 2007. Laos has started talks and proposed an accession package. In addition to that, all three ATEs are members of ASEAN. Thus, with increased participation in world trade, we examine the data to see if there has been increased trade to reflect the increased connectivity of these ASEAN7 countries.

From Table 8.5 we can see that both groups of ASEAN countries have significantly increased their agricultural exports. This is an important observation because the agricultural sector plays such an important part in their respective economies. In addition, in Panel A of Table 8.5 we can see that agricultural imports have shown a much slower rate of growth. Thus, we can conclude that the Green Revolution has allowed these countries to increase productivity. They are able to sustain themselves and earn foreign exchange by exporting their products without relying too much on imports.

Again, while the magnitude of the ATE exports have not reached that of the ASEAN4 countries, they show rates of growth that surpass the ASEAN4 countries and this indicates that they are rapidly catching up with their neighbours. This is impressive since they only opened their countries to the outside world in the earlier period of the analysis.

Overall, the effects of globalisation serve to improve technology used in the ASEAN countries, increasing productivity. Globalisation has also allowed these countries to become more cooperative and has given them cause to participate in world bodies to negotiate for a more competitive trading position. Furthermore, globalisation has allowed these countries to trade their surplus goods and provide more variety for their home consumers through increased trade.

CONCLUSION

This chapter has investigated the growth of the ASEAN7 countries of Cambodia, Vietnam, Laos, Malaysia, Thailand, the Philippines and Indonesia. These countries have developed significantly within the period of 1985 to 2007 and have achieved high average growth rates of nearly 5 per cent. The chapter aimed to study the effects of globalisation on the agricultural sector in these countries as they are developing economies and have a comparative advantage in agriculture. Furthermore, a comparison between the ATEs and the ASEAN4 countries sheds light on the growth of these two different groups to see if the ATEs are catching up with the ASEAN4.

Table 8.5   Agriculture imports and exports in the ASEAN7 countries

	1984–95	1996–2000	2001–07	% change
Panel A: Imports (millions)				
Cambodia**	0.00	49.81	158.35	15835.17
Lao PDR*	278.75	601.80	734.03	486.05
Vietnam**	0.00	806.72	2419.70	241970.36
ATEs	92.92	486.11	1104.03	86097.196
Malaysia	2620.97	4755.20	6960.92	165.59
Philippines	1459.72	3316.62	3668.71	151.33
Thailand	2891.20	4575.00	6442.16	122.82
Indonesia	2577.25	7011.86	8492.56	229.52
ASEAN4	2387.28	4914.67	6391.09	167.31
ASEAN7	1049.08	2084.47	3069.71	17.71
Panel B: Exports (millions)				
Cambodia**	0.00	10.65	20.33	2032.79
Lao PDR*	125.25	338.60	306.34	144.63
Vietnam**	0.00	2712.14	3086.59	308658.89
ATEs	41.75	1020.46	1137.77	103612.10
Malaysia	7784.04	9579.30	12908.65	65.84
Philippines	1826.25	2148.77	2530.49	38.56
Thailand	7361.30	12524.53	17285.47	134.82
Indonesia	4782.08	8309.20	13854.24	189.71
ASEAN4	5438.42	8140.45	11644.71	107.23
ASEAN7	5480.17	9160.91	12782.48	133.25

Notes:
*   The import and export data for Laos were not available for the World Deleopment
Indicators database. Hence the trade numbers displayed are the total amounts of
imports and exports for the Laos economy. While this may include items from other
sectors, the economy in Laos is predominately driven by the agricultural sector and
hence may be a close proxy for the actual agricultural trade.
**   Trade data for Cambodia and Vietnam are not available from the database for 1984–96
for Vietnam and 1984–99 for Cambodia. Hence the trade data for the period of 1996–
2000 for Cambodia reflects only one year of imports in Panel A and exports in Panel B.

Source: World Bank (2009).

In terms of globalisation, the chapter has examined the Index of Openness and the ratio of FDI to GDP. In addition, it also examined the participation of the countries in trade bodies and the diffusion of technology. Specifically, it was found that initially the ATEs were much less open compared to the ASEAN4 countries but have since caught up with their ASEAN4 neighbours within the period of analysis. The FDI–GDP ratio also increased significantly for the ATEs but the ratio was severely impacted due to the Asian Financial Crisis. Additionally, FDI flows were higher in the ATE countries compared to the ASEAN4 countries.

Hence, we have established that the ASEAN7 countries have embraced globalisation and openness, and in turn globalisation has helped the mainstay industry of agriculture via improved productivity. The ATEs play a role in ASEAN and the WTO but have yet to assert their position in other trade bodies. The ASEAN4 countries have membership of the WTO, ASEAN and the Cairns Group and have been active in trade talks. Thus, the ATEs are following closely in the footsteps of the ASEAN4 in terms of globalisation.

As mentioned, these ASEAN7 countries have an abundance of land and other mineral deposits and hence I focused my study on their agricultural sector. Once I established that globalisation was a growing influence in these counties, I examined the effects of globalisation on these countries and their agricultural sectors. It was found that agriculture has had a relative decline in terms of contribution to the GDP of the countries. However, this is underestimating the growth of the sector, where employment in agriculture has increased and productivity has grown even more.

One important finding is that the ATEs, Vietnam, Cambodia and Laos, have been growing at stellar rates compared to the ASEAN4 countries. I proposed that this is because the ATEs have only recently embraced market economics and hence have a lot to catch up on, in terms of growth, with their more developed counterparts in the ASEAN region. Their rate of productivity growth in the agriculture sector has also been very high which could be due to the steep learning curve the ATEs can enjoy, since the technology has already been developed. This high 'pick-up rate' can also be attributed to the quicker diffusion of technology in the agricultural sector, associated with globalisation.

Overall, agriculture is an important sector in a large number of developing countries in the Asia-Pacific region, and deserves attention since developing countries tend to have a high proportion of their population working in the sector. While industrialisation is an important step in developing the economy to improve living standards, the dispersion of technology in the agricultural sector through globalisation will also help to lower poverty levels. Hence, governments should not fully allocate resources to industrialisation at the expense of the agricultural sector. Globalisation has had a positive impact on the agricultural sectors in these ASEAN7 economies and this has improved living standards of the citizens.

NOTES

1. Asian transition economies (ATEs) countries consist of Cambodia, Laos and Vietnam.
2. ASEAN4 countries consist of Indonesia, Malaysia, the Philippines and Thailand.

REFERENCES

Bowles, P. and B. MacLean (1996), 'Understanding trade bloc formation: the case of the ASEAN Free Trade Area', *Review of International Political Economy*, **3**, 319–48.
Cheung, K. and P. Lin (2004), 'Spillover effects of FDI on innovation in China: evidence from the provincial data', *China Economic Review*, **15**, 25–44.
Johnson, D.G. (2004), 'Globalisation: what it is and who benefits', in C. Wiemer and C. Hepin (eds), *Advanced Research in Asian Economic Studies – Vol 1, Asian Economic Cooperation in the New Millenium: China's Economic Presence*, Singapore: World Scientific Publishing, pp. 27–42.
Tran, Thi Ut and K. Kajisa (2006), 'The impact of the Green Revolution on rice production in Vietnam', *Developing Economies*, **44**, 167–89.
World Bank (2009) *World Development Indicators*, accessed at http://data.worldbank.org/indicator.

9. Agriculture, development and Southeast Asian megacities

Brian J. Shaw

EARLY CITIES AND LATE URBANISATION

The history of urban forms within Southeast Asia can be traced back over a period of some 2000 years. Scholars have recognised the existence of two distinctive forms of indigenous settlement; namely the sacred city, generally located inland and designed according to cosmological principles; and the coastal or riparian trading city ideally placed to take advantage of the regional archipelago. While both forms prospered concurrently, the political fortunes of individual cities waxed and waned, and over time early inland centres such as Vyadhapura, capital of the Kingdom of Funan from the first century CE, gave way to Angkor, centre of the Khmer empire, which in turn was surpassed by Sukhothai, and then Ayutthaya in present-day Thailand. Of the maritime empires, Srivijaya flourished between the fourth and thirteenth centuries, with a 'golden age' between the seventh and eleventh centuries. Centred on present-day Palembang, it controlled trade in ports throughout the region, including Aceh, Makassar and Patani. Its successors included Kediri and Majapahit in Java, and later Malacca (McGee 1967; Osborne 2000; Reed 2000).

The inland centres have been characterised as hydraulic civilisations, situated in the great river valleys of mainland Southeast Asia, and also on Java, based upon wet rice (*sawah*) surpluses and bountiful fish harvests, overseen by all-powerful rulers, or god-kings (*deva raja*) (Wittfogel 1957). The most extensive and celebrated of these was the Khmer empire that flourished between the ninth and fifteenth centuries. Based on Angkor, but extending south to embrace the Mekong delta, northwards into present-day Laos and Thailand and westwards to the Indian Ocean, the kingdom owed its resilience to the careful and intricate management of fluvial resources. The unity between man and nature was reflected in the design of splendid city complexes, which reproduced the 'cosmological master plan configured to guarantee consonance between heaven and earth, and thereby promote harmony and prosperity' (Reed 2000, p. 46). When measured against contemporary environmental excesses, some 600 years would seem to be a period of remarkable sustainability, but it is instructive to note that the seeds of Angkor's dissolution have been traced to extensive forest clearance for rice growing. Such findings beg comparison with present-day experiences of severe flooding and reduced fish supplies (Asia-Pacific Focal Point 2005), and have implications for the present and future health of the region's ecosystem.

Notwithstanding their command of the archipelagic seas, which included the lucrative spice trade, the Java-based maritime empires also relied upon wet rice cultivation, irrigation schemes and integrated marketing networks for their prosperity (Reed 2000). Despite the aquatic settings in which many people lived, either in boats or in stilted houses along the shoreline, local interactions remained strong as most towns remained small in size and population and little distinction existed between urban and rural. This situation was to change somewhat with the advent of colonialism, as indigenously established port cities such as Batavia and Malacca became the lynchpins of an externally controlled trading system, and new colonial ports were established, most notably on the islands of Penang and Singapore. In addition, the intensification of colonial rule from about the beginning of the nineteenth century heralded a regional population explosion that still continues today. The population of Southeast Asia, variously estimated at around 25 million in the early 1800s, had reached 80 million by the end of the nineteenth century according to colonial census returns. By 1950 it had more than doubled again to 180 million and was to surpass 500 million before the end of the millennium (Fisher 1964; Hugo 2000; Owen 2005).

Population increases were supported through an expansion of wet rice cultivation in the region's fertile deltaic lowlands, and large-scale clearing of land elsewhere. In Java, Clifford Geertz (1963) coined the term 'agricultural involution' for the process of intensifying farming practices in the face of limited supplies of land as villages steadily increased in size. However, the reciprocities engendered by this custom of *gotong royong* were increasingly penetrated by a colonial system that replaced small-scale subsistence production with a cash economy. Private landownership, commercial rice cultivation and plantation agriculture for external markets transformed the nature of rural livelihoods. This, in turn, resulted in greater levels of rural–urban migration as traditional ownership was displaced and the burgeoning, multi-layered cities became theatres of apparent opportunity. Nowhere was this trend more evident than in Malaya, which from the mid-nineteenth century had attracted investments in tin mining and various plantation industries including coffee, gambier, pepper, sugarcane and tapioca, before the greatest catalyst of change came with the spectacular rise of rubber cultivation which was to transform both the economy and the rural landscape of the peninsula (Barlow 1978).

Rubber plants from the Amazon had been introduced into Southeast Asia via the Royal Botanic Gardens, Kew in London during the 1870s, but their impact was not felt until the end of the century when cultivation and harvesting practices refined by Henry Ridley, Director of the Botanic Gardens, Singapore, enhanced their appeal. Rising rubber prices led to a boom in rubber planting which took the area of planted rubber in the peninsula from 800 ha in 1898 to over 900 000 ha in 1921 (Barlow 1978, p. 26). Policies were introduced to stimulate the planting of rubber, shifting agriculture was discouraged and new land grants included 'a special clause stipulating additional planting of a "permanent" crop such as rubber or coconuts' (Barlow 1978, p. 28). The early dominance of European-owned plantations was challenged after rubber prices soared in 1909 by the emergence of Chinese and Malay-owned smallholdings in a 'frenzy of speculation' that disrupted the settled life of the *kampungs*. Accordingly, the colonial authorities legislated to preserve the integrity of Malay settlements, but nevertheless rubber became the dominant tree crop. By 1921 planted rubber under Asian ownership made up some 45 per cent of the crop's total area (Barlow 1978, p. 26).

Under the colonial mode of production the need for efficient transportation via roads, railways and seaports stimulated urban development. The western side of Malaya in particular experienced rapid development and that seaboard today is the more heavily urbanised area of peninsular Malaysia. Throughout Southeast Asia the spread of plantations, if somewhat less dramatic than in Malaya, fostered similar urbanisation impulses in the colonial areas of Java, Sumatra, Burma, North Borneo, Indochina and the Philippines during the first quarter of the twentieth century (Voon 1976). Yet, compared to other major world regions the pace of urbanisation was relatively slow. As late as 1950, barely 15 per cent of Southeast Asians were found in cities, with only Africa showing a lower level of urbanisation (see Table 9.1). Although colonialism had remoulded the Southeast Asian economy, the image of a rural idyll was still apparent throughout the region during the mid-twentieth century.

In the second half of the twentieth century urbanisation gathered momentum alongside post-colonial political sovereignty and then global integration. Within the rapidly developing market economies of Malaysia, Thailand, Indonesia and, to a lesser extent, the Philippines, annual urban growth rates of 4–5 per cent were experienced. Now, in the early twenty-first century, Brunei, Malaysia and the Philippines are predominantly urban societies, along with the city-state of Singapore. With urbanisation impulses accelerating in the former centrally controlled economies,

Table 9.1   Urbanisation in Southeast Asia, 1950–2025 (mid-year percentage of population defined as urban in each country)

	1950	1970	1990	2002	2025 (est)
Brunei	27	62	66	67	81
Burma	16	23	25	29	43
Cambodia	10	12	13	18	33
Indonesia	12	17	31	43	61
Lao PDR	7	10	15	20	34
Malaysia	20	34	50	59	71
Philippines	27	33	49	60	73
Singapore	100	100	100	100	100
Thailand	11	13	19	20	30
Timor-Leste	9	9	–	8	15
Vietnam	12	18	20	25	38
Region	15	20	30	36	54

Source: adapted from Wong et al. (2006), pp. 198, 271.

forward estimates suggest a dominantly urban Southeast Asia sometime around 2020, and an urban population of over 400 million by 2030 (Hugo 2006). This broad process of societal change has seen the accelerated growth of individual cities, notably the well-positioned trading capitals of Southeast Asia, which have maintained their relative advantage through to the present day. In 1950 there were just six cities with populations over 700 000 (Bangkok, Jakarta, Manila, Rangoon, Saigon and Singapore). By 2002 this number had increased to 20 and the first three had become megacities with populations of over 10 million (Hugo 2006). The region's most populous country, Indonesia, now has ten cities with populations of more than 1 million people and an estimated urban population of 95 million in 2006 (Firman et al. 2007). Such a rapid rural to urban transition has transformed the character of the region, and the image of the rural idyll is now in thrall to that of the burgeoning city.

MEGACITIES IN SOUTHEAST ASIA

The definition of a megacity has essentially been based on population size, rather than economic function. Thus, megacities are classified as urban agglomerations with exceedingly large populations, initially more than 8 million but now upgraded to more than 10 million (Lo and Yeung 1998). Globally the number of such megacities reached 22 by the first decade of the twenty-first century, two of which are generally accredited to Southeast Asia, namely Jakarta and Manila. To these we must add Bangkok, with around 10 million people, a population particularly subject to statistical under-enumeration and seasonal fluctuations. Yet, in terms of world city status, following the hierarchical scale devised by John Friedmann (1986), none of these cities would rate in the first order as operational nodes of the contemporary global economy with the interconnected financial, legal, marketing, media and other high-level services that characterise the headquarters of multi- or transnational corporations (TNCs). Indeed, the most obvious candidate for inclusion in terms of secondary order status is Singapore, with a population of just 4.6 million in 2007. Bangkok ranks behind Singapore but above Jakarta and Manila in secondary ranking, being an important centre for corporate and institutional headquarters. Not yet a megacity, or a global city, Ho Chi Minh City (HCMC) (formerly Saigon) with a population of some 5 million in 2000 has developed rapidly since the introduction of economic reforms and its future growth seems assured.

Jakarta is generally regarded as the largest of the three regional mega-cities with an estimated population of 21 million in 2000, spread over an area of 6175 square kilometres (Jones 2006). The Jakarta Metropolitan Area (JMA) consists of Jakarta province and the three surrounding regencies of Bekasi and Bogor in West Java and Tangerang in Banten, including the cities of Bogor, Depok, Tangerang and Bekasi, thus referred to as Jabodetabek as an acronym for the constituent urban areas, the last three all with populations over 1 million. Within this large area there is an obvious blurring of the distinction between 'urban' and 'rural' localities, with the Indonesian population census defining a locality as 'urban' when it meets three requirements. These are: a population density of 5000 people per square kilometre; having 25 per cent or less households working in the agricultural sector; and having eight or more kinds of urban facilities. This last criterion includes facilities such as primary, junior high and senior high schools; a cinema; a hospital or primary healthcare centre; a shopping centre; a bank; restaurants and the like (Firman et al. 2007). It can be seen that rapid population growth in fringe areas can lead to a reclassification of areas from rural to urban and thereby a disproportionate increase in urban numbers.

Metropolitan Manila's population is somewhat more difficult to estimate due to a very large area that includes eight cities and nine municipalities, extending between Manila Bay and Laguna de Bay, from Valenzuela and Caloocan City in the north, to Las Pinas and Muntinlupa City in the south. Gavin Jones gives a 2000 population of 21 million over 12 061 square kilometres based on provincial boundaries, but makes the point that the Philippines has 'a much more inclusive categorisation of urban areas' (Jones 2006, p. 252). The official classification is somewhat complex but includes cities and municipalities 'with a density of at least 500 persons per square kilometre; and all other administrative centres, with at least 1000 inhabitants which have predominantly non-agricultural occupations and possess certain minimal urban facilities' (ibid. p. 252). In comparison Thailand's definition of urban, despite some recent changes to include 'sanitary districts', still errs on the conservative side by not including distinctly urban subdistricts (*tambon*) located just outside municipalities (Jones 2006). Conventionally, the Bangkok Metropolitan Region (BMR) refers to the provinces of Bangkok and its neighbours Samut Prakan, Nonthaburi, Pathum Thani, Nakhon Pathom and Samut Sakhon, in order of urban population size. Jones (2006) estimates a population of 10 million over 7248 square kilometres for this region, a much lower density than Jakarta and comparable with Manila's extended area.

These three megacities, by virtue of their size, connectedness and disproportionate levels of foreign investment operate effectively as newly industrialising countries (NICs) within their respective national economies. In consequence, the economic and social changes associated with rapid industrialisation are impacting upon their surrounding countryside where traditional agricultural systems have, hitherto, sustained urban populations. Jones et al. (2000) stress the importance of analysing their population and employment structures in terms of zones, which follow a pattern of urban core, inner ring and outer ring areas. These co-authors make the point that, outside the urban core:

> The inner zone is the zone characterised by metropolitan 'overspill', a zone in transition from rural to urban settlement and land use patterns, experiencing very rapid growth in population and employment, and a rapid decline in its share of primary industry in total employment. The outer zone is also heavily influenced by the growth of the metropolis and likely to achieve 'inner zone' characteristics in future, but rural settlement patterns prevail, and agriculture continues to provide a significant share of employment. (Jones et al. 2000, pp. 122–3)

In Jakarta, as population and employment growth rapidly increased in peripheral areas between 1980 and 1990, the proportion of persons employed in farming fell from 19.1 to 5.6 per cent in the inner ring and 31.4 to 23.6 per cent in the outer ring. In Bangkok, over the same period, agricultural employment fell from 38.8 to 26.6 per cent in the inner ring and from 45.7 to 41.9 per cent in the outer ring. In Manila, where industrial and occupational classifications changed over the period, in 1990 9.3 per cent and 26.8 per cent of employed persons were recorded in the 'farmer, forestry etc.' category for inner and outer zones, respectively (Jones et al. 2000).

Such figures do not merely reflect a process of rural to urban migration and the transition of outlying megacity areas per se, but are indicative of a much broader transformation of relations between city and country-side redolent of the classical 'agrarian question' which resurfaced as an ongoing ideological battleground between, and within, Marxian and neo-classical schools in the context of twentieth-century Third World develop-ment (Watts and Goodman 1997). Simply expressed, the question relates to conditions that facilitate the penetration of capitalist relations into peasant agriculture and the prospects for capital accumulation therein. Writing at the beginning of the twentieth century, Lenin characterised such a transition as either a reactionary 'capitalism from above' domi-nated by feudal landlords, or a more acceptable 'capitalism from below' whereby the peasantry evolve into a capitalist farming class; the latter situation he saw as socially and politically progressive (Byres 1996). Now, at the beginning of the twenty-first century, the impact of globalisation has broken down earlier notions of a rural–urban dichotomy through improved transportation and increased mobility, creating opportuni-ties for off-farm work which, when coupled with the impact of changing desires and economic opportunities, have raised generational expectations beyond the family plot. As growing populations have increased the pres-sure on resource availability throughout Southeast Asia, there has been a widespread diversification of regional livelihoods, and the peri-urban areas of major megacities are just the most immediately visible and easily accessible manifestations of this process.

While the late-twentieth-century analysis of globalisation has pro-vided some scholars with an overarching answer to the agrarian ques-tion, others have been drawn towards a reconceptualisation of earlier assumptions. In rethinking globalisation and the agrarian question Philip McMichael focuses upon food security, environmental deterioration and agro-industrialisation exchanges as the debate passes 'from land tenure to food and green questions' (McMichael 1997, p. 654). Drawing from the work of Deborah Bryceson (1996), but writing specifically on Southeast Asia which currently ranks as one of the most dynamic areas of economic growth and structural transformation in the world, Jonathan Rigg (2001, p. 6) describes a process of 'de-agrarianisation' through occupational readjustment; income-earning reorientation; social re-identification; spatial relocation and spatial interpenetration. Factory work and non-farm activities have come to rural areas, but now heightened levels of mobility allow migrants to remain part of the village in socio-cultural terms whilst earning a living in the urban industrial sector. For Rigg (2001,

p. 27): 'the tendrils of globalization have reached further into the country-side and deeper into the lives and livelihoods of the region's inhabitants – the agrarian question is not dead but renewed'.

REGIONAL DISTINCTIVENESS

Following the lead of Terry McGee (1991; McGee and Robinson 1995; Kelly and McGee 2003), a number of geographers have portrayed the urbanisation process within parts of East and Southeast Asia as a region-ally distinctive phenomenon, whereby the densely populated lowland areas of wet rice cultivators have, over recent decades, been subjected to the dynamic attributes of rapidly expanding cities. Concentrated in national core regions, the key driving force has been the recent surge in export-oriented industrialisation driven by foreign investment, leading to the formation of extended metropolitan regions (EMRs). To describe the phenomenon of urban expansion occurring at the expense of surround-ing villages, McGee used the Bahasa Indonesia term *desakota* to indicate a fusion of both village (*desa*) and town (*kota*) qualities. The defining attributes of this process, in addition to elevated rural population densi-ties and the presence of a market economy, are: good transport networks; highly mobile populations; an increase in non-agricultural activities; juxtaposition of different and competing land uses; increased female participation in the workforce; and a lack of effective planning controls (McGee 1991). This combination of circumstances is seen to produce a juxtaposition of 'urban' and 'rural', particularly along major communi-cation lines between competing urban centres, of a type not experienced elsewhere within the so-called 'developing' world.

The corollary of *desakota* is the process of *kotadesasi* in which agricul-tural and non-agricultural activities occur side by side (McGee 1989). The scale of this juxtaposition extends from the subregional level, through the village level, to that of individual households, some members of which may be pursuing traditional agricultural activities while others (increas-ingly females) are working in local factories or commuting to the urban core. Initially, increases in individual mobility were achieved by virtue of the seemingly ubiquitous two-stroke motorcycle, later enhanced through an extension of public bus routes, subsidised company transportation and, somewhat inevitably, private vehicle ownership. The weakness of municipal regulations, or their lack of enforcement, fostered a variety of potentially conflicting peri-urban land uses with 'agriculture, cottage industry, and other uses existing side by side' (McGee 1989, p. 95). Much of the resulting economic activity can be characterised as small-scale and informal, occupying 'grey areas' between legality and illegality. Migrant or temporary workers are often housed in the most basic and communal 'squatter-like' conditions, some reflecting the continuing presence of well-established communities, and others as part of employment packages designed by agents to deliver low-cost labour to local entrepreneurs. Rather unsurprisingly, the collective impacts of such incompatible and unregulated land uses, which juxtapose noxious industry, substandard housing and urban subsistence agriculture, pose growing environmental concerns to local authorities equipped with limited resources (Williams 1997).

As the process of development has gathered pace, municipal authorities have increasingly turned their attention to the existence of such 'squatter problems', ostensibly on environmental and hygienic grounds. In reality, official action was more likely to be prompted by the need to free up land for new commercial, industrial and (prestigious) residential developments that were to be spawned by additional foreign direct investment. In this context, Tim Bunnell (2006, p. 328) has offered a further motive for action, namely the desire to '(re)image' the city, and by extension the state, 'as a suitable destination for hypermobile global investment capital'. In his profile on Kuala Lumpur, Bunnell links the construction of projects such as the Petronas Towers and the Kuala Lumpur Linear City (KLLC) to the clean-up of squatters along the Klang River. The Petronas Towers, constructed to be the tallest buildings in the world at that time, and the KLLC were symbols of Malaysia's advancement under Prime Minister Dr Mahathir bin Mohamad. The image of the future that accompanied their construction sat awkwardly with the continued existence of more traditional squatter *kampungs*. The clean-up of the Klang River was designed not only in terms of water quality but also to rid the city of 'riverine squatters' as 'polluting people in polluted places' (Bunnell 2006, p. 334.)

THE SUBORDINATION OF AGRICULTURE

The position of agriculture within this melange of somewhat contradictory developmental pressures has become increasingly tenuous. Growing demand has led to a revalorisation of land formerly used for purely agricultural purposes, and landowners have begun to see their properties as speculative assets rather than as working farms. Smallholders wishing to expand increasingly find the cost of land prohibitive. Its conversion for real estate, commercial or industrial purposes, or merely to stand idle, flows through to tenant farmers and agricultural workers who are displaced from both livelihood and residence. Such trends are illustrated by the expansion of Bangkok into its former hinterland, the rich rice-growing region of the Chao Phraya river basin, where an estimated one-third of cultivable land has been bought by land speculators (Bello et al. 1998). Rising prices have made it difficult for Thailand's Agrarian Land Reform Office (ALRO) to purchase private land for distribution to farmers as part of a land reform programme, and even agro-industrial enterprises were forced to relocate to cheaper land in Thailand's upper central and lower northeast regions. 'It seems at times as though the entire country is being bought by the ever growing wealthy, by the rapidly expanding middle class, and by foreign investors' (Charles Mehl, quoted in Bello et al. 1998, p. 161).

Central to the well-being of agricultural systems is the issue of water supply. In a time when the world was waking up to the prospect of a crisis in water availability, localised demands for water supply within Southeast Asia's EMRs have been skyrocketing. This essential resource has, in a similar way to that of land, been squeezed between the needs of farmers, the demands from industry and the desires of housing developers. To this list we must also add recreation, most specifically the excessive water demands generated by the 'green menace' in which the Asian golf boom has come to symbolise the unjust monopolisation of natural resources by a wealthy few (Ing and Bennett 1993). Growing affluence within the region has raised the demand for potable water supplies and efficient sewerage systems, large factories are insatiable consumers of clean water and commercial operations such as restaurants make their own heavy demands. In many such cases the first casualty of this heightened situation has been a reduction in the supply of dry-season water destined for the irrigation of a second rice crop. In Thailand, a country which can be described as a 'water-oriented society', farmers in the central plain were discouraged by the government from planting a second rice crop, and instead told to plant vegetables or other less water-intensive crops (Bello et al. 1998).

At the local level farmers have seen their water supplies shut off to meet competing demands from industry and have faced the prospect of increasingly contaminated canals, rivers and coastal waters. The dumping of untreated domestic sewage, chemicals from agricultural run-off, industrial effluents and oil spills are the prime causes of such pollution, leading to widespread environmental degradation. One such case is that of Manila Bay, an important fishing ground and aquaculture site, now suffering from increasing levels of pollution caused by the combination of domestic and industrial wastes that have degraded local rivers. The Pasig River, linking Manila Bay and Laguna de Bay, has been described as: 'an open sewer, a stinking dumpsite and as waste depository not only of 820 industrial factories along its bank but also of the 70 000 urban poor dwellers whose houses line its length' (Florentino-Hofilena, quoted in Hingco 1999). Such conditions hark back to the graphic descriptions of the River Irk, recorded by Frederick Engels in his treatise on mid-nineteenth-century England (Engels 1969 [1845], pp. 81–3). In contemporary Manila such conditions led to the 1997 privatisation of the Manila Metropolitan Waterworks and Sewerage System (MWSS).

Within the EMRs, those farmers who still endeavour to extract a return from the soil face another set of problems relating to the declining terms of trade between farm and non-farm activities. As the costs of farm inputs such as feed, fertiliser, fuel and pesticides rise without corresponding increases in farm-gate price, this leads to a real decline in the value of agricultural commodities. The relatively high wages that can be obtained from off-farm and non-farm work, coupled with the increasingly low status of farming compared to factory or even informal-sector employment, make it difficult to keep younger generations on the farm. Rigg (2007, pp. 120–21), links these factors to the 'mobility revolution' in the Global South, having also made the point that, 'in a functional sense there is no "edge" to the EMR', a view that leaves us with the rather sobering thought that Jakarta's influence can be seen to extend throughout the island of Java, and that of Bangkok everywhere within the limits of an 18-hour bus journey (Rigg 2001, p. 59).

QUO VADIS?

This chapter began with a notion of 'cosmological consonance', stressing the unity of man and nature, but just as the introduction of private landownership combined with commercial and plantation cultivation for external markets transformed Southeast Asian rural livelihoods about a century ago, we can today recognise similar forces of change with equally far-reaching consequences. The presence of large-scale, vertically integrated food production or agribusiness has relegated the individual smallholder both literally and metaphorically to the end of the agri-food chain. Such commodity chains extend beyond national boundaries and typically provide powerful TNCs with access to land, cheap labour and government support in developing countries. While immediate benefits are seen to accrue to smallholders through access to capital, new technology and minimum prices, over time there are a number of negative downsides that result from an unequal power relationship. Agribusiness has the power to squeeze smaller growers through a gradual reduction of farm-gate prices, whilst at the same time raising product standards and overpricing its own corporate services (Rigg 2007, p. 102).

In global terms, this corporate shift has moved former 'shallow' trade-based linkages between countries towards 'deep' international production-based intrafirm linkages (Watts and Goodman 1997, p. 4). During the 1980s and 1990s, leading European and US-registered TNCs operating in Asia, such as Carrefour, Royal Ahold and Wal-Mart, accelerated their planned investments in the region, often increasing their shares in existing joint ventures or buying out their Asian partners. Others such as Delhaize, Auchan and Tesco established their presence within the region's rapidly modernising system of agri-food processing and distribution. The onset of the Asian economic crisis 1997–98 found such companies well placed to take advantage of major asset depreciation and operational cost reductions, resulting in a near doubling of their operational presence in Asia between 1995 and 2001 (DFAT 2001). In addition, Asia-registered, highly vertically integrated, agri-food giants such as Charoen Pokphand Group (CP Group) of Thailand, the San Miguel conglomerate of the Philippines and the Salim Group of Indonesia are also major players within Southeast Asia, supplying both domestic and overseas markets.

The complex links between urban and rural became starkly evident with the advent of the Asian economic crisis. The ensuing recession impacted severely upon the 'wannabe' tiger economies of Indonesia, Malaysia, the Philippines and Thailand. Urban employment prospects quickly diminished as factories closed and construction work dried up, with the result that many workers temporarily reverse-migrated back to their home villages and re-engaged in agriculturally related pursuits. In Thailand, King Bhumibol (Rama IX) officially encouraged such movement, exhorting a return to 'traditional' subsistence ethics (Askew 2002, p. 94). This solution could only be a short-term palliative, as rural households were deprived of their urban-generated remittance payments and rural economies still retained the disadvantaged structures that had fostered the migration imperative. However, despite the severity of the crisis, a potential catastrophe was avoided as a rural safety valve was opened to accommodate the poorest migrant workers.

From the above discussion we might easily reach the conclusion that the uncertain future for agriculture within Southeast Asia extends far beyond the limits of megacities and other EMRs within the region. The all too common incidence of apparently 'idle' land, changes in production methods to overcome labour shortages and 'cost squeezes', coupled with an absolute decline in the numbers of those actively engaged in agricultural production, are not just features of expanded city-regions. Within the wider context, the challenges of continued population growth, increasing and evolving consumer demand for food supplies, and the prospect of severe and ongoing changes in world climates makes the position of agriculture even more critical if widespread, rather than presently localised, famines are to be avoided. One grassroots organisation drawing attention to these problems is La Via Campesina. Established in 1993 as an international movement of peasants, small and medium-sized producers and the landless, and with representation in at least seven Southeast Asian countries, it advocates the decentralisation of food production and supply chains, arguing that many TNCs have increased their profits during the food crisis and have played a major role in increasing world hunger by excluding family farmers from food production (La Via Campesina 2009). If its predictions of a corporately induced deepening hunger crisis prove accurate, then Southeast Asia, and the world, may need to revisit the rural safety valve sometime in the not too distant future. To paraphrase two nineteenth-century social commentators and a more recent discussion by Richard Walker (1997, p. 283): 'Primary producers of the world unite! You have nothing to lose but your commodity chains.'

REFERENCES

Asia-Pacific Focal Point for World Heritage Management in the Asia-Pacific Region (2005), 'The limits of pre-industrial, urban growth in Angkor', accessed at http://acl.arts.usyd.edu.au/research/angkor/angkor.html.

Askew, M. (2002), *Bangkok: Place, Practice and Representation*, London and New York: Routledge.

Barlow, C. (1978), *The Natural Rubber Industry: Its Development, Technology, and Economy in Malaysia*, Kuala Lumpur and Oxford: Oxford University Press.

Bello, W., S. Cunningham and Li Kheng Poh (1998), *A Siamese Tragedy: Development and Disintegration in Modern Thailand*, London and New York: Zed Books.

Bryceson, D. (1996),'De-agrarianization and rural employment in sub-Saharan Africa: a sectoral perspective', *World Development*, **24**, 97–111.

Bunnell, T. (2006), 'Out of place in the global cityscape: moral geographies of squatting in Kuala Lumpur', in T. Wong, B.J. Shaw and K. Goh (eds), *Challenging Sustainability: Urban Development and Change in Southeast Asia*, Singapore: Marshall Cavendish, pp. 323–39.

Byers, T. (1996), *Capitalism from Above and Capitalism from Below: An Essay in Comparative Political Economy*, Basingstoke: Macmillan.

Department of Foreign Affairs and Trade (DFAT) (2001), *Agrifood Globalization and Asia*, Canberra: Commonwealth of Australia.

Engels, F. (1969), *The Condition of the Working Class in England St Albans*, (German edn first published in 1845), Oxford: Panther Books.

Firman, T., B. Kombaitan and P. Pradono (2007), 'The dynamics of Indonesia's urbanisation', *Urban Policy and Research*, **25**, 433–54.

Fisher, C.A. (1964), *South-east Asia*, London: Methuen.

Friedmann, J. (1986), 'The world city hypothesis', *Development and Change*, **17**, 69–84.

Hingco, T. (1999), 'Waste disposal problems in metro Manila and the response of the urban poor', in G. Chapman, A.K. Dutt and R. Bradnock (eds), *Urban Growth and Development in Asia Volume II: Living in the Cities*, Aldershot: Ashgate, pp. 269–86.

Hugo, G. (2000), 'Demographic and social patterns', in T. Leinbach and R. Ulack (eds), *Southeast Asia Diversity and Development*, Upper Saddle River, NJ: Prentice Hall, pp. 74–109.

Hugo, G. (2006), 'Population development and the urban outlook for Southeast Asia', in T. Wong, B. Shaw and K. Goh (eds), *Challenging Sustainability: Urban Development and Change in Southeast Asia*, Singapore: Marshall Cavendish, pp. 268–98.

Ing, K. and B. Bennett (1993) *Green Menace: The Untold Story of Golf* (video recording), Bundoora VIC: La Trobe University.

Jones, G. (2006), 'Urbanisation in Southeast Asia', in T. Wong, B. Shaw and K. Goh (eds), *Challenging Sustainability: Urban Development and Change in Southeast Asia*, Singapore: Marshall Cavendish, pp. 247–67.

Jones, G., Tsay Ching-Lung and B. Bajracharya (2000), 'Demographic and employment change in the mega-cities of South-east and East Asia', *Third World Planning Review*, **22**, 119–46.

Kelly, P. and T. McGee (2003), 'Changing spaces: Southeast Asian urbanization in an era of volatile globalization', in Sien Chia Lin (ed.), *Southeast Asia Transformed: A Geography of Change*, Singapore: ISEAS, pp. 257–85.

La Via Campesina, (2009), 'Transnationals contribute to hunger farmers provide solutions', accessed at www.viacampesina.org/main_en/index.php?option=com_contentandtask=blogsectionandid=5andItemid=27.

Lo, F. and Y. Yeung (1998), *Globalization and the World of Large Cities*, Tokyo: United Nations University Press.

McGee, T.G. (1967), *The Southeast Asian City: A Social Geography of the Primate Cities of Southeast Asia*, London: Bell.

McGee, T.G. (1989), 'Urbanisasi or Kotadesasi? Evolving patterns of urbanization in Asia', in F. Costa, A. Dutt, L. Ma and A. Noble (eds), *Urbanization in Asia: Spatial Dimensions and Policy Issues*, Honolulu: University of Hawaii Press, pp. 93–108.

McGee, T.G. (1991), The emergence of *desakota* regions in Asia: expanding a hypothesis, in N. Ginsberg, B. Koppell, and T. McGee (eds), *The Extended Metropolis: Settlement Transition in Asia*, Honolulu, HI: University of Hawaii Press, pp. 3–25.

McGee, T.G. and I. Robinson (1995), *The Mega-Urban Regions of Southeast Asia*, Vancouver, BC: University of British Columbia Press.

McMichael, P. (1997), 'Rethinking globalization: the Agrarian question revisited', *Review of International Political Economy*, **4**(4), 630–62.

Osborne, Milton (2000), *Southeast Asia: An Introductory History*, St Leonards, NSW: Allen & Unwin.

Owen, N.G. (2005), *The Emergence of Modern Southeast Asia: A New History*, Honolulu, HI: University of Hawaii Press.

Reed, R. (2000), 'Historical and cultural patterns', in T. Leinbach and R. Ulack (eds), *Southeast Asia: Diversity and Development*, Upper Saddle River, NJ: Prentice Hall, pp. 35–73.

Rigg, J. (2001), *More than the Soil: Rural Change in Southeast Asia*, Harlow: Pearson Education.

Rigg, J. (2007), *An Everyday Geography of the Global South*, London and New York: Routledge.

Voon, P.K. (1976), *Western Rubber Planting Enterprise in Southeast Asia 1876–1921*, Kuala Lumpur: Penerbit Universiti Malaya.

Walker, Richard A. (1997), 'Commentary on Part IV: fields of dreams, or the best game in town', in David Goodman and Michael Watts (eds), *Globalising Food: Agrarian Questions and Global Restructuring*, London and New York: Routledge, pp. 273–84.

Watts, M. and D. Goodman (1997), 'Agrarian questions: global appetite, local metabolism: nature, culture, and industry in *fin-de-siècle* agro-food systems', in D. Goodman and M. Watts (eds), *Globalising Food: Agrarian Questions and Global Restructuring*, London and New York: Routledge, pp. 1–32.

Williams, S. (1997), '"The Brown Agenda": urban environmental problems and policies in the developing world', *Geography*, **82**, 17–26.

Wittfogel, Karl (1957), *Oriental Despotism: A Comparative Study of Total Power*, New Haven, CT: Yale University Press.

Wong, T., B. Shaw and K. Goh (2006), *Challenging Sustainability: Urban Development and Change in Southeast Asia*, Singapore: Marshall Cavendish, pp. 268–98.

10. Contract farming and technology transfer: perspectives from the Philippines' oil palm industry

Paul Huddleston

INTRODUCTION

The purpose of this chapter is to examine how contract farming systems in the Philippines' oil palm sector have influenced the adoption of new agricultural technologies. Contract farming is generally part of a wider process of vertical integration within a commodity system, whereby a farmer grows a commodity as part of an agreement with an external party. In most cases this contract is with a processing company, which agrees to purchase the commodity. While the form of contract varies considerably, it usually involves agreements around price, quality and time of delivery. In some cases, the contracting firm also offer access to agronomic advice, new technologies, and economic or other forms of assistance. This access to technology is often regarded as critical in the promotion of wider processes of rural development (Eaton and Shepherd 2001). Technology is often seen as the path to a more productive and efficient farming sector, improved incomes, and increased levels of household well-being. Noteworthy are major bio-technological advances, as well as improvements in transport, storage and packaging technologies. Meanwhile, the use of sophisticated equipment that improves product quality, reduces labour demand and ensures consistency in quality has expanded significantly, to such an extent that the implications for the small farmer in developing countries cannot be underestimated (Narayanan and Gulati 2002, p. 49). In this regard, Mayer (2002, p. 62) noted: 'One of the main opportunities, which globalization is said to offer to developing countries, is that they would have better access to the technological advances in developed countries.'

In order to meet domestic and export agricultural targets, developing countries need improved technologies within the entire commodity chain from production to processing and distribution. Reardon and Barrett

(2000, pp. 202–3) summed up the discussion on the transfer of technology when they stated: 'The necessity of agro-industrialization is almost indisputable . . . [A] plethora of questions remains as to how to get the right kind of agro-industrialization . . . to yield broad-based environmentally sustainable growth that creates wealth and improves human well-being.' Reardon argued that environmental sustainability is the key criterion on which to judge the success of any contract farming scheme, even in the face of a successful transfer of technology.

Ehui and Delgado (1999) argued that while technology need not crowd out smallholders through substitution of capital for labour, there is evidence that an increase in the share of processed products in the agri-food sector implies an increase in capital to labour ratios. This could result in small farmers losing the benefits of contract farming to larger farmers or corporate farms, with the latter able to reap the economies of scale offered by technological advances. Where technology is appropriate to their resource base and constraints, the speed of adoption is not significantly different between small and large farmers (Narayanan and Gulati 2002). The issue, therefore, becomes the degree of access to technology rather than the technology per se.

The transfer of technology is frequently viewed as being critical to the relationship between the outgrower and the processor. Vellema (2002, p. 3) supported this contention when he stated: 'Technology transfer through the introduction of artefacts [agricultural inputs] and through the guidelines and rules prescribed by the contract and technicians is, in the case of contract farming, a major determinant in the relationship between the contract grower and the trans-national corporation.' Beyond the biological suitability of the introduction of a contracted crop into an area, the relationship forged between the outgrower and the contractor is a key factor in the determination of economic results and the subsequent general influence on local and regional socio-economic development (Carney 1994).

Technology used in oil palm cultivation is relatively basic when compared to other crops farmed under contract. Nevertheless, it is significant as a viable strategy for increasing the productivity of smallholder outgrowers as it includes the transfer of both technical and managerial processes. This view, whereby the transfer of technology and managerial processes increases the productivity of smallholder agriculture, was the focus of the research on oil palm outgrowers in the Philippines based on field work undertaken in 2005. The research examined the variations in technology used by the interviewed outgrowers before and after entering into contracts with the local oil palm processor, along with the benefits that accrued to the outgrowers, including improvements in their farming systems and agricultural practices. The research variables included access to technology, credit, soil and nutrient sampling, agricultural inputs, agricultural extension and the use of mechanisation before and after entering into contract. Finally, the research assessed the benefits of technology transfer under contract as perceived and articulated by the outgrowers, along with the specific training related to land care and land conservation that they received.

CONTRACT FARMING AND TECHNOLOGY

The industrialisation of agriculture has resulted in significant and widespread institutional, technological and social changes to agricultural production at a global level. These changes, according to Schrader (1986), are largely the result of advances in biological and information technologies along with general economic growth, the increasing scale of organisation and the relative modernisation of production, processing and distribution systems (Kirsten and Sartorius 2002). Drabenstott (1995) argued that there are two forces driving the process of agro-industrialisation: namely, a new consumer and a new producer. The focus of the present discussion is on the new producers who are utilising new technological and managerial processes. These technologies allow processors to produce customised products, under agricultural contracts, to meet the changing lifestyle and food safety concerns of the consumer. The harnessing of technology ensures that the consumer gets the quality, consistency and value and other characteristics they demand (Drabenstott 1995). The resultant increased levels of technology being utilised in the manufacture and processing of agricultural commodities has resulted in the expansion of product uses and in the development of additional products (Von Braun and Kennedy 1994).

Contract farming systems are quickly replacing spot markets for domestic agricultural crops, export agricultural crops and other agricultural products, and have heralded an increase in product quality and safety along with the use of more consistent technology (Vellema 2002). Production contracts are increasingly linking small, medium-sized and large Third World farmers more directly to consumers in both domestic and foreign markets. These linkages are being made possible through the increased vertical coordination of agricultural firms or retail distributors as represented by both transnational corporations and indigenous bodies – national corporations – that cater to the changing demands of society (Kirsten and Sartorius 2002). At the heart of these changes are the technological advances and processes that allow for the increased industrialisation of the agricultural sector.

Kirsten and Sartorius (2002, p. 506) offered some cautionary advice: 'Although this sounds like an ideal situation, traditional markets do not handle these [changing] circumstances well'. Indeed, changes in agricultural systems throughout the world are resulting in social, cultural and economic impacts. There is considerable debate on the positive and negative impacts of technology transfer by agribusiness to the developing world (Dicken 1986; Poulton et al. 1998). In this regard, some researchers have questioned the appropriateness of technology transfer to developing countries by multinational corporations, citing unspecified adverse effects on the social and political environment (Dicken 1986; Little and Watts 1994).

Notwithstanding these concerns, the use of contract farming systems is rapidly increasing in developing countries. The global sourcing of agricultural products in the developing world is resulting in the rapid replacement of more traditional forms of agriculture along with the social interrelationships that supported them. Efficient agricultural production requires contracted farmers to have timely crop cultivation techniques, and such considerations as how and when to fertilise, weed, water, apply pesticides and fungicides are crucial to this process. It also requires that outgrowers have information on the product requirements of the processor, such as export standards related to chemical use (Key and Runsten 1999). This is of particular importance since the cultivation regime varies considerably in accordance with the technological requirements of the specific crop.

The contracted crop is frequently an important determinant of the socio-economic characteristics of the outgrower sought by processors (Glover 1987). Larger farmers have a distinct advantage over smaller farmers if processors rely on the contracted farmers to acquire technological and production information on their own. This is because larger producers are frequently better educated and can subtract the fixed costs of acquiring knowledge from a broader revenue base (Key and Runsten 1999). In the case of labour-intensive crops, such as oil palm, the small farmer has an advantage in that he can access labour from a much greater base, often at no cost, from within the extended family structure. The processor, in the case of the small farmer, however, must ensure that they mount an effective extension programme both to transfer the optimal cultivation techniques to their outgrowers and to ensure that the contracted farmers are fully aware of their product requirements.

None of this negates the frequently reported rationale of farmers in developing countries that they enter into production contracts to gain access to technology, technical skills and managerial processes. Other reasons that farmers enter into contracts include the security of contracted sale and access to credit. To realise these benefits, farmers are prepared to surrender some of their independence in order to acquire new facets of production (see Carney 1988; Clapp 1994; Glover 1994; Jackson and Cheater 1994; Rehber 2000; Kirsten and Sartorius 2002; Vellema 2002). Through the application of new technology and the use of modern managerial systems, outgrowers can increase production, reduce costs and augment their incomes (Clapp 1994; Watts 1994b; Baumann 2000).

While contract farming schemes are increasingly being developed within the context of an agro-industrial environment characterised by increasing vertical coordination, the attempt to control production through the introduction of new technology rarely involves a standardisation of social relations in production (Little and Watts 1994). This is important because it affirms that there is no established 'outgrower technology' programme that can be universally applied. As Vellema (2002, p. 3) indicates: 'the institutional and organizational configurations of contract farming are extremely varied. There are many ways in which companies . . . organize production, both technically and socially.'

The economic liberalisation and institutional reform that has taken place in the agricultural sector has occurred alongside a decline in the role of government in the provision of agricultural services and the dissemination of agricultural research via government extension services. Within this new economic order, it is the private sector that has to assume the responsibility for the provision of agricultural research, extension, production and marketing services via outgrower contracts (Coulter et al. 1999; World Bank 2001). As a direct result, the institutional absorption and integration of farmers into new production systems has taken place (Little and Watts 1994). Watts (1994a) argues that contract farming leads to the 'deskilling of labour', but Grossman (1995, p. 204), while agreeing that this could be the case in highly regulated schemes, indicates that it is by no means a certainty. He postulates that: 'in many cases, peasants modify technical packages to suit local needs'.

Benziger (1996) indicates that the success of liberalisation and institutional reform in the agricultural sector is contingent upon the willingness of the farmers to learn new technology. Glover (1987, p. 446), while pointing out that contract farming had negative features, indicates that: 'one of contract farming's most promising features is its effectiveness in transferring technology to small farmers. To exclude small farmers from contract farming involving technologically dynamic crops is to exclude them from one of their few opportunities for exposure to new techniques.' Glover and Kusterer (1990) conclude that improvements to the farming and management skills of small farmers are possible over relatively short periods.

PERSPECTIVES ON TECHNOLOGY TRANSFER UNDER CONTRACT

In theory, contractors can provide better extension programmes than governments because they have a more direct financial interest in the success of their outgrower programmes. While accepting this as a basic premise, Baumann (2000) argues that the transfer of technology under contract is varied both in its quality and in its sustainability. He feels, however, that there is more likelihood of both success and sustainability where a contract farming scheme's implementation is not subject to a constant reinvention of its technology, its means of dissemination to outgrowers or the cropping procedures involved. In this regard, Baumann (2000), citing from Ellman's (1986) evaluation of the Commonwealth Development Corporation (CDC) outgrower schemes, agrees with Ellman's conclusion that the CDC projects have been successful in their transfer of technology due to these factors. Ellman (1986) had argued that this success was principally because the CDC concentrated on a limited number of crops and developed an expertise based upon a refined and simple technology that was consistently disseminated to outgrowers.

Baumann (2000) is concerned that a repetitive monocropping system could adversely affect the environment. Technology developed for many contract farming schemes is highly crop-specific and often fails to include the transfer of knowledge on how to manage the crop as part of an integrated farming system. The insistence of contractors on the use of standardised agricultural inputs and input quantities can lead to conflict between themselves and their outgrowers, who have a more intimate knowledge of their own micro-environments. The contractors may transfer technology but the danger remains that this alone may not contribute to the outgrower's development as an agriculturalist, nor will it contribute to local, regional or national knowledge development or to environmental protection.

The continuity, quality and sustainability of extension services are other questions that arise during the analysis of contract farming schemes. Glover and Kusterer (1990) note that there is a rapid transfer of technology when the new crop is first introduced into an area. Attention given to the new outgrowers is more intense at these times, but tends to fade away over time as the contractors direct their attention to more recently recruited outgrowers. Instructional written memoranda to the outgrowers replace direct farm-level assistance and this can lead to feelings of abandonment amongst less secure outgrowers. The training itself can vary from formal to informal, but usually consists of general orientations, on-farm demonstrations in planting, weeding and harvesting, on-farm inspections, and skills training in managerial systems such as the record-keeping of costs and sales. Glover (1987) reports that there are benefits to outgrowers beyond the training associated with the transfer of technology. He points out that outgrowers, through a direct association with the contractor's staff, learn about the business environment beyond their farm fields, including a better understanding of how the market works or how to run their farms as a business. Glover (1994) indicates that even if there are less than successful contractual results, outgrowers still apply the knowledge and experience gained under contract to other future situations.

Vellema (2002) studied the relationship between technology transfer and organisational change in agriculture in the Philippines. While recognising the importance of technology in contract farming, he held that institutional and cultural fundamentals were the basic ingredients in the success of any contract farming scheme. Vellema (2002, p. 3) sees the transfer of technology as being the 'central element mediating the relationship between the contract grower and the company'. He considers that the provision of agricultural inputs, instructions and rules prescribed under the contract or emanating from technicians, hired by processors, as being essential for creating an environment in which the relationship between the parties can nurture, evolve and finally mature into a successful scheme. Vellema (2002, p. 14) points out that the management of this knowledge and technology is transient because the entire process is: 'imperfect and firm [processor] and commodity specific'. It allows for the conclusion that decision-making related to the introduction and use of technology is institutionally removed from the farm level (see Clapp 1988; Glover 1994; Little and Watts 1994; Burch et al. 1996). In spite of the fact that processors dominate the process, Vellema (2002, p. 15) postulates that: 'success or failure in growers' fields not only depends on individual crop management but is interrelated to the design of cropping systems and the selection of (new) technologies inside the company'.

TECHNOLOGY TRANSFER AND TRAINING

In the Philippines, the transfer of technology to oil palm outgrowers was undertaken using informal training methodologies. Structured training materials were not employed in the transfer of either general or specific information on the cultivation or management of the crop. Potential outgrowers were identified at 'outgrower information workshops' organised by the processor (Agumil Industries Inc.) in its palm oil mill's catchment area. These farmer orientation meetings were, in reality, an occasion for the processor to ascertain whether the interested farmers met the criteria established for the selection of outgrowers.

The outgrower selection criteria used by Agumil includes not only land ownership and financial considerations but also the applicant's reputation as a farmer and businessperson. In terms of the financial variable, the company looked for any impediment that would obstruct the prospective outgrower from meeting the financial costs of establishing and maintaining an oil palm farm. To be an outgrower, a farmer is expected to either have his or her own financial resources or be eligible to obtain a bank loan and, more importantly, to be seen as someone who would repay their loans.

Farmers are also expected to have the title to their agricultural land or, as a minimum, have a legal lease for its use for the next 25 years. Finally, farmers must possess a positive reputation, often indicated by word of mouth from 'trusted' members within their community. These personal references form a strong basis for the farmer's acceptability as an Agumil outgrower (Narciso 2003; Chang 2005).

Following the selection of outgrowers, Agumil used initial group meetings to introduce the farmers to oil palm cultivation and to basic managerial techniques. These sessions were undertaken orally, had limited structure and contained no written 'course material' for the outgrowers to retain and review later. Following these group trainings, on-farm instructions were subsequently provided to the outgrowers by the processor's extension agents on matters such as seedling spacing, weeding, harvesting, pruning and land conservation techniques (Narciso 2003). The training was not extended beyond the oral level and, once again, no written materials were presented to the outgrowers.

The participation of Agumil in these on-site activities varied from activity to activity but it was common for Agumil to lay out the pattern for the planting of the oil palm seedlings and to supervise their planting. The outgrowers received instructions on business management, including record-keeping, but the adoption of these business processes varied with many outgrowers relying upon Agumil's record-keeping. Once the outgrowers had completed the full cycle of training related to the key functions involved in oil palm cultivation, they continued to receive on-site visits and instructions from the processor's agricultural demonstrators. This training waned over time and was replaced by written memoranda sent by post to the outgrowers with instructions on when to undertake cyclical tasks such as brush or circle weeding and pruning (Jaquias 2004).

CHANGES IN THE USE OF TECHNOLOGY

Among the issues concerning the appropriateness of technology transfer via contract farming schemes in developing countries are the cultural, social and economic costs to the host country. These can arise from problems associated with the imposition of a profit-motivated agribusiness corporate system on rural societies that cultivate land under traditional and frequently communal modes of production (Eaton 1997). Contract farming schemes are designed on the basis of crops that are most appropriate in terms of their chances of agronomic success, market acceptance and their ease of adaptation in order to diversify the farmer's cash crop base (Glover and Ghee 1992; Baumann 2000; Eaton and Shepherd 2001). These introduced innovations may include technological changes involving both managerial processes and new production processes including the use of fertilisers, new cultivars and pesticides (Eaton and Shepherd 2001). Material inputs may require additional finance on the part of farmers and, under contract farming schemes, agribusiness may be not only the source of innovative technical change but also the source of the farm credit required by the outgrowers. Harvey (1985), supporting contract farming systems, proposes that smallholder farmers gain access to technology, agricultural inputs, farm credit and management processes in this manner. In this sense, contract farming systems can foster agricultural development (Eaton 1997).

The main perception of the interviewed Filipino farmers was that their overall use of technology had not increased due to their exposure to the technology inherent in oil palm cultivation. When requested to indicate the level of use of 'technology' after entering into contract, 75 per cent of the Filipino outgrowers indicated that their use of technology had not changed since entering contract. Twenty per cent of the Filipino farmers under contract, however, did indicate that their use of technology had subsequently increased. Clearly, the adaptation of new technology was not the primary benefit sought after by outgrowers in the research area.

Table 10.1 presents the responses of the outgrowers to specific questions on their changing use of farm inputs, credit, soil and leaf nutrient sampling, agricultural machinery and extension services. In terms of agricultural credit, entering into contract did change the source of the outgrower's funds. There was a switch away from self-financing (85 per cent to 48 per cent) as 45 per cent of the outgrowers availed themselves of the commercial financing from the First National Bank of the Philippines. There was, however, a significant improvement in the utilisation of agricultural extension services under contract. Previously, only 16 per cent of the Filipino farmers indicated that they benefited from extension services. After entering into contract, 100 per cent of the outgrowers indicated that they now benefited from agricultural advisory services. The use of fertiliser did not change after the farmers' entry into oil palm production contracts, as the use of fertiliser before contract farming was already high in any

Table 10.1   Philippine oil palm outgrower's sources of funds, services and supplies before and after contract

Farming components	Before (%)	After (%)
Financing		
Self financed	85.2	48.1
Institutional	7.4	4.4
Local money lender	0.0	0.0
Oil palm processor	0.0	0.0
Extension services		
Not used	84.0	0.0
Min. of Agr.	8.0	0.0
Other Sources	8.0	0.0
OP processor	0.0	100.0
Fertiliser source		
None used	12.0	0.0
Min of Agr.	0.0	0.0
Local market	76.0	64.0
Other sources	12.0	0.0
OP processor	0.0	36.0
Soil/leaf sampling		
Not done	64.0	32.0
Min. of Agr.	12.0	0.0
Commercial labs	24.0	24.0
OP processor	0.0	44.0
Machinery use		
None used	8.0	8.0
Rented	60.0	32.0
Owned	32.0	60.0

case. Local market purchases remained high at 64 per cent, down from 76 per cent, before the outgrower scheme commenced. Thirty-six per cent indicated that they now purchase their fertiliser directly from the processor, Agumil.

Nutrient sampling of both soils and vegetation has increased significantly since the farmers became oil palm outgrowers. Previously, 64 per cent of the Filipino outgrowers indicated that they had never had their soil or plants tested for nutrients. After entering into outgrower contracts, 64 per cent of the outgrowers indicated that they have received this service from Agumil, but the number of farmers who still do not test for nutrients was 32 per cent. Twenty-four per cent of the outgrowers in the Philippines still use private laboratories, a proportion that remained unchanged from the period before they entered into contracts with Agumil.

While the incidence of machinery use has not changed, the rental versus ownership ratio has reversed with more outgrowers (60 per cent) reporting that they now own machinery, versus 32 per cent who indicated that they rent. Before entering into contract these two percentages were reversed, with 60 per cent renting and 32 per cent owning. This reflects greater farm incomes derived from the cultivation of oil palm, coupled with the fact that the outgrowers, if they can afford it, would find a small tractor of benefit in the transport of the oil palm fruits to Agumil's central collection points.

PERCEIVED BENEFITS FROM THE TRANSFER OF TECHNOLOGY

Based upon outgrowers' perceptions in the Philippines, 56 per cent felt that the major benefit from the technology transfer was the training itself, and 27 per cent believed that the benefit was in the transferability of the technical and managerial lessons to their farming in general. This 'transferability' benefit increased to 65 per cent when outgrowers provided a secondary response. Training in its own right was indicated as the major benefit in their first response (71 per cent), while 50 per cent saw the benefit of 'transferability' of the technical and managerial lessons to their farming in general as the major benefit in their secondary response.

In general, little difference exists between 'training' and 'transferability'. The outgrowers saw being a contract farmer as an opportunity to improve both their cultivation and managerial processes, resulting in an opportunity to improve their farming and increase their profits. In terms of the outgrower's perceptions on what they saw as the negative or positive benefits arising from the transfer of technology, outgrowers were primarily positive with 91 per cent indicating that they had benefited overall. Ninety-six per cent of the outgrowers felt that their entry into oil palm contract farming had provided them with enhanced farming skills. This was reflected in their responses to a secondary question concerning their views on whether their farming practices had improved, with 88 per cent agreeing that this was the case.

At a more specific level, 65 per cent of the outgrowers indicated that the primary improvement to their agriculture rested in the fact that they now knew how to produce a crop that they were not familiar with before. In other words, they had diversified their agriculture. Twenty-three per cent indicated that they used the techniques acquired from Agumil extension agents to improve the husbandry of their other commercial tree crops. In terms of the secondary responses, 62 per cent of the Filipino outgrowers provided an ambiguous response to the effect that 'the transfer of technology made them better farmers'.

LAND CONSERVATION AND THE TRANSFER OF TECHNOLOGY

Environmental protection plays a critical role in contract farming systems (Burch et al. 1992; Little and Watts 1994; Miller 1995). Deforestation, the depletion of water resources and soil degradation are major ecological concerns that frequently accompany agricultural development (Eaton 1997). The nature of the crop produced and the physical environment determine the degree of environmental problems that can be associated with a contract farming scheme. While the economic rationale for the development of contract farming schemes can be quite well understood, physical and biological environmental degeneration may become a major economic threat to rural societies (Eaton 1997). In the Philippines, environmental concerns did not receive the same attention as other elements of the training programme in the outgrower programme. This, however, does not necessarily imply a lack of concern on the part of the Filipino processor.

In view of national and global concerns related to environmental protection, it is ethically and economically crucial that sponsors, their extension staff and the outgrowers themselves address environmental issues during the implementation of outgrower schemes. The most practical way that sponsors can ensure ecological compatibility within contracts is to ensure that projected outgrower areas are selected in consultation with the farmer and qualified extension staff (Eaton 1997). The farmer's knowledge of the local historical and production performance of his land, including local micro-environmental factors, should ultimately form a considerable part of the decision-making process on agronomic and land care issues. The willingness by outgrower scheme managers to incorporate local knowledge is imperative for the success of the outgrower system, but sponsors are not always astute enough to follow this advice (Cinco 2004).

During the interviews conducted in the Philippines, outgrowers were asked if, in their view, the processor (Agumil) was concerned about the long-term viability of their land. Only 65 per cent of the Filipino outgrowers shared the belief that Agumil was prepared to provide the appropriate transfer of technical knowledge, through training, on land care techniques. Fifty-two per cent of the outgrowers, however, indicated that they had received training specifically related to land care. In interviews, the managers of Agumil indicated that the preservation of the environment and the outgrowers' farms was of paramount importance to them.

In an open-ended follow-up question, outgrowers were asked to indicate what training they had received, if any, from Agumil. Fifty-eight per cent of the outgrowers indicated that they had received land care training and that the primary training received was on how to construct terraces and drainage canals to prevent slope erosion (26 per cent). The second most cited training was on the planting of nitrogen-fixing cover crops (23 per cent), to decrease erosion while at the same time nourishing the oil palms. The use of the pruned palm fronds to construct 'banks', again with the intent of preventing rapid run-off and soil erosion, was also cited by 7 per cent of the outgrowers who received training on land care from Agumil's extension agents. Forty-two per cent of the outgrowers reported that they had not received any training on land care.

CONCLUSION

Contract farming is increasing rapidly in developing countries, affecting traditional agricultural practices and the supporting social interrelationships. The fact remains that contract farming in developing countries will increase in the future in response to the globalisation of agricultural systems. As such, care must be exercised to ensure that new technology is introduced within a well-organised and effective development framework. It must involve proper transfer mechanisms in conjunction with technical and managerial processes that directly benefit smallholder outgrowers.

Outgrower contracts allow contract farming scheme sponsors to maintain a desired level of quantity and quality of production. In turn, the sponsors of contract farming schemes in developing countries must provide technical advice to farmers on all facets of the production, transportation and handling of the crop that they market. These improved techniques are required to upgrade and promote agricultural commodities into markets that demand high quality standards (Eaton and Shepherd 2001). Inherent in this system is the requirement for outgrowers to be given information on the product requirements of the processor, such as export standards related to chemical use and other crop characteristics (Key and Runsten 1999). This is of particular importance since the cultivation regime varies considerably in accordance with the technological requirements of each specific crop. These introduced agronomic adaptations, production techniques and managerial and financial processes may actually increase productivity and quality. In order to achieve these increases, private sector companies may offer more focused technological advisory services than government agricultural extension services have in the past, as they have a direct financial interest in improving farmers' production, in terms of both quantity and quality (Glover and Kusterer 1990).

With the exception of the oil palm seedlings, a product of extensive hybridisation, the transfer of knowledge required for the production of oil palms represents the transfer of a relatively low level of technology. Outgrowers in the research area have readily accepted the technology that was tendered as part of the outgrower scheme and they support Drabenstott's (1995) definition of 'new producers'. The data collected during the course of this research has provided little evidence to support the cautionary advice of Kirsten and Sartorius (2002) on the capacity of traditional systems to cope with increasing levels of technology. Similarly, there was no evidence of any of the adverse effects on the social and political environments that were postulated by Dicken (1986) or Little and Watts (1994). The production of oil palm under contract in the Philippines does not lend itself to the situation portrayed by Ehui and Delgado (1999), wherein small rural farmers have difficulty in coping with the transfer of technology necessitated by agro-industrialisation that mandates an increase in the capital to labour ratio. In the research area, it has been more a question of the access to technology rather than the technology per se, as suggested by Narayanan and Gulati (2002).

As indicated in the literature, research into other outgrower schemes has led to considerable conflict between the sponsor and the outgrower, but in the research area investigated as part of this research, the outgrowers were prepared to surrender some of their independence to gain access to technology (see, for example, Carney 1988; Clapp 1994; Glover 1994; Jackson and Cheater 1994). Virtually all (91 per cent) of the outgrowers felt that they had benefited from being under contract and that they had improved as farmers. This finding is supported by Baumann (2000) in his analysis of outgrower schemes and outgrower crops. It is important, however, to bear in mind that the benefits derived from being under contract will vary depending upon the specific crop and the technology associated with it (Vellema 2002). In the case of the oil palm, while only the pruning and harvesting functions are unique to it, the managerial, financial and weeding systems and tree planting schematic layouts have proven useful to the outgrowers in their production of other tree cash crops.

The present research found that the transfer of technology, simple as it is in the case of oil palm cultivation, was frequently a central issue in the determination of the relationship between the processor and the outgrower. For example, the frequency and intensity of weeding or the level of fertilisation was frequently cited by the interviewed outgrowers as a valid cause for questioning the processor's understanding of the local agricultural environment in the Philippines. This lack of understanding was also evident in relation to cultural norms, and was not restricted to technological aspects of oil palm production.

Contract farming systems can introduce adverse consequences to the environment (Burch et al. 1992; Little and Watts 1994; Miller 1995; Eaton 1997). Variations, dependent upon the crop that is under production, do occur and it is imperative that the views of the extension staff coupled with those of the outgrowers themselves be taken into consideration during the design and implementation of outgrower schemes (Eaton and Shepherd 2001). Agumil, in the Philippines, was prepared to address environmental issues, but training in this area did not seem to be a central facet of its outgrower education programme. These results are interesting given that Filipino outgrowers virtually all have title to their properties. One might expect the focus on environmental land care training to be quite a central issue to both them and the processor under the oil palm contract farming scheme.

Contract farming has received the endorsement of multilateral and bilateral donors in part because the proponents (contractors or processors) of outgrower schemes in developing countries are prepared to work closely with and transfer agricultural technology to smallholder farmers. Their actions are not entirely altruistic as these transnational or national corporations have considerable self-interest involved in ensuring outgrowers' success in achieving product quality, quantity and the timeliness of product delivery. If the outgrower scheme is in its early stages, there is also an opportunity to use the success of earlier outgrowers as a means of attracting further farmers into the scheme (Cinco 2004). This was certainly the case with the development of Agumil's outgrower scheme in the Philippines, where early outgrowers were hand-picked to achieve almost certain success. Agumil's objective was for these successful farmers to serve as examples to lure further smaller farmers into the outgrower scheme. The regular supply of fruit from the outgrowers is required to maximise the economic efficiency of the contractor's processing mills, even where a nucleus estate exists. In this respect, the profitability of the firm depends on its ability to operate the plant at full capacity (Chang 2005).

The significance of the transfer of knowledge involved in the oil palm industry in the Philippines is that it generally allows for its adaptability and transferability into the outgrowers' farming businesses. Benziger (1996) noted that the success of an outgrower scheme was, at least in part, based upon the willingness of outgrowers to adopt new technology.

This has certainly taken place in the scheme investigated as part of this research. The outgrowers' acceptance of new technology has resulted in their increasing self-confidence and ability to transfer this knowledge into other facets of their lives. Examples of this were apparent, given the propensity of the outgrowers to enter into other business ventures using the business acumen that they obtained as oil palm farmers.

In conclusion, the evidence reported here supports Glover's (1987, 1994) contention that outgrowers benefit beyond the actual content of the technology transferred to them, and that the outgrowers use the knowledge and experience of living under contract in other situations. As such, the introduction of new technology, as part of a contract farming scheme, can open up new markets and create economic benefits for smallholder farmers. The development and transfer of technology remains a central component of all contract farming schemes. While outgrowers may resent not being included in the deliberations on the application of technology in their own fields, their contributions are more likely to be fine-tuning rather than a true contribution to technology use per se. Contract farming should be seen as integral to the developmental process since, as Kirsten and Sartorius (2002, p. 516) note: 'the educational experience of interacting with an agricultural partner can provide a platform for farmers in developing countries . . . to convert from subsistence to commercial farming'. The value of contract farming, at least in part, rests in the benefits derived from the transfer of technological and farm management processes.

REFERENCES

Baumann, P. (2000), Equity and efficiency in contract farming schemes: the experience of agricultural tree crops, Overseas Development Institute working paper no. 139.

Benziger, V. (1996), 'Small fields, big money: two successful programs in helping small farmers make the transition to high value-added crops', *World Development*, **24**, 1681–93.

Burch, D., R.E. Rickson and R. Annels (1992), 'The growth of agribusiness: environmental and social implications of contract farming', in G. Lawrence, F. Vanclay and B. Furze (eds), *Agriculture, Environment and Society: Contemporary Issues for Australia*, Melbourne VIC: Macmillan Company of Australia, pp. 12–30.

Burch, D., R. Rickson and G. Lawrence (eds) (1996), *Globalization and Agri-food Restructuring: Perspectives from the Australasia Region*, Singapore: Avebury.

Carney, J.A. (1988), 'Struggles over crop rights and labour within contract farming households in a Gambian irrigated rice project', *Journal of Peasant Studies*, **15**, 334–49.

Carney, J.A. (1994), 'Contracting a food staple in the Gambia', in P. Little and M. Watts (eds), *Living Under Contract: Contract Farming and Agrarian Transformation in Sub-Saharan Africa*, Madison, WI: University of Wisconsin Press, pp. 167–87.

Chang, C.K. (2005), personal interview – Chief Executive Officer, Agumil Philippines Inc. Davao, Mindanao, Philippines.

Cinco, C. (2004), personal interview – Community Relations Manager, Filipinas Palmoil Plantations Industries, San Francisco, Agusan del Sur, Philippines.

Clapp, R.A. (1988), 'Representing reciprocity, reproducing domination: ideology and the labour process in Latin American contract farming', *Journal of Peasant Studies*, **16**, 5–39.

Clapp, R.A. (1994), 'The moral economy of the contract', in P. Little and M. Watts (eds), *Living Under Contract: Contract Farming and Agrarian Transformation in Sub-Saharan Africa*, Madison, WI: University of Wisconsin Press, pp. 78–96.

Coulter, J., A. Goodland, A. Tallontire and R. Stringfellow (1999), 'Marrying farmer cooperation and contract farming for agricultural service provision in sub-Saharan Africa', London: Overseas Development Institute (ODI) Natural Resources Perspectives, no. 48.

Dicken, P. (1986), *Global Shift: Industrial Change in a Turbulent World*, London: Harper & Row.

Drabenstott, M. (1995), 'Agricultural industrialization: implications for economic development and public policy', *Journal of Agricultural and Applied Economics*, **27**, 13–20.

Eaton, C. (1997), 'Adaption performance and production constraints of contract farming in China', PhD thesis, Department of Geography, University of Western Australia.

Eaton, C. and A. Shepherd (2001), *Contract Farming: Partnerships for Growth*, Rome: Food and Agriculture Organization of the United Nations.

Ehui, S. and C. Delgado (1999), 'Economy-wide impacts of technological change in the agro-food production and processing sectors of sub-Saharan Africa', International Food Policy Research Institute of the World Bank MSSD discussion paper no. 38.

Ellman, A. (1986), *Nucleus Estates and Smallholder Outgrower Schemes*, London: Overseas Development Administration.

Glover, D.J. (1987), 'Increasing the benefits to smallholders from contract farming: problems for farmers' organizations and policy makers', *World Development*, **15**, 441–8.

Glover, D. (1994), 'Contract farming and commercialization of agriculture in developing countries', in J. von Braun and E.T. Kennedy (eds), *Agricultural Commercialization, Economic Development, and Nutrition*, Baltimore, MD: International Food Policy Research Institute, Johns Hopkins University Press, pp. 166–75.

Glover, D. and L.T. Ghee (1992), *Contract Farming in Southeast Asia: Three Country Studies*, Kuala Lumpur: Institute for Advanced Studies, University of Malaya.

Glover, D. and K. Kusterer (1990), *Small Farmers, Big Business: Contract Farming and Rural Development*, London: Macmillan Press.

Grossman, L. (1995), 'Book review – Living under contract: contract farming and agrarian transformation in sub-Saharan Africa', *Annals of the Association of American Geographers*, **85**, 204–6.

Harvey, C. (1985), *Rural Development and Administration in the Third World: Development Methods and Alternate Strategies*, Aldershot: Ashgate.

Jackson, J.C. and A.P. Cheater (1994), 'Contract farming in Zimbabwe: case studies of sugar, tea, and cotton', in P. Little and M. Watts (eds), *Living Under Contract: Contract Farming and Agrarian Transformation in Sub-Saharan Africa*, Madison, WI: University of Wisconsin Press, pp. 140–66.

Jaquias, D.D. (2004), personal interview, President of the Agusan del Sur State College of Agriculture and Technology, Butuan, Agusan del Sur, Philippines.

Key, N. and D. Runsten (1999), 'Contract farming, smallholders, and rural development in Latin America: the organization of agro processing firms and the scale of outgrower production', *World Development*, **27**, 381–401.

Kirsten, J. and K. Sartorius (2002), 'Linking agribusiness and small-scale farmers in developing countries: is there a new role for contract farming?', *Development Southern Africa*, **19**, 503–29.

Little, P.D. and M.J. Watts (1994), *Living Under Contract: Contract Farming and Agrarian Transformation in Sub-Saharan Africa*, Madison, WI: University of Wisconsin Press.

Mayer, J. (2002), 'Globalization, technology transfer and skill accumulation in low-income countries', in S.M. Murshed (ed.), *Globalization, Marginalization and Development*, London: Routledge, pp. 62–79.

Miller, L. (1995), 'Agribusiness, contract farmers and land-use sustainability in North-West Tasmania', *Australian Geographer*, **26**, 104–11.

Narayanan, S. and A. Gulati (2002), 'Globalization and the smallholders: a review of issues, approaches and implications', International Food Policy Research Institute of the World Bank MSSD discussion paper no. 50.

Narciso, P.P. (2003), personal interview, Manager of the Outgrower Division, Manat, Trento, Agusan del Sur, Philippines.

Poulton, C., A. Dorward, J. Kydd, N. Poole and L. Smith (1998), 'A new institutional economics perspective on current policy debates', in A. Dorward, J. Kydd and C. Poulton (eds), *Smallholder Cash Crop Production under Market Liberalization: A New Institutional Economics Perspective*, Wallingford: CAB International, pp. 1–55.

Reardon, T. and C.B. Barrett (2000), 'Agro industrialization, globalization, and international development: an overview of issues, patterns and determinants', *Agricultural Economics*, **23**, 195–205.

Rehber, E. (2000), 'Vertical coordination in the agro-food industry and contract farming: A comparative research of Turkey and the USA', Food Marketing Policy Centre Research Report Series, Storrs, CT: University of Connecticut.

Schrader, L.F. (1986), 'Responses to forces shaping agricultural marketing: contracting', *American Journal of Agricultural Economics*, **68**, 1161–7.

Vellema, S. (2002), *Society and Technology in Philippine Transnational Agribusiness*, Maastricht, Netherlands: Shaker Publishing.

Von Braun, J. and E.T. Kennedy (1994), *Agricultural Commercialization, Economic Development, and Nutrition*, Baltimore, MD: Johns Hopkins University Press.

Watts, M.J. (1994a), 'Life under contract: contract farming, agrarian restructuring, and flexible accumulation', in P. Little and M. Watts (eds), *Living Under Contract: Contract Farming and Agrarian Transformation in Sub-Saharan Africa*, Madison, WI: University of Wisconsin Press, pp. 248–57.

Watts, M.J. (1994b), 'Epilogue: contracting, social labour, and agrarian transitions', in P. Little and M. Watts (eds), *Living Under Contract: Contract Farming and Agrarian Transformation in Sub-Saharan Africa*, Madison, WI: University of Wisconsin Press, pp. 21–77.

World Bank (2001), *Building Institutions for Markets*, Washington, DC and Oxford: Oxford University Press.

11. Agriculture, land use and conservation initiatives in Indonesia: implications for development and sustainability

Julian Clifton

INTRODUCTION

This chapter describes the interplay between global, regional and local forces governing land use and resource extraction in an area of central Buton Island in southeast Sulawesi, Indonesia, during the period 2002–07. Through integrating first-hand observations and research with critical reviews of international conservation efforts, this chapter presents an illustration of how globalisation, as represented through international conservation programmes, may interact with the socio-economic and political environment in developing countries targeted by such activities. The outcomes are illustrated through analysis of initiatives designed to reduce pressure on forest resources through creating new management institutions, altering household income-generating strategies, and reducing forest clearance for crop cultivation in villages surrounding two forest reserves. These demonstrate the increasing scope of intervention associated with contemporary global conservation programmes and the extent to which local livelihoods are being affected by this process.

DESCRIPTION OF THE STUDY AREA

Sulawesi is the fourth-largest island in Indonesia, with a total area of around 190000 km^2 and a population of 14.1 million in 2000 (Badan Pusat Statistik 2001). It is divided for government purposes into six provinces (*propinsi*), which are further subdivided into districts (*kabupaten*), subdistricts (*kecamatan*) and villages (*desa*). The province of southeast Sulawesi is administered from the town of Kendari on mainland Sulawesi and includes Buton Island, which is divided into two districts (Buton and North Buton) with a total area of around 6200 km² and a total population of 461 000 in 2000 (Badan Pusat Statistik 2001). Buton district covers the central and southern areas of the island and includes 12 subdistricts.

Buton Island has been described as containing one of the most pristine remaining areas of lowland evergreen rainforest in Sulawesi, with the presence of endemic species to Sulawesi including the endangered 'flagship' anoa (*Bubalus depressicornus*) and the Buton macaque (*Macaca ochreata brunnescens*) enhancing its profile in conservation terms. Scientific interest in the area has been enhanced by the discovery of numerous hitherto unknown species, principally herpetofauna, by researchers in recent years (Operation Wallacea 2006). Two of southeast Sulawesi's 15 protected areas are found in central Buton, comprising the Lambusango Wildlife Reserve and the Kakenauwe Nature Reserve, both of which were gazetted in 1982 and which cover around 28 000 ha in total. Conservation and management of these protected areas is undertaken by the provincial branch of the Natural Resources Office (Konservasi Sumber Daya Alam or KSDA) which is based in Kendari. The KSDA is a department of the Directorate General for Forest Protection and Nature Conservation (PHPA), which itself is situated within the Ministry of Forestry. The forest reserves are surrounded by forest designated as 'production forest' (49 800 ha) and 'protection forest' (1900 ha) which are managed by Ministry of Forestry officials operating at the district level of government. Under the Forestry Law of 1999, licences are required for all activities within production and protection forests which may include agriculture, mining and collection of forest products. The location of the study area, including selected villages and the borders of the forest reserves, is illustrated in Figure 11.1.

Detailed census data for the region are not available, but the population of the largest village of Lawele was estimated at around 2650 people in 2005 (Malleson 2007, p. 24), with the population of other villages ranging from 200 to 1700. The population is predominantly Butonese in origin, with most settlements being established in the period of relative stability in rural areas following the political unrest of the late 1960s. In addition, the national policy of transmigration has resulted in an estimated total of 210 000 people being moved to southeast Sulawesi between 1968 and 1997, representing 12.6 per cent of the provincial population in 2000 (Saragih and Yoshida 2002, p. 2). Transmigrants in central Buton mainly consist of groups from Bali and Java, with villages mostly being located in fertile areas along river valley bottoms where rice cultivation can be practiced. More recently, smaller villages in more remote locations have been established in response to the needs of refugees fleeing the Moluccas in the late 1990s. Approximately 150 000–170 000 displaced persons from

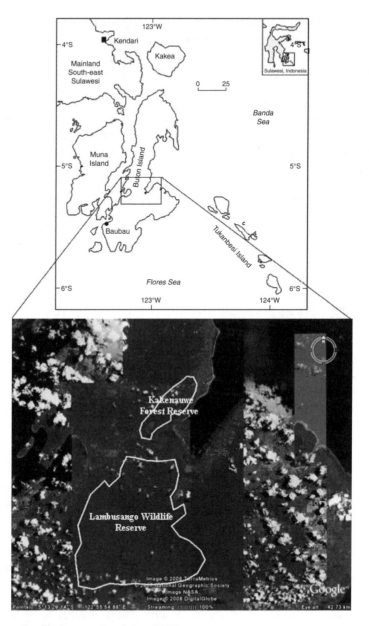

Source: Satellite image – Google Inc. (2009).

Figure 11.1   Location map of villages and conservation areas in Buton Island, South East Sulawesi

the Moluccas are considered to be present in southeast Sulawesi (Waas et al. 2003, p. 329), with Buton Island providing a destination for many Muslim refugees claiming Butonese ancestry. This combination of factors lies behind the province of southeast Sulawesi recording one of the fastest annual increases in population of 5.35 per cent between 1971 and 2000, far exceeding the national average of 2.52 per cent per annum over this period (Badan Pusat Statistik 2001).

Data collected in 2007 indicated that annual household incomes in the villages of central Buton ranged from IDR6 million to IDR18 million, or US$660–1990.[1] Agriculture was the most significant source of income, providing up to 40 per cent of annual household income. Cash crops include rice, cashews, coconuts and coffee, being located in plots adjacent to settlements, whilst various fruit and vegetables are cultivated for subsistence purposes in home gardens. Forest products including timber, rattan and, less frequently, honey, represented up to 11 per cent of annual household income, although this varied as a function of distance from the forested areas (Malleson 2007, p. 4).

The situation regarding agricultural land use and ownership rights in rural Indonesia is rendered exceedingly complex by a host of legal and administrative contradictions and irregularities relating to forested and agricultural land, which have been covered in detail elsewhere (Contreras-Hermosillo and Fay 2005; McCarthy 2000; Peluso 1996). These range from simplistic or misleading official definitions of 'clearance', unclear jurisdiction within government departments over matters relating to land ownership and use, and the requirements of individuals to 'prove' ownership of land or the existence of traditional agricultural practices. More recently, uncertainties over administrative responsibilities have been enhanced by the devolution of administrative responsibilities as part of the move towards regional autonomy in the post-Suharto period, often referred to as *reformasi*. Interviews conducted in central Buton enabled clarification of the local procedures involved in clearing and using land for agriculture. In cases where the land lay within the production or protection forests, permission for clearance would be required from the provincial branch of the Ministry of Forestry, which would entail considerable cost and time delays and hence rarely occurred. It was far more common for the village head to grant permission, which theoretically should only apply where the land lay outside zoned forested areas, but in practice took place in all cases.

A combination of factors were noted which have generated increased demand for forest clearance for agricultural purposes within the villages of central Buton. Foremost amongst these is the growing population and number of villages in central Buton, reflecting both transmigrants and refugee populations being resettled in this area. The stipulation that individual farmers begin to pay taxes on cleared land after two years of cultivation, in combination with the low fertility of the shallow leached soils developed on Buton's karst limestone slopes (Whitten et al. 1996, p. 468), will serve to maintain demand for forest clearance. Furthermore, the presence of crop-raiding forest animals such as macaques and wild pigs often underpinned the perceived need for forest clearance amongst farmers.

Under these circumstances, there is evident pressure for clearance which has impinged upon the forest reserves and adjacent forested areas. Recent analysis of satellite imagery has indicated that 6 per cent or approximately 1700 ha of the total forest reserve area experienced degradation between 1991 and 2004, almost all of which had taken place in proximity to settlements. A further 25 per cent (7000 ha) was classified as 'growth' forest, which included areas recovering from degradation during this period (Widayati and Carlisle 2007). Furthermore, 19 per cent (9285 ha) of the production forest was degraded between 1991 and 2004 and 15 per cent (7533 ha) was classified as 'growth' forest.

More recently, the nature and severity of the threats to the forest reserves in central Buton have been exacerbated by events at the international level. The increase in global oil prices and growing domestic demand led the government to cap the national oil price subsidy in late 2005. Amongst other widespread impacts, this caused the price of paraffin (kerosene), widely used in Buton for cooking purposes by rural communities and poorer households, to increase overnight by 186 per cent, leading to an immediate surge in demand for firewood as an alternative fuel source. In addition, Buton is distinctive in that the island contains Indonesia's sole known reserves of natural asphalt or bitumen, estimated at around 120 million tonnes (Siswosoebrotho et al. 2005, p. 858). The expansion of the Chinese economy has resulted in demand for asphalt growing at a rate of 12 per cent per annum (Research and Markets Limited 2008), with state-owned and private companies now exporting Butonese natural asphalt to China. The scale of this activity is reflected by the recent leasing of 24000 ha in northern and central Buton for bitumen exploration to a joint Chinese–Indonesian company in a venture worth approximately US$50 million over 30 years (Sino Prosper Holdings Limited 2006). In the post-Suharto *reformasi* period, the new tax regime places greater emphasis on district governments securing their own funding base through taxes on activities including mining and tourism (Seymour and Turner 2002, p. 39). Therefore, the continued expansion of the asphalt mining sector is of considerable importance to the district government, particularly since a redrawing of administrative boundaries in 2007 resulted in the loss of the district's jurisdiction over popular tourist destinations in the islands off Buton's east coast. Whilst the full extent of natural asphalt deposits in central Buton is uncertain, the likely expansion of open-cast mining of this product clearly poses a hazard to the integrity of the forest reserves. Longer-term potential threats to the forest are also associated with the national government's plans to substitute 10 per cent of fossil fuel consumption with biofuel products by 2010 (Reuters 2008). This will entail the planting of an estimated 5.25 million ha of oil palms, cassava, sugarcane and jatropha, with Sulawesi being one of the likely centres of cultivation (United States Department of Agriculture 2007).

This brief summary demonstrates that a variety of actors, including individual farmers, households, commercial operators and government departments, are subject to diverse socio-economic forces at the local, regional and international level. Together these sectors result in an increasing diversity and severity of threats to forest reserves in this area. Furthermore, the maintenance of these reserves is fundamentally weakened by chronic underfunding of the state bodies responsible for their management. Information relating to domestic spending on conservation is limited in terms of timescales and coverage, but data covering the period 1994–2000 show that total expenditure on national parks declined in real terms, equating to approximately US$2 million in 1999/2000 (Rhee et al. 2004, pp. 2–16). Moreover, the allocation of funds to individual protected areas is biased in favour of a restricted number of sites, predominantly in Java (MacAndrews 1998, p. 133). In the case of central Buton, the lack of funding and staff shortages result in an absence of boundary markers, enforcement or awareness-raising activities, with just one ranger being responsible for policing the two forest reserves. Consequently, the strict rules regarding the reserves, which preclude all access and product extraction other than under permitted scientific research, simply cannot be implemented by the KSDA. Research has demonstrated that the majority of villagers in settlements adjoining the reserves were either unaware of the reserves' existence or the location of the reserve boundaries (Clifton 2002).

GLOBALISING CONSERVATION: THE GEF INITIATIVE

This state of affairs, with increasing pressure to exploit protected forest resources set against a virtually powerless domestic conservation institution, changed significantly as a result of external intervention in 2005. It is this intercession, involving an alliance of overseas organisations pursuing an agenda of active participation in forest management and protection, which will form the basis of the ensuing discussion. The objectives of the programme will be described and its impacts examined with reference to changes to livelihoods and land use practices that are currently taking place amongst villages surrounding the reserves.

The Lambusango Forest Conservation project is a four-year programme with total funds of US$4.5 million which commenced in July 2005.[2] It is co-financed by the Global Environment Facility or GEF (US$1 million), a UK-based research tourism operator (Operation Wallacea) active in Buton (US$1.6 million) together with the provincial departments of the Forestry Office and the KSDA, which contribute US$0.95 million and US$0.93 million respectively. This project identified the primary threats to the forest reserves as clearance by an expanding local population, selective logging, rattan collection and hunting. Attention was also drawn to the contrast between the forest reserves which are run by the provincial branch of the KSDA for conservation purposes, and the adjacent production and protection forests managed by forestry offices at the district level, that are responsible for maximising tax revenue through regulating forest product usage. It was suggested that this reduces the utility of the production and protection forests to act as buffer zones for the forest reserves, and that an alternative management situation was required to combat the above threats effectively.

This programme therefore proposed to amalgamate the forest reserves, production forest and protection forest into a single management unit covering around 60 000 ha, referred to as the Lambusango Forest Management Area (LFMA). A management plan for the LFMA would be produced by a forum consisting of equal numbers of governmental and non-governmental representatives. The plan specified that strict rules would continue to apply to those areas formerly designated as forest reserves, but the Forum would work with adjacent villages to identify and demarcate areas of nearby production forest that could be used by residents of each village, termed 'village-managed forests'. Within these, residents would be permitted to extract resources including timber and non-timber forest products (NTFPs) such as rattan or honey at predetermined sustainable levels of usage. Rattan could also be harvested from outside the village-managed forests, including the former reserve areas, but all rattan collectors would need to be licensed and work to annual quotas. In order to participate in the scheme, each village would need to sign a contract agreeing, amongst other things, to halt all hunting and logging outside of the village-managed forests, stop all conversion of forest to agricultural land, and ensure that the extraction of timber and NTFPs from the village-managed forest stayed within predefined limits. Enforcement activities would involve the KSDA rangers in conjunction with district forestry officials but would essentially rely upon 'village guardians' appointed by each village to ensure that the regulations described above were adhered to. Failure to comply would ultimately result in the village being excluded from participation in these activities for a 12-month period. A set of performance criteria are described to monitor the impact of the programme, which include targets of increased total income from legally collected forest products (5 per cent increase above inflation per year), awareness of the LFMA's existence (90 per cent recognition in participating villages by the end of the project) and enforcement (10 per cent decline in reported offences per annum for the project's duration).

Analysis of the GEF Programme

Since its inception in 1991, the GEF has been the subject of detailed scrutiny from academics, governments and non-governmental organisations, with many reviews of its structure and policies (Sharma 1996; Streck 2001; Young 2002). Fundamental to many of these critiques is the perceived control of the World Bank and its principal donors over the funding of the GEF, the extent to which GEF sponsored programmes further the economic interests of these donors and, more recently, the introduction of selection criteria that effectively render certain countries ineligible for GEF funding (Ervine 2007, p. 132). The effectiveness of GEF programmes is also a focal point of attention, with a recent review indicating that only 17 out of 210 biodiversity projects funded by the GEF had sufficient monitoring programmes to evaluate their impact (Saterson et al. 2004, p. 597). A full evaluation of the Lambusango Forest Conservation project would require a lengthy discussion of the political, social and economic assumptions of the programme and would only be appropriate following the project's completion. For the purposes of this discussion, attention will be focused upon the implications for agricultural activity, income diversification and non-timber forest product usage amongst village communities.

Rattan regulation

An increased degree of regulation over the extraction of rattan from the forested areas of central Buton receives high priority in this project and the establishment of a formalised sustainable harvesting regime is seen as crucial in this respect. Rattan, also referred to as cane or wicker, are climbing plants of the Palmae family with around 600 different genera, the largest being *Calamus* which includes around 370 species. The strength and flexibility of rattan results in its widespread use in furniture, matting, housing construction, thatching, basket-making and other diverse products. The harvesting of rattan as a non-timber forest product is widely perceived as beneficial for conservation. This is based on the grounds that it imparts a quantifiable value to forested areas, thereby aiding the economic argument for forest conservation, it is less destructive than other forest uses, and makes a significant contribution to the economic and social livelihoods of people living in proximity to the forest (Arnold and Perez 2001). The Lambusango Forest Conservation project proposal reports that a total annual extraction of 1500 tonnes takes place from within the forest reserves, providing an annual return equivalent to IDR1.2 billion (US$130000).[3] This calculation is an upper estimate based upon the highest-quality rattan (*Calamus zollingeri*) which, according to personal observations in 2004, is sold locally to traders for around IRD 80000 per 100 kg, although prices can be as low as IDR30000 per 100 kg for lower-quality species such as *Calamus ornatus*. Therefore, a lower boundary estimate for the annual value of rattan harvested would be in the order of IDR450 million (US$53000). Assuming a median household income of IDR12 million (Malleson 2007, p. 4), rattan collection from inside the forest reserves would equate to the total annual income of between 40 and 100 households. However, the number of households indirectly dependent upon rattan income through multiplier effects is likely to be high in this remote rural location, suggesting that the total number of households directly and indirectly dependent upon rattan is likely to far exceed this range of values.

It is therefore apparent that the effects of tighter regulation of this sector through licences and quotas will have economic implications for a considerable number of individuals and households living near to the forested areas of central Buton. These regulations are justified through the description of 'large teams of collectors operating throughout the reserve' which have had noticeable impacts on the remaining rattan stocks, although the extent of these impacts is not further quantified (GEF 2004, p. 6). However, the driving forces and conditions governing rattan collection are such that there are grounds to argue that this form of management may be ineffective. A sample of 60 collectors interviewed in 2005 reported that rattan constituted one of up to three income sources (Lumley-Holmes 2006, p. 78), with participation being significantly influenced by conditions of increased economic hardship or lack of alternative incomes. Participation was, however, seen to be limited by a range of factors including the need to undertake agricultural activities, personal fitness levels, access difficulties during the wet season and the irregular presence of traders.

Maintaining a diversity of income sources is commonplace in developing countries to combat uncertainty arising from seasonality in income and lack of credit facilities, among other causes (Ellis 1998, p. 10). The period of financial instability in the late 1990s in southeast Asia was compounded in Indonesia by a combination of factors, including excessive foreign debt amongst the private sector, poor governance in the banking system and the overvaluation of the currency (Firman 1999, p. 70). This resulted in the economic crisis or *krismon* having a particularly severe effect on the value of the rupiah and domestic inflation rates. In rural communities, staples such as rice and sugar doubled in price, whilst rattan and other export commodities increased in value (Angelsen and Resosudarmo 1999, p. 3). Given the limitations on capital and labour, restricting small farmers' ability to increase output to take advantage of increased food prices, diversification into rattan collection as a means to supplement income is a rational choice under these circumstances, particularly as minimal investment in materials is required.

Since this time, inflation has continued to reach double-digit figures whilst the world demand for rattan has continued to grow. Indonesia is the leading exporter, with rattan exports worth approximately US$700 million in a global market valued at around US$4 billion (International Network for Bamboo and Rattan 2004). Hence rattan continues to represent a viable additional source of income for Butonese villages. This combination of market forces is reflected in the fact that three-quarters of the rattan collectors interviewed in 2005 had begun collecting in the preceding ten years, underlining the recent nature of economic events driving participation. Furthermore, the practice amongst Butonese rattan traders of offering cash loans amounting to IDR300 000 as advance payment to collectors indicates that participation can lead to instant credit, which will evidently be a significant stimulus to individuals in periods of financial instability.

This analysis suggests that rattan collection in central Buton represents a locally significant activity in overall economic terms, but one which constitutes an occasional source of income for individuals, predominantly farmers. Additionally, it is driven mainly by short-term financial needs whilst being constrained by factors including seasonal labour requirements and the dependence on traders to purchase the rattan. Aside from the lack of biological data from which sustainable quotas could be derived, the enforcement of quotas and licences would therefore be problematic as rattan collection is not a simple matter of choice but one which is dictated by external socio-economic conditions. This situation would only be exacerbated in periods of increased economic hardship or uncertainty. These times seem to have afflicted Indonesia at regular intervals, with the poorer residents of local villages being more likely to experience the adverse effects of these regulations as they seek to diversify their income sources under these circumstances. Furthermore, daily monitoring and enforcement activities are envisaged to rest largely with local residents appointed as 'forest guardians', that could well serve to increase the degree of conflict associated with rattan collection at the individual and village level. The net effect of quotas and licences in the rattan sector can therefore be construed as being at odds with the stated goal of 'promoting sustainable livelihoods in rural communities' (GEF 2007) due to the lack of recognition accorded to the driving forces at the local scale which are seen as influential in this case study.

Agricultural diversification
The Lambusango Forest Conservation project has also undertaken activities designed to reduce the reliance on income generated through illegal logging amongst villages surrounding the reserves, through promoting the cultivation of cash crops. Such promotion has taken the form of grants and technical assistance to villages, selected on the basis of criteria including sufficient road access and a history of illegal logging (Purwanto 2006, p. 6). Aside from the potential animosity generated by focused interventions that may be seen to be benefiting villages associated with illegal activities, the project encountered significant problems through the promotion of ginger as an alternative cash crop. Ginger may be seen to offer positive prospects for cultivation in this region as it does not require irrigation and is in demand both domestically and at the international level. The most recently available data indicate that the producer price of ginger in Indonesia was IRD 9 million (US$960) per tonne in 2005, representing an increase of 10 per cent since 2003 (Food and Agriculture Organization 2007).[4]

However, this neglects the considerable risk factors associated with ginger production both from an agricultural and an economic point of view. Ginger is particularly prone to bacterial diseases and insect infestation, with bacterial wilt caused by the prokaryote *Ralstonia solanacearum*, which is endemic in tropical environments, being particularly virulent, causing potential complete crop loss within months (Kumar and Hayward 2004). It should also be mentioned that ginger cultivation in Buton requires fertiliser and insecticide inputs which would render the crop ineligible for the more lucrative organic ginger market. Furthermore, the international price for ginger is notoriously volatile, being subject to periodic gluts and adverse effects associated with poor product quality. These problems of disease and profitability are manifest in a recent survey that ranked ginger the most risk-laden spice crop for cultivation (Vinning 1990).

Given the emphasis on demonstrating quantifiable improvements in village incomes within the project time scales, the selection of ginger can be justified in strict economic terms. However, the local producer price fell dramatically from IDR6800 per kilogram in 2005 (US$0.7) to IDR1560 per kilogram in 2006 (US$0.17)[5] as a result of domestic oversupply

(Purwanto 2006, p. 36). This resulted in the project being forced to buy back all the cultivated ginger from participants at an estimated cost of around US$4000. Efforts have since focused on marketing cashew nuts under a Fair Trade label, but these have encountered difficulties in gaining certification due to the lack of processing capacity and institutional weaknesses of the newly created cashew farmers' association.

These examples serve to underline the potential pitfalls of promoting conservation through the realisation of economic benefits, which are themselves contingent upon external economic conditions as well as the marketing criteria for Fair Trade or organic produce. The selection of ginger as an alternative cash crop to reduce reliance on income generated through logging is evidently a high-risk option and owes its origin to the economic performance criteria contained in the original LFMA proposal. The failure of these activities in the early stages of the programme could well have significant deleterious effects on future participation in activities sponsored by the project, with some villagers blaming the conservation project for the lack of success in obtaining a suitable price for their ginger (Purwanto 2007, p. 7). This has evident wider implications for conservation in the region. This situation can be related to critiques of GEF-sponsored activities which identify the dangers of relying upon achieving conservation through the opening up new markets for capital investment and accumulation (Ervine 2007, p. 129). In a developing-country context, this often equates to increasing the risks faced by individuals through altering land use practices which render them more vulnerable to external economic conditions, this being clearly demonstrated in the case of ginger cultivation in the forests of central Buton.

Controlling forest clearance for agriculture
The third element of this discussion relates to the stipulations of the LFMA programme relating to forest clearance for agricultural purposes. This is clearly defined as a problem to be remedied at the village level, with the implication that each village head should be responsible for implementing a veto on further permits for clearance. As stated beforehand, however, the Ministry of Forestry is the state entity responsible for the utilisation and extraction of forest resources and in theory should be the authority responsible for these decisions. Due to lack of resources and, arguably, the mistrust between different levels of government – common throughout Indonesia as power is contested in the period of greater autonomy – the village head has been the de facto authority in these matters, albeit without any legal basis. Therefore, any decisions made by the village head regarding forest clearance for agricultural or other purposes are potentially without legal foundation. Whilst this situation would probably have

endured without undue attention under other circumstances, the introduction of considerable amounts of conservation funding directly involving the village heads has raised the profile of this uncertain legal situation. The effects of a ban on clearance would evidently also impinge upon the operation of other national policies, including transmigration, whilst reducing the capacity of the region to accommodate future refugee influxes. These are clearly areas of jurisdiction over which the central government would wish to retain authority. It is, therefore, problematic as to whether the programme has the ability to implement this proposed ban which conservationists see as fundamental to the integrity of the forested area.

The GEF Programme in Its Wider Context

The Lambusango Forest Conservation project clearly identifies the construction of transmigrant and refugee settlements as a conservation issue when they are located in proximity to the forested areas. Continued government investment in facilities, including paved roads, water supplies and building infrastructure, is framed as a threat to nearby forested areas, given the potential for such investments to result in the continued expansion of these settlements. This issue raises the final point for discussion in this chapter, which relates to the scale of the conservation agenda in developing countries. The Lambusango Forest Conservation programme, with its agenda including issues relating to individual income-generating strategies and agricultural activities, alongside housing and infrastructure provision at the wider scale, clearly has a broad remit with regard to the economic and societal development of the area. The programme itself results from an alliance between the GEF and an international non-governmental organisation. This organisation is in the form of a research ecotourism operator (Operation Wallacea) and provided the scientific stimulus and co-financing for the project. Such an arrangement is increasingly common, with the private and non-governmental sector becoming increasingly influential in the global conservation arena, as their funding base has expanded, whilst that of multilateral agencies such as the GEF has diminished (Rodriguez et al. 2007, p. 755). The joint activities of developed-country institutions in this regard has led to the recognition of the 'globalisation of conservation', whereby strategies are applied to specific locales in the developing world, irrespective of local natural, cultural and socio-economic systems (Zimmerer 2006, p. 64).

This facet of globalisation draws upon scientific data, identifying global biodiversity 'hotspots' or 'ecoregions'. These regions are seen as priority areas for intervention, in order to deliver the global benefits of conservation required by international agreements such as the

Convention on Biological Diversity. Sulawesi is a prime example of this, including tropical moist forest categorised as critical or endangered in the Global 200 Ecoregions, used to allocate World Wide Fund for Nature resources (Olson and Dinerstein 2002, p. 202). It is also central to the Wallacea biodiversity hotspot, utilised in a similar manner by Conservation International (Conservation International 2007; Myers et al. 2000, p. 854) and constitutes one of the Endangered Bird Areas prioritised by Birdlife International (Birdlife International 2003). This historic association with the work of Alfred Russel Wallace, a contemporary of Darwin, credited with being the co-founder of the theory of evolution, further distinguishes Sulawesi as being the 'biogeographic crossroads' of East Asia and Australasia (Cannon et al. 2007, p. 747). This focus on terrestrial conservation activities is mirrored in the marine environment, with Sulawesi constituting one of the areas receiving World Bank loan funding for conservation of coral reefs via the 15-year COREMAP programme initiated in 1998 (Moosa 2004).

Given these associations, it is evident that the influence of a globalised conservation agenda will increase in the future in this part of Indonesia, and that the rationale for this intervention will continue to reflect the priorities of developed-world agencies and organisations. This analysis has underlined, however, the extent to which this agenda can be at odds with the local economic, political and socio-cultural context, leading to adverse consequences for residents and limiting the effectiveness of these conservation strategies. This point has additional relevance in light of the Resources Allocation Framework adopted by the GEF, which will be used to distribute funding during the current (2006–10) replenishment period. This framework, the focus of much debate amongst donors and recipients, utilises a Performance Index and Benefits Index, weighted 80:20 respectively, as the basis for determining whether countries are eligible for GEF funding. The Performance Index includes criteria measuring the country's capacity to implement GEF programmes successfully based on its past performance (GEF 2005). Thus, problems in delivering outcomes under current GEF-funded activities will negatively impact upon a country's eligibility to apply for future funds, underlining the potential ramifications of the issues raised in this discussion.

CONCLUSION

This analysis has outlined the implications of initiatives designed to improve the effectiveness of forest management and conservation in a remote rural location in eastern Indonesia. The rationale for this intervention reflects the institutional weaknesses of biodiversity con- servation at the national level, set against the growing range of threats associated with population pressure and economic development at the local level. However, the design and implementation of the programme has been shown to have adverse consequences for maintaining a diversity of income sources, and negative implications for achieving sustainable livelihoods amongst communities. These problems reflect the assump- tions inherent in global conservation programmes relating to individuals' ability and willingness to adopt new practices, and the potential weak- nesses of these assumptions in the context of local economic and political circumstances. It is apparent that, whilst the rhetoric of globalised con- servation is supportive of community participation and empowerment, the reality can be that individuals and households are exposed to greater risk and conflict generated as a result of these policies. Indeed, there is an evident need for the conservation agenda to reflect the decentralisation of power and decision-making taking place in countries such as Indonesia, in order to ensure that their programmes are sensitive and attuned to the local environment, economy and society on which they depend for their success.

NOTES

1. This exchange rate is calculated using the 2007 average rate of US$1 = IDR9056. Source: https://www.cia.gov/library/publications/the-world-factbook/fields/2076.html.
2. Full details of the project can be found on the GEF Project Database at http://gefonline. org/home.cfm.
3. This exchange rate calculated using the 2003 average rate of US$1 = IDR8577. Source: https://www.cia.gov/library/publications/the-world-factbook/fields/2076.html.
4. Exchange rates calculated using average rates of US$1 = IDR8577 (2003) and IDR9705 (2005). Source: https://www.cia.gov/library/publications/the-world-factbook/fields/2076. html.
5. This exchange rate calculated using the 2006 average rate of US$1 = IDR9159 (2006). Source: https://www.cia.gov/library/publications/the-world-factbook/fields/2076.html.

REFERENCES

Angelsen, A. and D.P. Resosudarmo (1999), '*Krismon*, farmers and forests: the effects of the economic crisis on farmers' livelihoods and forest use in the outer islands of Indonesia', Centre for International Forestry Research, Bogor, Indonesia, accessed at www.cifor.cgiar.org/publications/pdf_files/krismon.pdf.
Arnold, J. and M. Perez (2001), 'Can non-timber forest products match tropical forest conservation and development objectives?', *Ecological Economics*, **39**, 437–47.

Badan Pusat Statistik (2001), population statistics, accessed at www.bps.go.id/sector/population/index.html.

Birdlife International (2003), 'BirdLife's online World Bird Database: the site for bird conservation', accessed at www.birdlife.org.

Cannon, C., M. Summers, J.R Harting and P.J.A. Kessler (2007), 'Developing conservation priorities based on forest type, condition and threats in a poorly known ecoregion: Sulawesi, Indonesia', *Biotropica*, **39**, 747–59.

Clifton, J. (2002), 'Forest management in the Kakenauwe and Lambusango Forest Reserve areas', unpublished report for Operation Wallacea, accessed at www. opwall.com.

Contreras-Hermosillo, A. and C. Fay (2005), 'Strengthening forest management in Indonesia through land tenure reform: issues and framework for action', accessed at http://www.forest-trends.org.

Ellis, F. (1998), 'Household strategies and rural livelihood diversification', *Journal of Development Studies*, **35**, 1–38.

Ervine, K. (2007), 'The greying of green governance: power politics and the Global Environment Facility', *Capitalism, Nature, Socialism*, **18** (4), 125–42.

Firman, T. (1999), 'Indonesian cities under the krismon', *Cities*, **16**, 69–82.

Food and Agriculture Organization (2007), FAOSTAT, accessed at.http://faostat. fao.org.

Global Environment Facility (2004), 'Lambusango Forest Conservation Project', accessed at www.gefweb.org.

Global Environment Facility (2005), 'The GEF Resource Allocation Framework', accessed at www.gefweb.org.

Global Environment Facility (2007), 'About the GEF', accessed at www.gefweb. org.

Google, Inc. (2009), *Google Earth* (Version 5), software, available at: www.earth. google.com.

International Network for Bamboo and Rattan (2004), 'Bamboo and rattan facts', accessed at www.inbar.int.

Kumar, A. and A.C. Hayward (2004), 'Bacterial diseases of ginger and their control', in P.N. Ravindran and K.N. Babu (eds), *Ginger: The Genus Zingiber*, Boca Raton, FL: CRC Press, pp. 341–66.

Lumley-Holmes, C. (2006), 'An assessment of the economic stability of the commercial rattan trade for the communities surrounding the Lambusango Forest Management Area, south-east Sulawesi, Indonesia', unpublished BA dissertation, Department of Geography, University of Portsmouth.

MacAndrews, C. (1998), 'Improving the management of Indonesia's national parks: lessons from two case studies', *Bulletin of Indonesian Economic Studies*, **34**, 121–37.

Malleson, R. (2007), 'Socio-economic baseline surveys of communities bordering the Lambusango Forest, south-east Sulawesi, Indonesia', accessed at www. opwall.com.

McCarthy, J.F. (2000), 'The changing regime: forest property and *reformasi* in Indonesia', *Development and Change*, **31**, 91–129.

Moosa, M.K. (2004), 'Implementing policy and strategy for coral reef rehabilitation and management: lessons learnt from an Indonesian effort', in M. Ahmed, C.K. Chong and H. Cesar (eds), *Economic Valuation and Policy Priorities for Sustainable Management of Coral Reefs*, Penang, Malaysia: World Fish Center, pp. 159–69.

Myers, N., R.A. Mittermeier, C.G. Mittermeier, G.A.B. da Fonseca and J. Kent (2000), 'Biodiversity hotspots for conservation priorities', *Nature*, **403**, 853–8.

Olson, D.M. and E. Dinerstein (2002), 'The Global 200: priority ecoregions for global conservation', *Annals of the Missouri Botanical Garden*, **89**, 199–24.

Operation Wallacea (2006), 'Summary of biological and sociological research carried out by Operation Wallacea in the forest of Central Buton', accessed at www.opwall.com.

Peluso, N.L. (1996), 'Fruit trees and family trees in an anthropogenic forest: ethics of access, property zones and environmental change in Indonesia', *Comparative Studies in Society and History*, **38**, 510–48.

Purwanto, E. (2006), 'Lambusango Forest Conservation Project: summary of eighth progress and implementation plan report', accessed at www.lambusango.com.

Purwanto, E. (2007), 'Lambusango Forest Conservation Project: which way forward?', accessed at www.lambusango.com.

Research and Markets Limited (2008), 'Massive infrastructure expansion paving the way for growth in the Asian asphalt market', accessed at http://biz.yahoo.com/bw/080117/20080117005464.html?.v=1.

Reuters (2008), 'Indonesia to switch 10 pct petroleum to biofuel', accessed at www.reuters.com.

Rhee, S., D. Kitchener, T. Brown, R. Merrill, R. Dilts and S. Tighe (2004), 'Report on biodiversity and tropical forests in Indonesia', USAID, accessed at.www.irgltd.com.

Rodriguez, J.P., A.B. Taber, P. Daszak, R. Sukumar, C. Valladares-Padua, S. Padua, L.F. Aguirre, R.A. Medellin, M. Acosta, A.A. Aguirre, C. Bonacic, P. Bordino, J. Bruschini, D. Buchori, S. Gonzalez, T. Mathew, M. Mendez, L. Mugica, L.F. Pacheco, A.P. Dobson and M. Pearl (2007), 'Globalization of conservation: a view from the South', *Science*, **317**, 755–56.

Saragih, H. and S. Yoshida (2002), 'Assessment of food crop production associated with transmigration schemes in southeast Sulawesi-Indonesia', *Japanese Journal of Tropical Agriculture*, **46**, 1–13.

Saterson, K.A., N.L. Christensen, R.B. Jackson, R.A. Kramer, S.L. Pimm, M.D. Smith and J.B. Wiener (2004), 'Disconnects in evaluating the relative effectiveness of conservation strategies', *Conservation Biology*, **18**(3), 597–9.

Seymour, R. and S. Turner (2002), '*Otonomi daerah*: Indonesia's decentralization experiment', *New Zealand Journal of Asian Studies*, **4**, 33–51.

Sharma, S. (1996), 'The World Bank and the Global Environment Facility: challenges and prospects for sustainable development', *Brown Journal of World Affairs*, **3**, 275–87.

Sino Prosper Holdings Limited (2006), announcement in relation to the Buton bitumen mine project, accessed at www.sinoprosper.com.

Siswosoebrotho, B.I., N. Kusnianti and W. Tumewu (2005), 'Laboratory evaluation of Lawele Buton rock asphalt in asphalt concrete mixture', *Proceedings of the Eastern Asia Society for Transportation Studies*, **5**, 857–67.

Streck, C. (2001), 'The Global Environment Facility: a role model for international governance?', *Global Environmental Politics*, **1**, 71–94.

United States Department of Agriculture (2007), 'Indonesia: palm oil production prospects continue to grow', accessed at www.pecad.fas.usda.gov.

Vinning, G. (1990), *Marketing Perspectives on a Potential Pacific Spice Industry*, Canberra: Australian Centre for International Agricultural Research.

Waas, J., A. van der Kwaak and M. Bloem (2003), 'Psychotrauma in Moluccan refugees in Indonesia', *Disaster Prevention and Management*, **12**, 328–35.
Whitten, T., G.S. Henderson and M. Mustafa (1996), *The Ecology of Sulawesi*, Hong Kong and Singapore: Periplus.
Widayati, A. and B. Carlisle (2007), 'Land cover change in Lambusango Forest and vicinity from 1991 to 2004: initial results from the analysis of satellite imagery', accessed at www.opwall.com.
Young, Z. (2002), *A New Green Order? The World Bank and the Politics of the Global Environment Facility*, London: Pluto.
Zimmerer, K.S. (2006), 'Cultural ecology: at the interface with political ecology – the new geographies of environmental conservation and globalization', *Progress in Human Geography*, **30**(1), 63–78.

12. Globalised agriculture, development and the environment

J.N. Callow and Julian Clifton

INTRODUCTION

An analysis of the processes and impacts of an increasingly globalised economy with regard to agriculture, development and environment in the Asia-Pacific is inevitably complicated by numerous factors, including the varied history, politics, societies and cultures of the region's states, their often unique environmental conditions and the vastly differing socio-economic circumstances which affect populations and ethnic minorities within each country. Consequently, the study of the environmental impacts of globalisation in the context of agriculture, also referred to variously as 'agro-industrialisation' or 'agro-industrial modernisation' (Reardon and Barrett 2000), in this region is often undertaken through a case study approach (Burch et al. 1996). Reflecting the spatial complexity and different experiences of globalisation within the Asia-Pacific, this chapter will seek to provide a broad overview and introduction to relevant themes, with reference being made to more detailed readings wherever appropriate.

Any discussion of globalisation raises questions over definition, interpretation and subjectivity with regard to an individual's perception of such a complex and contested term. Bearing in mind the focus of this text, we describe globalisation from an economic viewpoint, referring to its association with 'internationalisation', defined here as the 'large and growing flows of trade and capital investment between countries' (Hirst and Thompson 1996, p. 48); and 'liberalisation', or the removal of government-imposed restrictions on trade to create an open world economy. Together with technological advances, particularly in relation to biotechnology, the globalisation of agriculture describes processes of integration linking suppliers and consumers within the agricultural sector around the world. This creation of a global mass food production system facilitated by major transnational corporations can be broadly characterised as the production of high-value goods such as fruit and horticultural produce for export from developing countries, with a return flow of low-value products such as grains from the developed world which undercut domestic food production through capital-intensive production systems (Robinson 2004). Whilst this may describe the prevailing trends in developed countries during the 'productivist' phase of agriculture since the Second World War, factors including the reduction in protectionist state support and the rise of agri-environmental policies, along with burgeoning interest in organic produce and consumer safety, have led to the recognition of a 'post-productivist' phase in agriculture since the 1990s (Wilson 2001). This concept of distinct 'food regimes' can serve as a framework to describe changing trends in food production, but has been criticised for its overtly structuralist approach, failing to recognise the complexity of factors affecting agricultural policy at the individual nation level (Goodman and Watts 1994) and the processes by which individual farmers adapt to new economic constraints and opportunities (Rigg 2005).

The environmental consequences of an increasingly globalised agricultural sector with regard to the developing countries in the Asia-Pacific will reflect the rate and extent of the penetration of commercially oriented agriculture into the pre-existing predominantly subsistence-oriented sector. These will evidently differ between countries, but there are certain overall trends which can be identified. The expanding international market for produce has been shown to result directly in increased rates of forest clearance, resulting in a cycle of soil degradation, erosion and further clearance in increasingly marginal agricultural environments (Barbier 2000). The negative impacts of this process with regards to biodiversity are exacerbated by the greater use of chemicals in crop production. Herbicides are increasingly relied upon as the alternative to manual weeding as the opportunity cost of farm labour rises in response to employment opportunities in urban areas, whilst cultivation of high-value crops such as fruit requires regular application of pesticides and fungicides to maintain output levels (Pingali 2001). Excessive use of irrigation water in areas of poor drainage will induce increasing soil salinity, to the detriment of both crop productivity and, eventually, the suitability of the land for continued agriculture. These and other impacts of globalised agricultural production are described in more detail elsewhere (Doorman 1998; Coleman et al. 2004; Robinson 2004)

However, these forms of environmental degradation are by no means new phenomena which have emerged in association with a globalised agricultural sector. Rather, land degradation has long been associated with agricultural development, often with serious implications for the environment as well as the economic and social functioning of societies. Examples of the impact of unsustainable agricultural development on societies can be traced back to at least 2400 BC, when the ancient Mesopotamians altered the hydrology of the rich alluvial plains of the Tigris and Euphrates rivers, resulting in salinisation of the floodplain, a form of degradation that ultimately contributed to the decline of the Mesopotamian kingdoms (Jacobsen and Adams 1958; Diamond 2004). There is therefore a long history of agricultural intensification, environmental degradation and impacts for civilisations, which needs to be considered in the context of globalised agriculture in the Asia-Pacific.

GLOBALISED AGRICULTURE AND ENVIRONMENTAL DEGRADATION IN THE ASIA-PACIFIC

The Asia-Pacific region exemplifies widespread changes in agricultural systems and subsequent impacts on the environment that are associated with globalised agriculture. Environmental degradation takes many forms, and is typically caused by numerous, complex and interdependent processes. While anthropogenic action is the primary cause of degradation, natural processes such as extreme climatic events or climatic shifts are also key drivers in association with the impact of humans. Ecological systems, soils, waterways and estuaries are all degraded by natural events such as fires started by lightning, large rainfall and flood events. Over longer time frames, climate changes and natural erosive processes have also significantly altered ecological systems, landscape geomorphology and degraded the nutrient content of soils. It is important to recognise that these natural processes have deleterious impacts with respect to potential agricultural activity, but the impact that humans have had on the natural environment has increased the rate of these processes, and also caused types of changes that have not been previously experienced. It is also important to be cognisant of the linkages between natural environmental variability, the occurrence of extreme events and human influence upon natural processes. An area of land cleared for agriculture may undergo various changes under the pressure of animal grazing of pastures. In an average rainfall year, pasture growth will be good, and the soil surface will be well covered, as long as grazing pressures are well managed. Natural events such as low rainfall cause poor pasture growth, and the pressure to maintain animal herds over the dry periods means that the soil cover is often overgrazed. Under these conditions, extreme rainfall events will cause severe degradation compared to a similar event when the soil surface is well protected by good pasture growth. Thus, environmental degradation is caused by an interaction between anthropogenic and natural processes, but it is often the inadvertent result of human attempts to modify and manage the environment which enhances the scale of degradation beyond the degree associated with 'normal' natural events. Degradation of the environment is therefore a complex process, with many drivers. While the process of degradation is primarily driven by human action, natural processes are an important ingredient in contributing to degradation processes or specific events. Environmental degradation constitutes a wide range of processes involving complex systems and linkages, whereby feedback and amplification may induce unforeseen changes, both positive and negative, in associated components of the natural environment.

As mentioned earlier, it is important to recognise that adverse environmental impacts associated with agriculture are not a new phenomenon. Many of the processes of degradation that are observed through the Asia-Pacific and elsewhere are caused by processes resulting from traditional agricultural systems. Deforestation of the tropical rainforest and orang-utan habitat in Borneo and salinisation of agricultural land in southern Australia were initiated long before a globalised agricultural sector evolved from domestically focused colonial or rural subsistence agricultural systems. There are, however, some key changes that a globalised agricultural system has introduced. Intensification, mechanisation, increasing fuel, fertiliser and pesticide inputs, plant breeding and genetic modification, decreased agricultural crop biodiversity, corporatisation and changes in trade networks have all affected the rate, severity and extent of environmental degradation caused by agriculture. The following sections explore examples of this by examining the ways through which globalised agricultural systems impact on soil, water and biodiversity degradation.

Soil

Soil degradation poses a significant direct risk to agricultural production, as ultimately agriculture is reliant on soil, along with rainfall, as the medium for production. Degradation of the soil takes many forms, most related to the exploitation of soils beyond their natural capacity. Soil can be removed through physical erosion, leading to the productive capacity of the remnant soils being exceeded, causing changes in soil structure, biology and soil chemistry. In this context, soil degradation can be envisaged as reflecting the transition of agriculture from a sustainable enterprise to a mining operation, as resource exploitation becomes the driver of economic gain, rather than sustainable use of a renewable or non-degrading resource. Soil degradation poses significant costs to the maintenance of agriculture competitiveness in a globalised market.

Declining soil health causes reduced productivity, and requires either cuts in production to more sustainable levels or, more commonly, an ever-increasing investment in fertiliser, chemicals and other inputs to compensate for the loss of productivity.

Soil is also degraded through removal by wind and water. Agricultural lands at greatest risk to wind erosion in the Asia-Pacific are the dryland agricultural areas with the driest and most unpredictable climate, and those with deep sandy soils that retain little water and have less cohesive soils strength to resist erosional forces. Wind erosion is determined by wind strength (as the shearing force), and resistance factors such as crop cover, surface roughness (stoniness), and the soil strength and moisture content. While uncontrollable climate patterns affect wind strength and rainfall which influence soil moisture and erosional forces, land management practices such as planting windbreaks, managing livestock grazing of pasture and retaining stubble can change the risk of wind erosion occurring.

Management of wind erosion is an interesting example of ways that globalised agriculture, and in particular the increasing availability of technology, has helped to assist better management decisions and to reduce wind erosion risk. Remote sensing satellites such as Landsat and MODIS allow crop cover to be estimated at high resolution over large areas. Using these data in combination with rainfall, soil maps and predicted medium-term rainfall outlook, crop growth rates, soil cover, soil moisture and, as a consequence, the risk of wind erosion can be predicted (for example McTainsh et al. 2009). This allows a more precautionary approach to land use management, enabling informed decisions to be made prior to any degradation taking place. Globalised agricultural systems have not, however, been without blame for contributing to wind erosion. The process of farm amalgamation in broadacre agricultural areas of Australia has resulted in a shift from 'traditional' individualistic, hands-on management, with a diverse range of produce on family-owned farms, towards 'modern' homogenised corporate monoculture operations characterised by higher levels of absentee landownership. Less people on the ground, greater pressures to maintain production and contract farming arrangements which mandate how land is managed during the production cycle all serve to compromise the extent to which agricultural activity can be adapted to reflect local environmental conditions and constraints. Ironically, this process of farm amalgamation and increasing absentee ownership is typically greatest in the areas of least-reliable rainfall which are consequently at greatest risk of wind erosion.

Of the soil that remains in enclosures under conditions of wind and water erosion, declining soil health is one of the most complex but critical forms of soil degradation. Soil health is determined by many factors, such as soil composition or parent material (for example geology), soil texture and structure, soil chemistry and biological activity. Declining soil health is caused by many different anthropogenically induced processes including leaching of nutrients, soil acidification caused by fertiliser use, burning crop residue and organic matter, soil compaction by machinery and harvesting, and chemical (pesticide and fungicide) use and concentration in the soil.

Soil acidification is one of the most serious processes affecting soil health and productivity of agricultural land and is now recognised as one of the most spatially extensive land degradation problems facing agricultural activity in the Asia-Pacific. The process of soil acidification is chiefly driven by the growth and harvesting of crops and the intensification of agriculture. Whilst many soil types are naturally acidic (von Uexküll and Mutert 1995), the removal of buffering alkaline elements such as potassium, calcium, magnesium and sodium through their incorporation into agricultural crops all result in a gradual increase in the hydrogen ion content of the soil through plant secretion in order to maintain ionic balance (Helyar and Porter 1989; Moore et al. 1998). This process is enhanced through practices such as the application of nitrogenous fertilisers (CSIRO 1997). The widespread cultivation of leguminous crops, pasture and trees tolerating a range of climatic conditions as a means to enhance soil productivity through nitrogen fixation is now recognised as a major cause of soil acidification and consequent land degradation throughout the Asia-Pacific region.

As discussed earlier, a key feature of globalised agriculture is the intensification of agriculture and increasing inputs of fertiliser in order to maintain production levels in soils with diminished natural nutrients. Figure 12.1 shows trends in fertiliser consumption for the major agricultural producers in the Asia-Pacific, illustrating the scale and rate of growth since the late 1970s (Indonesia) and 1980s (Vietnam, Thailand, Malaysia, Philippines). Given that the area of agriculture in New Zealand and Australia has actually contracted since the 1980s, overall fertiliser use in these countries can be seen to have doubled.

Whilst soils have been identified as acidic for many decades, understanding the mechanisms of soil acidification and identifying how management methods can be changed to manage soil health better is a more recent development. Whilst the intensification of production systems and increasing inputs is one aspect of globalisation, the advances in understanding gained through scientific research are a parallel outcome. It is evident that research into soil chemistry, plant nutrition and nutrient content have significantly improved our knowledge of the causal processes

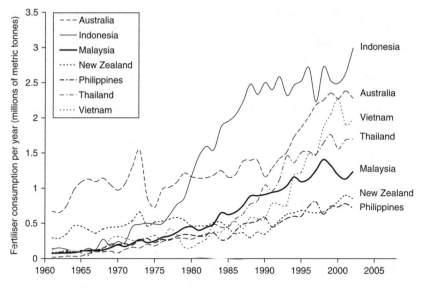

Source: UNEP (2007).

Figure 12.1   Fertiliser consumption of selected Asia-Pacific countries from 1961–2002

behind acidification, and induced changes such as improved crop rotation, identifying trace element deficiencies caused by acidification and the use of lime as an ameliorate for soil acidity, along with a greater awareness of the adverse impact of traditional approaches such as stubble burning.

The sugar industry is an interesting study in globalised agriculture and soil degradation. Sugarcane is native perennial grass from the Asia-Pacific (Southeastern Asia) of the genus *Saccharum*. It was introduced to ancient agricultural civilisations by traders and is now found throughout the world, particularly through the wet and dry tropics and subtropical areas with sufficient water for irrigation. Intensification of production through the mid-twentieth century was also associated with a period of declining yields, despite increasing input of fertilisers. Research identified a number of factors that were affecting soil health: adverse impact of pesticides and inorganic fertilisers on beneficial soil biota; monocultures causing build-up of detrimental soil pathogens; cane burning causing no retention of organic matter, and exposure of the soil surface to erosion; and uncontrolled traffic (particularly associated with heavy machinery on wet soils) causing soil compaction (Garside et al. 2005). These impacts were associated with a plateauing of yield increases from the 1960s through to the 1990s in the Australian sugar industry. However, the adoption of no-till legume crop rotations to reduce inorganic fertiliser reliance and break the monoculture cycle, green cane harvesting and trash blanketing (returning of green and brown leaves to cover the soil surface), controlled traffic farming – that is using Global Positioning System (GPS) to drive over the same area each time to reduce soil compaction), and improved soil health have all improved crop yields while reducing inorganic fertiliser inputs (Garside et al. 2005).

The expansion of agriculture in developing economies, involving the intensification and increased mechanisation of production systems, increased use of fertilisers and chemicals, corporatisation and farm amalgamation have all played a role in increasing the rates of soil degradation. Managing soil health is fundamental to maintaining the production medium required for agriculture, which has seen a series of divergent approaches and philosophies adopted. Techno-optimists have looked towards emerging technology epitomised by 'precision agriculture' which utilises advances in GPS, geographic information systems (GIS) and computing power to improve crop quality and food safety, to improve environmental protection through targeted use of chemicals and, of course, to enhance economic profitability (Robert 2002). However, the need for improved decision-support systems and training of individual farmers, and the incorporation of natural spatial and temporal variability in crop production, has limited the application of techniques associated with precision agriculture within developing countries. The exception to this lies with plantation agriculture, wherein the close involvement of transnational corporations, highly mechanised production systems and exacting product quality standards have been conducive to the adoption of precision agriculture (McBratney et al. 2005).

Water

Whereas soil is the medium for production, water remains the most critical input for both dryland and irrigated agriculture. Dryland or rain-fed agriculture is wholly reliant on rainfall, whereas irrigated agriculture is based on manipulating the spatial and temporal availability of water to optimise its supply for growing agricultural crops. Unfortunately, the Asia-Pacific is one of the most unreliable and seasonal regions for rainfall and streamflow in the world (Finlayson and McMahon 1988), and faces many challenges for both dryland and irrigated agriculture. El Niño and La Niña cycles have long been associated with the oscillating fortunes of agriculturalists in the east of Australia and adjacent areas of the Asia-Pacific. Much of the rest of the Asia-Pacific region receives a large proportion of rainfall from monsoonal and cyclonic activity, with high inter- and intrayear variability in rainfall, streamflow and the amount of water available for dryland and irrigated agriculture. Unreliable rainfall, periods of flooding and waterlogging of crops and long periods of drought, all present many challenges to globalised agricultural systems.

Dryland agriculture faces challenges due to highly variable rainfall regimes in many areas of the Asia-Pacific, particularly in relation to drought, removal of surface vegetation, and exposure to wind erosion and desertification. Ironically, these agricultural areas also suffer from issues associated with excess water in many dryland areas that has resulted in waterlogging and secondary salinity (Ghassemi et al. 1995). Seasonal agricultural crops are a poor hydrologic substitute for the perennial forests that they have replaced. In the more arid areas of the Asia-Pacific, this form of degradation is particularly pronounced, as the difference in the proportion of rainfall used by both traditional and globalised agricultural crops in comparison to the endemic vegetation systems is most acute. It is in these areas that these forms of degradation are the greatest threat.

In the cereal-growing area or 'Wheatbelt' region of Western Australia, native vegetation systems intercepted, evaporated and transpired over 99.95 per cent of rainfall (George 1992). Modern crops now only use around 90 per cent of rainfall and as a result groundwater tables are rising, and large areas of the landscape are now waterlogged and affected by secondary salinity (Hatton and Nulsen 1999; National Land and Water Resources Audit 2001; Hatton et al. 2003; Peck and Hatton 2003). A key feature of globalised systems is the movement toward homogenised methods of production and decreased diversity of crop types. Growing cereal crops in these landscapes has caused significant environmental damage. However, this remains a more profitable enterprise than alternatives such as tree crops, which are known to use more water and which help alleviate problems of waterlogging and secondary salinity (Stolte et al. 1997; Hatton and Nulsen 1999; Dunin 2002). This presents a problem for landowners who have invested in land and capital equipment and need to derive the maximum short-term profit to service the large debt they have consequently incurred. Traditional agricultural systems were smaller in scale and did not rely on such large investments in technology and inputs. It is predicted that, as a result of land clearance for agriculture, up to 30 per cent of the Wheatbelt landscape may turn saline and be unsuitable for broadacre cropping (Ferdowsian et al. 1996; National Land and Water Resources Audit 2001). Landowners are forced to find a solution that maintains the productivity of the business whilst sustaining some margin of profitability. This has largely resulted in farm amalgamation to compensate for land lost to salinity and waterlogging, instead of directly addressing the threat and environmental cost, given the costs of such interventions and the relatively cheap price of land.

Irrigated agriculture is able to withstand short periods of drought. Longer-term climate variability, particularly the notable decrease in rainfall for many regions of the southern Asia-Pacific, in combination with increasing pressure on existing allocated supplies, have begun to alter the access of agriculture to sufficient quantities of water. Access to and the development of water resources have been described by Aplin et al. (1995) in terms of three phases: the pre-industrial phase, the development phase and the mature phase. Whilst the pre-industrial phase was characterised by gravity-fed exploitation of water resources proximal to their source, the development phase saw efforts to alter the spatial and temporal availability of water resources intensify. Industrialisation allowed gravity to be conquered with pumping, and the building of structures such as dams to manipulate formerly unreliable water supplies for the benefit of agriculture and urban drinking water supplies.

The challenges of the mature phase facing many developed countries involves a change of emphasis from resource exploitation towards licensing and managing water allocations to agriculture from regulated rivers. This phase of the water development cycle is also associated with the growing recognition of the broader importance of applying sustainability principles to water allocation, and in particular to the provision of water for the environment and a prioritising of water allocations on the basis of economic and social importance for other users. However, the ever-increasing scale of water demand, particularly in urban areas, has led to the development of increasingly expensive water supply options such as desalination, along with greater rates of groundwater extraction and usage. Whilst recycling of water is practiced extensively in some countries, this requires a considerable investment in technology along with the gaining of public support, which can be particularly problematic, particularly where recycled water is proposed for human consumption.

The Asia-Pacific faces perhaps the greatest challenges in managing water of any region on Earth. Whilst climate change will be associated with new levels of uncertainty regarding water supply, economic growth in countries experiencing high rates of population increase within this region may be the most important factor driving increased rates of water withdrawal and the greater incidence of water stress by 2050 (Alcamo et al. 2007). Whilst agriculture accounts for around 70 per cent of water consumption in Australia (Department of Environment and Heritage 2000), demand for domestic water consumption as income levels increase is considered pivotal to increased rates of consumption elsewhere in the

Table 12.1   Consumption and export of virtual water embedded in agricultural produce by countries of the Asia-Pacific

Country	Internal consumption of domestic virtual water Gm³/year	Exported virtual water Gm³/year	Internal consumption of imported virtual water Gm³/year
Australia	14.03	68.67	0.78
Indonesia	236.22	22.62	26.09
Malaysia	36.58	18.47	12.73
Philippines	99.09	7.61	11.74
Thailand	120.17	38.49	8.73
Vietnam	85.16	11.00	2.27

Note: no data exist for New Zealand.

Source: Hoekstra and Chapagain (2008).

Asia-Pacific. However, the situation in Australia is acute, with increasing conflict in key locations such as the Murray–Darling Basin over rights and allocations of an increasingly scarce resource.

Linked to this issue of increasing water scarcity in the region is the use and export of water used to create agricultural products in the Asia-Pacific, and in particular the export of embedded or 'virtual' water. The concept of virtual water (Allan 1998) is used to account for the water required to grow crops, or in the case of livestock the water they drink plus the water required to grow the grain and pasture that they consume, while growing the food or fibre product. While the water inputs required to grow specific food crops or meat and fibre differ between regions, production systems and with the ways used to account for water use, there are some key factors that are critical for globalised agricultural systems of the Asia-Pacific. Chief amongst these is the surprisingly high amount of water required to produce many agricultural goods. Data from Hoekstra and Chapagain (2008) indicate that 1 kg of lettuce requires an average of 130 litres of water; a single 250 ml glass of beer 75 litres (mostly associated with growing the barley); 1 kg of beef requires 15 500 litres; and a single 250 gram cotton T-shirt involves around 2700 litres. The Asia-Pacific is a significant net exporter of virtual water (Table 12.1). While Malaysia and the Philippines are slight net importers of virtual water, this is a small percentage of overall consumption and they can be considered almost self-sufficient. Australia, Thailand and Vietnam are significant players at a global level as net exporters of virtual water.

A critical component of the globalisation of water resources through the movement of agricultural products is the outsourcing of the water needs and the environmental impacts associated with production. Chapagain et al. (2006) identify three types of water required to produce products: 'green water' or rainfall inputs transpired by crops; 'blue water', that is surface and groundwater extracted for irrigation and processing; and finally 'grey water' which represents the pollution of water resources caused during growth and processing (or water required to dilute pollution). In the case of the export of Australian cotton to Japan, a total of 328 Mm^3 of virtual water is transferred, comprising 184 Mm^3/yr of blue water, and 101 Mm^3/yr of green water, and causes impacts (grey water) amounting to 43 Mm^3/yr of water that would be required to dilute the pollution (Chapagain et al. 2006). Globally, the flow of virtual water is from countries of Central and Southeastern Asia and Africa to the Middle East and Western Europe (Hoekstra and Chapagain 2008). As such, the countries of the Asia-Pacific need to consider carefully the use of their water and the associated impacts as an export-orientated player in a globalised virtual water market. In the case of Australian cotton industry, with its geographical location in some of the more arid areas of the Murray–Darling Basin, the issues of water scarcity and overallocation in the basin need to be weighed against the higher profit per litre of water of cotton compared to crops such as sugar, or summer pastures, but its lower profit for the water input compared to fruit, vegetables and grape production (based on data from Australian Bureau of Statistics 2006, 2008), as well as the environmental consequences of the water use and 'export'.

To the north of the Asia-Pacific, China is a country that may point to the future for many other populous countries which rely heavily upon irrigated agriculture to meet domestic food requirements. Increasingly larger and more expensive projects are required to supply water to meet the demand for direct human consumption, and for agriculture to grow sufficient food to supply and generate export returns to sustain economies and populations. Interbasin transfers of water already occur in many countries of the Asia-Pacific, but not yet at the scale of those operating and planned across China. The recent development of desalination for drinking water supply across many Australian major capital cities means that the cost of water is rising significantly. Increasing development and extraction of water from systems has caused significant changes to rivers and wetland systems. Reduction of floods and reduced annual flow has resulted in adverse environmental changes, with wetlands infilled with sediment, fish populations severely affected, and changes in river width and navigability, to name but a few (Osborne 2004). The association of economic development with increased per capita water use (Hoekstra and Chapagain 2008) is another key issue for the region. Providing water to both agricultural and domestic consumers as demand for the resource increase is a major challenge for the region, particularly given the combined impacts of population growth and agricultural intensification.

Biodiversity

Development for agriculture has impacted greatly on the natural ecology and biodiversity of the Asia-Pacific. Large areas of native forests and woodlands have been replaced by seemingly endless tracts of agricultural monoculture. Many areas of the Asia-Pacific have only remnant islands of the mega-biodiverse native ecological systems that once characterised the region. Agricultural development by definition involves the destruction of the remnant vegetation communities and their replacement with agricultural crops. Different types of development and, in particular, the transition from traditional subsistence to globalised agricultural systems have altered both the rate and style of agricultural development, and consequently the impact on biodiversity.

This process is most clearly evident in tropical rainforests in developing countries of the Asia-Pacific. Traditional slash-and-burn systems have persisted for millennia, where families felled and burned the forest, planted agricultural crops for periods of only several years, and then abandoned these areas, allowing the forest to regenerate while they moved on to a new area. This patchwork of clearing, cropping and bush regeneration during fallow periods has been replaced by a transition towards more continuous cropping and the permanent conversion of forest to agricultural crops. Whilst the impacts of slash-and-burn with regards to soil properties may be regionally variable (Obale-Ebanga et al. 2003), native biodiversity would inevitably be degraded, whilst invasion of introduced species across the agricultural frontier would be facilitated. However, the impact of globalised agricultural systems is far greater than that of traditional systems. This transition is driven by population growth to increase crop productivity through intensification and continued forest clearance for agricultural land, facilitated by new opportunities to access capital through contract and corporatised farming arrangements (Mather and Needle 2000; Lambina et al. 2001).

Across the developing countries in the Asia-Pacific, the face of agriculture has changed markedly since the 1960s (Figure 12.2). In Australia and New Zealand there was only minor clearing of forest and woodlands for agriculture during the latter part of the twentieth century, while in developing counties of the Asia-Pacific, the area of agriculture has increased significantly over the same period, particularly in the Philippines and Thailand. Whilst these data suggest that rates of forest clearing have

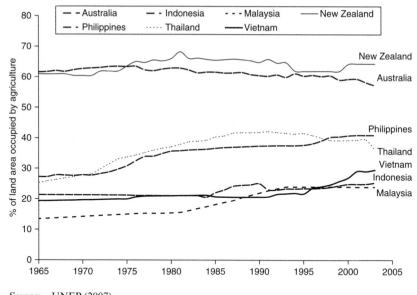

Source: UNEP (2007).

Figure 12.2   Changes in the percentage of countries' land mass that is cropped for agriculture

slowed somewhat in recent years, large areas of forest in countries such as Vietnam, Indonesia and Malaysia are rapidly being cleared for agriculture.

A particularly good example of the changes in agricultural systems and the place of globalised agricultural systems in these developing countries is the oil palm plantation industry. While originally an African plant, the oil palm (*Elaeis guineensis*) was introduced into Malaysia in the early twentieth century. The potential for the high-yielding and valuable crop to provide a steady and high income source for people drove the development of the oil palm industry in Malaysia and Indonesia, which together accounted for 80 per cent of the world's oil palm output in 2005 (Basiron et al. 2004).

The production of oil palm occurs on a variety of farms, from small-scale, grower-owned and controlled plantations, through to larger-scale corporatised operations. The oil palm yields large quantities of oil compared to other plants, with application to the (fast) food, cosmetics and biofuels industries. Because of the application of the products, and their importance in particular to the food industry, large global firms are now buyers of oil palm products and control the market for the product. Increases in the world demand for oils, and biofuels in particular, have driven up the global price, and consequently the Indonesian and Malaysian government have strongly supported activities to meet the increasing global demand. Projections indicate that the combined oil palm output from Indonesia and Malaysia will increase by over 160 per cent to around 47.4 million tonnes in the period 2005–12, with most new plantations being established in Borneo, particularly in the Indonesian province of Kalimantan and the Malaysian provinces of Sabah and Sarawak (Carter et al. 2007).

The significance of oil palm as a driver of tropical forest removal is reflected in recent research indicating that between 55 per cent and 60 per cent of the area converted to oil palm in Malaysia and Indonesia between 1990 and 2005 involved primary or secondary forests and the loss of their associated biodiversity (Koh and Wilcove 2008). This reflects a shift away from agricultural development through a state-subsidised smallholder approach, towards incentives encouraging private investment and development of 'frontier' lands largely consisting of forested areas claimed by the state (McCarthy and Cramb 2009). Furthermore, Malaysia recently announced the purchase of a total of 250 000 hectares of land in Indonesia, Papua New Guinea and Brazil, with the intention of establishing oil palm plantations (Butler 2008), underlining the potential continued threat to tropical forests worldwide associated with oil palm cultivation. Forest clearance for plantation agriculture in the tropics has direct and severe impacts on biodiversity, with orang-utans, tigers and rhinoceros being examples of charismatic megafauna in imminent danger of extinction through loss of habitat. Whilst these are focal areas of campaigns run by international environmental non-governmental organisations (NGOs), these losses are paralleled by unknown rates of decline in other species dependent upon tropical forest habitats. Furthermore, oil palm plantations have been shown to harbour distinctly lower species diversity than other plantation crops such as rubber, cocoa and coffee (Fitzherbert et al. 2008). This has culminated in oil palm being cited as possibly the 'single most important threat to the greatest number of species' (Koh and Wilcove 2009, p. 68).

EMERGING ENVIRONMENTAL AND SOCIAL DIMENSIONS OF GLOBALISED AGRICULTURAL SYSTEMS

At the other end of the management continuum are the moves by some producers away from large-scale, homogenised globalised systems towards organic farming and 'fair trade' markets. Globally, organic production accounted for around 30.4 million hectares in 2008, of which

12.3 million ha was in Australia, followed in the Asia-Pacific by China (2.3 million ha), Indonesia (41 400 ha) and Thailand (21 700 ha) (Willer 2008). Within Australia, the organic sector is dominated by extensive pastoral grazing, primarily involving beef cattle for the domestic market, which represents 97 per cent of the total area certified as under organic production. However, this accounts for less than half of the total value of organic produce, with grains, oilseeds and horticulture mainly for export representing significant areas of production. Elsewhere in the Asia-Pacific, the growth of the organic sector has been hampered by conflicting goals between the NGOs and business entrepreneurs that constitute the main sponsors and promoters of organic farming. However, with the ongoing rapid pace of development within China, and to a lesser extent India, the urban-centred middle-class market for organic produce is projected to continue to expand (Ong 2008). The entry of 'fair trade' products, which emphasise the producer's receipt of a greater proportion of the product's selling price, into the mainstream supermarkets in Europe and the United States has facilitated the rapid growth and diversification of this market. Whilst the selling point of fair trade produce is therefore rooted in the socio-economic benefits to small-scale producers rather than being couched in environmental terms, some products such as coffee, bananas and chocolate may be dual-branded as both organic and fair trade.

The organic sector therefore offers considerable potential to ameliorate some of the adverse environmental effects associated with 'mainstream' agriculture, whilst its own expansion has arisen through opportunities presented by a globalised system of agricultural production and consumption. Specifically, the benefits to biodiversity are associated with a reduction in chemical pesticide and inorganic fertilisers, sympathetic management of hedgerows and other non-cropped habitats, and the preservation of habitat heterogeneity through the encouragement of mixed farming practices, all of which have been shown to enhance populations of native plants, invertebrates, mammals and birds on organic farms in comparison to conventional farming (Hole et al. 2005).

Both organic and fair trade options, however, may only be suitable options for producers under certain conditions. Similar to conventional agriculture, a reliable and quick distribution network is essential to avoid product despoilation, whilst close linkages between producers and marketing agents operating in destination countries are fundamental towards securing some degree of demand stability. These will lead to distinct localised differences in terms of the scale and intensity of production and its socio-economic and environmental impacts (Agergaard et al. 2009). Additionally, stringent criteria relating to certification of organic produce must be met, which may be duplicated or multiplied where produce is destined for an international market. Through the Food and Agriculture Organization and the World Health Organization, the United Nations provides guidelines for national legislation defining organic produce under the Codex Alimentarius process. As of 2008, these have been fully implemented in the Asia-Pacific by China, Japan, South Korea, Taiwan and Thailand, with guidelines for export produce only implemented in Australia and New Zealand. All other countries in the region have either not adopted the guidelines or, as in the case of the Philippines, are in the process of doing so (Huber et al. 2008). Organisations such as the International Federation of Organic Agricultural Movements (IFOAM) recommend criteria to assist private organisations in developing certification mechanisms. The alignment of regulations utilised by state authorities and private certification companies is consequently of high priority in terms of facilitating customer confidence in the value of organic produce and future growth in the sector.

MANAGING ENVIRONMENTAL DEGRADATION IN GLOBALISED AGRICULTURAL SYSTEMS

In order to summarise policy responses to the threats outlined above, examples from outside the Asia-Pacific can be identified which offer potential for adoption within the region. Within the European Union, 'agri-environmental policies' whereby individual farmers can access funds designed to support environmentally sensitive modes of production have been progressively introduced and refined since the mid-1980s. This reflects a changing emphasis from farmers as food producers to 'custodians' of the land, implying a greater responsibility on the individual to maintain biodiversity. The efficacy of the raft of agri-environmental policies with respect to biodiversity is difficult to evaluate, reflecting regional differences in adoption, the limited time scale of policy operation, and the practical issues associated with linking biodiversity indicators to specific farming practices (Hanley et al. 1999; Kleijn and Sutherland 2003). Whilst these problems would doubtless be accentuated in the highly contrasting socio-economic and environmental contexts of agriculture in the Asia-Pacific, the environmental benefits of relatively simple measures such as set-aside have been clearly established (Van Buskirk and Willi 2004) and offer potential for adoption within the region.

However, policies such as these require large amounts of financing, which in the European case has been made possible through reallocating a relatively small fraction of money previously destined to subsidise agricultural practices under the Common Agricultural Policy. With its relatively low rate of agricultural production subsidy, Australia has not been able to follow this path, instead opting for a system of central government support and assistance to farmers' groups established under the Landcare programme initiated in the 1990s. At its peak, this involved around 30 per cent of the national farming community, with around 4000 groups undertaking diverse activities designed to raise community awareness of degradation issues and to implement measures to address these (Curtis 1998). Reform of this policy has been undertaken to address perceived inefficiencies of the programme, resulting in a regionalised approach towards addressing environmental problems associated with agriculture as part of the 'Caring for Our Country' programme introduced in 2007. Whether this will enable mitigation of the ongoing large-scale and severe environmental issues facing agriculture in Australia is unclear. However, Landcare and its associated programmes (Natural Heritage Trust I and II), have consistently faced criticisms of being unable to demonstrate 'value for money'; hence methods of evaluation which adequately reflect the varied social, economic and environmental benefits associated with management intervention are required (Hajkowicz 2009).

Policies designed to mitigate the environmental impacts of resource use almost inevitably involve extra production costs, which are usually passed on to the consumer either directly in the form of prices, or indirectly through tax or other mechanisms. The globalised agricultural system is no exception to this rule, as reflected in the 'organic premium' reflecting the additional production costs associated with organic food, which frequently amounts to an additional 100 per cent for fruit and vegetables in the US organic market (Oberholtzer et al. 2007). Whilst the nature and extent of additional organic production costs will obviously differ according to the product, long-term monitoring of farm trials in the US indicates that the true organic premium may be much lower, with a value of 10 per cent being cited for grain production (Pimentel et al. 2005). The organic sector has been characterised by rapid growth in terms of land area, product diversity and the total global market for organic food and drink, which increased by over 70 per cent to US$38.6 billion from 2002 to 2006 (Sahota 2008). It may be that this is characteristic of a youthful sector and that, once full market penetration (estimated at around 2–3 per cent in developed economies) is achieved, growth rates will level off.

However, the willingness of consumers to pay a premium for organic produce or for any additional cost related to mitigating the environmental impacts of agriculture will to some extent be determined by external economic factors. It is too early to discern the implications of the current economic slowdown in this respect or to comment upon the wider consequences for the globalised agricultural sector. Similarly, previous widespread global economic recessions have not taken place in circumstances similar to the modern globalised economy, hence comparisons with earlier experiences are largely inappropriate. With regard to the Asia-Pacific region and Indonesia in particular, the economic crisis of the late 1990s can be used as a yardstick to assist in identifying implications of the current economic situation with respect to agriculture.

A detailed overview of the combined effects of rapid currency depreciation, extreme climatic events and political unrest on Indonesian smallholders is provided by Gérard and Ruf (2001). This shows that the price of virtually all agricultural commodities fell heavily during the economic crisis, reflecting the inability of smallholders to diversify and the oligopolistic concentration of buyers who could dictate prices. Consequently, an increase in the area of land cultivated was the only viable option for farmers seeking to maintain income in the face of declining prices, with inevitable adverse outcomes for the environment. Whilst the circumstances leading to the regional economic crisis of the late 1990s differ in many respects to the current global situation, the likelihood of instability and uncertainty with respect to product prices may induce a similar response, although obviously this will be dependent upon the conditions of supply and demand relating to each product. A further difference rests with the roots of the current global economic decline lying in developed countries' economies, which could evidently lead to a retrenchment of globalised corporations' activities in developing countries, with individual farmers under contract farming agreements being most at risk.

The most appropriate conclusion that can be drawn at this stage is that, under the current globalised system of agriculture, farmers worldwide and particularly in developing countries are exposed to new and unpredictable hazards directly affecting their livelihoods, which will in turn determine the environmental impacts of their agricultural activities. Whilst globalisation evidently offers some opportunities to enhance the environmental sustainability of agriculture, the need to satisfy growing consumer demand will inevitably compromise and probably negate the net worth of any such beneficial outcomes.

REFERENCES

Agergaard, J., N. Fold and K.V. Gough (2009), 'Global–local interactions: socioeconomic and spatial dynamics in Vietnam's coffee frontier', *Geographical Journal*, **175**, 133–45.
Alcamo, J., M. Florke and M. Marker (2007), 'Future long-term changes in global

water resources driven by socio-economic and climatic changes', *Hydrological Sciences Journal*, **52**, 247–75.

Allan, J.A. (1998), 'Virtual water', *Ground Water*, **36**, 545–6.

Aplin, G., P. Mitchell, H. Cleugh, A. Pitman and D. Rich (1995), *Global Environmental Crises: An Australian Perspective*, Melbourne VIC: Oxford University Press.

Australian Bureau of Statistics (2006), *Water Account, Australia, 2004–05*, Canberra: Commonwealth of Australia.

Australian Bureau of Statistics (2008), *Water Use on Australian Farms, 2006–07*, Canberra: Commonwealth of Australia.

Barbier, E.B. (2000), 'Links between economic liberalization and rural resource degradation in the developing regions', *Agricultural Economics*, **23**, 299–310.

Basiron, Y., N. Balu and D. Chandramohan (2004), 'Palm oil: the driving force of world oils and fats economy', *Oil Palm Industry Economic Journal*, **4**, 1–10.

Burch, D., R.E. Rickson and G. Lawrence (eds) (1996), *Globalization and Agri-food Restructuring: Perspectives from the Australasia Region*, Aldershot: Ashgate.

Butler, R. (2008), 'Amazon palm oil: palm oil industry moves into the Amazon rainforest', accessed at http://news.mongabay.com/2008/0709-amazon_palm_oil.html.

Carter, C., W. Finley, J. Fry, D. Jackson and L. Willis (2007), 'Palm oil markets and future supply', *European Journal of Lipid Science and Technology*, **109**, 307–14.

Chapagain, A.K., A.Y. Hoekstra, H.H.G. Savenije and R. Gautam (2006), 'The water footprint of cotton consumption: An assessment of the impact of worldwide consumption of cotton products on the water resources in the cotton producing countries', *Ecological Economics*, **60**, 186–203.

Coleman, W., W. Grant and T. Josling (2004), *Agriculture in the New Global Economy*, Cheltenham, UK and Northampton, MA, USA: Edward Elgar.

CSIRO (1997), Acidification of cropping soils in South Australia – causes and effects, series no. 1, Glen Osmond, SA: CSIRO – Land and Water

Curtis, A. (1998), 'Agency–community partnership in landcare: lessons for state sponsored citizen resource management', *Environmental Management*, **22**, 563–74.

Department of Environment and Heritage (2000), *Water in a Dry Land*, Canberra: Department of Environment and Heritage.

Diamond, J. (2004), *Collapse: How Societies Choose to Fail or Succeed*, New York: Viking Press.

Doorman, F. (1998), *Global Development: Problems, Solutions, Strategies*, Utrecht, Netherlands: International Books.

Dunin, F.X. (2002), 'Integrating agroforestry and perennial pastures to mitigate water logging and secondary salinity', *Agricultural Water Management*, **53**, 259–70.

Ferdowsian, R., R. George, F. Lewis, D. McFarlane, R. Short and R. Speed (1996), The extent of dryland salinity in Western Australia, in *Proceedings of the 4th National Conference and Workshop on the Productive Use and Rehabilitation of Saline Lands*, Perth: Promaco Conventions, pp. 89–97.

Finlayson, B.L. and T.A. McMahon (1988), 'Australia v the world: a comparative analysis of streamflow characteristics', in R.F. Warner (ed.), *Fluvial Geomorphology of Australia*, Sydney: Academic Press, pp. 17–40.

Fitzherbert, E.B., M.J. Struebig, A. Morel, F. Danielsen, C.A. Brühl, P.F. Donald and B. Phalan (2008), 'How will oil palm expansion affect biodiversity?', *Trends in Ecology and Evolution*, **23**, 538–45.

Garside, A.L., M.J. Bell, B.G. Robotham, R.C. Magarey and G.R. Stirling (2005), 'Managing yield decline in sugarcane cropping systems', *International Sugar Journal*, **107**, 16–26.

George, R. (1992), 'Estimating and modifying the effects of agricultural development on the groundwater balance of large wheatbelt catchments, Western Australia', *Journal of Applied Hydrogeology*, **1**, 41–54.

Gérard, F. and F. Ruf (2001), *Agriculture in Crisis: People, Commodities and Natural Resources in Indonesia, 1996–2000*, Richmond: Curzon Press.

Ghassemi, F., A.J. Jakeman and H.A. Nix (1995), *Salinisation of Land and Water Resources: Human Causes, Extent, Management and Case Studies*, Sydney NSW: University of New South Wales Press.

Goodman, D. and M.J. Watts (1994), 'Reconfiguring the rural or fording the divide? Capitalist restructuring and the global agro-food system', *Journal of Peasant Studies*, **22**, 1–49.

Hajkowicz, S. (2009), 'The evolution of Australia's natural resource management programmes: towards improved targeting and evaluation of investments', *Land Use Policy*, **26**, 471–8.

Hanley, N., M. Whitby and I. Simpson (1999), 'Assessing the success of agri-environmental policy in the UK', *Land Use Policy*, **16**, 67–80.

Hatton, T.J. and R.A. Nulsen (1999), 'Towards achieving functional ecosystem mimicry with respect to water cycling in southern Australian agriculture', *Agroforestry Systems*, **45**, 203–14.

Hatton, T.J., J. Ruprecht and R.J. George (2003), 'Preclearing hydrology of the Western Australia wheatbelt: target for the future?', *Plant and Soil*, **257**, 341–56.

Helyar, K.R. and W.M. Porter (1989), 'Soil acidification, its measurement and the processes involved', in A. Robson (ed.), *Soil Acidity and Plant Growth*, Sydney NSW: Academic Press, pp. 61–101.

Hirst, P. and G. Thompson (1996), *Globalization in Question: The International Economy and the Possibilities of Governance*, Cambridge: Polity Press.

Hoekstra, A.Y. and A.K. Chapagain (2008), *Globalization of Water: Sharing the Planet's Freshwater Resources*, Oxford: Blackwell Publishing.

Hole, D.G., A.J. Perkins, J.D. Wilson, I.H. Alexander, P.V. Grice and A.D. Evans (2005), 'Does organic farming benefit biodiversity?', *Biological Conservation*, **122**, 113–30.

Huber, B., O. Schmid and L. Kilcher (2008), 'Standards and regulations', in H. Willer, M. Yussefi-Menzler and N. Sorensen (eds), *The World of Organic Agriculture: Statistics and Emerging Trends 2008*, London: Earthscan, pp. 59–70.

Jacobsen, T. and R.M. Adams (1958), 'Salt and silt in ancient Mesopotamian agriculture', *Science*, **128**, 1251–8.

Kleijn, D. and W.J. Sutherland (2003), 'How effective are European agri-environment schemes in conserving and promoting biodiversity?', *Journal of Applied Ecology*, **40**, 947–69.

Koh, L.P. and D.S. Wilcove (2008), 'Is oil palm agriculture really destroying tropical biodiversity?', *Conservation Letters*, **1**, 60–64.

Koh, L.P. and D.S. Wilcove (2009), 'Oil palm: disinformation enables deforestation', *Trends in Ecology and Evolution*, **24**, 67–68.

Lambin, E.F., B.L. Turner, H.J. Geista, S.B. Agbola, A. Angelsen, J.W. Bruce, O.T. Coomes, R.G.F. Dirzo, C. Folke, P.S. George, K. Homewood, J.

Imbernon, R. Leemans, X. Li, E.F. Moran, M. Mortimore, P.S. Ramakrishnan, J.F. Richards, H. Skanes, W. Steffen, G.D. Stone, U. Svedin, T.A. Veldkamp, C. Vogel and J. Xu (2001), 'The causes of land-use and land-cover change: moving beyond the myths', *Global Environmental Change*, **11**, 261–9.

Mather, A.S. and C.L. Needle (2000), 'The relationships of population and forest trends', *Geographical Journal*, **166**, 2–13.

McBratney, A., B. Whelan, T. Ancev and J. Bouma (2005), 'Future directions of precision agriculture', *Precision Agriculture*, **6**, 7–23.

McCarthy, J.F. and R.A. Cramb (2009), 'Policy narratives, landholder engagement and oil palm expansion on the Malaysian and Indonesian frontiers', *Geographical Journal*, **175**, 112–23.

McTainsh, G., J. Leys, G. Bastin, K. Tews, C. Strong and H. McGowan (2009), *Wind Erosion Risk Management for More Environmentally Sustainable Primary Production*, Alice Springs, NT: Desert Knowledge Cooperative Research Centre.

Moore, G., P. Dolling, B. Porter and L. Leonard (1998), 'Soil acidity. Soilguide: a handbook for understanding and managing agricultural soils', bulletin no. 4343, Perth, WA: Agriculture Western Australia.

National Land and Water Resources Audit (2001), *Australian Dryland Salinity Assessment 2000*, Canberra: National Land and Water Resources Audit.

Obale-Ebanga, F., J. Sevink, W. de Groot and C. Nolte (2003), 'Myths of slash and burn on physical degradation of savannah soils: impacts on vertisols in north Cameroon', *Soil Use and Management*, **19**, 83–86.

Oberholtzer, L., C. Dimitri and C. Greene (2007), 'Price premiums hold on as US organic produce market expands', in A.J. Wellson (ed.), *Organic Agriculture in the US*, New York: Nova Science Publishers, pp. 71–96.

Ong, K.W. (2008), 'Organic Asia 2007', in H. Willer, M. Yussefi-Menzler and N. Sorensen (eds), *The World of Organic Agriculture: Statistics and Emerging Trends 2008*, London: Earthscan, pp. 102–10.

Osborne, M.E. (2004), *River at Risk: The Mekong and the water politics of China and Southeast Asia*, Sydney, NSW: Lowy Institute for International Policy.

Peck, A.J. and T. Hatton (2003), 'Salinity and the discharge of salts from catchments in Australia', *Journal of Hydrology*, **272**, 191–202.

Pimentel, D., P. Hepperly, J. Hanson, D. Douds and R. Seidel (2005), 'Environmental, energetic and economic comparisons of organic and conventional farming systems', *Bioscience*, **55**, 573–82.

Pingali, P.L. (2001), 'Environmental consequences of agricultural commercialization in Asia', *Environment and Development Economics*, **6**, 483–502.

Reardon, T. and C.B. Barrett (2000), 'Agroindustrialization, globalization and international development: an overview of issues, patterns and determinants', *Agricultural Economics*, **23**, 195–205.

Rigg, J. (2005), 'Poverty and livelihoods after full-time farming: a south-east Asian view', *Asia Pacific Viewpoint*, **46**, 173–84

Robert, P.C. (2002), 'Precision agriculture: a challenge for crop nutrition management', *Plant and Soil*, **247**, 143–9.

Robinson, G.M. (2004), *Geographies of Agriculture: Globalization, Restructuring, and Sustainability*, Edinburgh: Pearson Education.

Sahota, A. (2008), 'The global market for organic food and drink', in H. Willer, M. Yussefi-Menzler and N. Sorensen (eds), *The World of Organic Agriculture: Statistics and Emerging Trends 2008*, London: Earthscan, pp. 53–8.

Stolte, W.J., D.J. McFarlane and R.J. George (1997), 'Flow systems, tree plantations, and salinisation in a Western Australian catchment', *Australian Journal of Soil Research*, **35**, 1213–29.

von Uexküll, H.R. and E. Mutert (1995), 'Global extent, development and economic impact of acid soils', *Plant and Soil*, **171**, 1–15.

United Nations Environment Programme (UNEP) (2007), UNEP GEO data portal, accessed at geodata.grid.unep.ch/.

Van Buskirk, J. and Y. Willi (2004), 'Enhancement of biodiversity within set-aside land', *Conservation Biology*, **18**, 987–94.

Wilson, G.A. (2001), 'From productivism to post-productivism . . . and back again? Exploring the (un)changed natural and mental landscapes of European agriculture', *Transactions of the Institute of British Geographers*, **26**, 103–20.

13. Globalisation, agriculture and development in the Asia-Pacific: reflections and future challenges

M.A.B. Siddique and Matthew Tonts

INTRODUCTION

Globalisation is a highly contested concept that is open to a diversity of interpretations. However, whether one defines globalisation in scalar terms or otherwise, it is clear that it is far more than just an overused term coined for the board room. Globalisation has had an enormous impact on all sectors of the economy, with Asia-Pacific agriculture just one of the many sectors affected. Globalised agriculture has brought with it a myriad of new and more complicated features, impacting on economies, social systems and environment alike. As developing countries like India and China use agriculture to improve economic growth and sustenance for their overpopulated countries, developed countries like Australia and New Zealand continue to rely heavily on the sector for economic stability.

The main aim of this book has been to (re-)explore the links between globalisation, agriculture and development in the Asia-Pacific region, with special focus on Australia, New Zealand, China, India, the Philippines and Vietnam. It has demonstrated that globalised agriculture has had a significant impact on the region in terms of the economy, as well as the social and environmental condition of constituent countries. The book has considered a number of the important issues surrounding a globalised agricultural system, and augments knowledge of the effects of the sector on the major economies in the Asia-Pacific region. Currently, while a number of case studies have offered an insight into some of these issues, there are few recent resources that synthesise or interpret the processes and implications of these shifts within the case study areas. This book contains new material relating to the subject, providing a broad interpretation of the globalisation of agriculture in the Asia-Pacific.

SUMMARY OF THE KEY FINDINGS

Chapter 2 by Argent explores the Australian agricultural sector in the context of a scaled conceptualisation of globalisation. He shapes globalisation as a set of tendencies, through which relative states of networks and flows, as well as places and people, are acknowledged. Additionally, furthering this robust depiction of globalisation, the international permeation of cultural ideals and norms as well as an increasing environmental consciousness, and banking presence, are recognised. Through this contemporary interpretation, an in-depth analysis of the impact of globalisation on the Australian agricultural sector is given. An emphasis is placed on the role of neoliberalism, the growing force of transnational corporations, the global environmental crises and associated problems, as well as the impact and scope of global finance and banking, as powerful aspects of globalisation in Australia.

This is augmented by Pritchard and Tonts's assessment of agricultural change and regional development in Australia. In Chapter 3, they argue that improved market efficiency and productivity has not necessarily contributed to a more prosperous set of regional communities and economies. Indeed, they provide evidence to suggest that the globalisation of Australian agriculture has had a deleterious effect on many places.

New Zealand, like much of the Australasian region, has traditionally placed a great emphasis on agriculture, with particular superiority surrounding the sheep industry, as the country supposedly rode the sheep's back into the new globalised era. In Chapter 4, Jackson considers the extent to which the agricultural sector has influenced the New Zealand economy and examines its likely impact into the future. The evolution of free trade is also considered, beginning with an analysis of the various measures of openness that are commonly utilised. He continues with an in-depth look at the degree of protection and openness of New Zealand's economy, considering the exchange rate as an important indicator of the country's integration on a world scale. Moving from the early, heavily protectionist, post-Second World War economy through to the liberalised economic conditions of today, the national dependence on agriculture is explored. Jackson illustrates a marked shift from the sheep industry to that of dairy, with the rise of the processing giant Fonterra illustrative of a vertically integrated globalised agri-food complex.

In Chapter 5 the focus shifts to China and India. Here, Siddique assesses the impact of agriculture on economic development in China and India. The chapter examines agriculture in both countries in terms of its composition, and gives a brief outline of the different regions in which principal agricultural crops are cultivated. Contribution of the agricultural sector to gross domestic product (GDP) and foreign exchange is also examined, as well as the significant transformation in terms of development and sector reform that agriculture has undergone in these countries. The chapter details the numerous country-specific policy changes implemented and the effect these adjustments have had on production with regard to worker incentives and efficiency of output. The findings show a significant rise in yield within the context of numerous obstacles. Additionally, Siddique demonstrates that differential pace of agricultural development, such has been the case with seed fertiliser technology as well as mechanisation, has subsequently influenced change in the pace of agricultural growth between the countries, and hence economic growth and development for the regions as a whole. Gauging the importance of different plan and policy initiatives provides important insights into future endeavours that should perhaps be executed in the agricultural development effort in both China and India, as well as in other countries that are reliant on the agriculture sector for economic development.

In Chapter 6 Chatterjee, Rae and Ray explore the agricultural sector in India since the inception of change and subsequent growth in the region. They find that since the implementation of reforms, trade in agriculture has increased significantly from US$5.8 billion in 1990 to US$15.7 billion in 2003. However, despite total trade increasing, agriculture's trade balance has shown a declining trend, reflecting strong growth in agricultural imports over exports. While import growth has slowed down in recent years, the Indian market still has important implications for future trade prospects with Australia and New Zealand, both major agricultural exporters. Imports from these two countries started to grow from 2003, gaining 187 per cent and 65 per cent in the three years from 2003 to 2006, for Australia and New Zealand respectively. Given that India's agricultural imports started to decline during this period, this increased trade is impressive. Furthermore, the authors point out that with increased affluence within India there has been a change of preferences away from cereals toward meat, fish, fruit and vegetables, and that this supply is likely to come from imports due to local constrictions on land. Therefore, with a greater focus, the Indian market could yield even more significant returns for the Australasian exporters.

Chatterjee, Rae and Ray also illustrate that while India's trade in agriculture has increased, and its importance both as a source of employment and local food security is questionable, since the implementation of reforms the level of food per capita has actually declined. This is due to rising prices of staples such as wheat and rice. This is an issue of national priority in India; achieving and maintaining food security has been a major plank of India's development efforts since Independence, due to a large proportion of the populace living below the poverty line. Additionally, given supply constraints on India's home soil, due in part to the ever-increasing presence of the private sector, the Indian government has had to import grains from overseas, conflicting with its aim of food self-dependence. The authors emphasise that this decreasing food security seems to have occurred as a consequence of the changes the country has implemented since the 1990s, and is a matter that needs urgent attention.

In Chapter 7, Wu and Dingtao provide an assessment of China's integration into the world and the impact that this has had on agricultural performance within the country. China has increasingly pervaded the world market, with indicators suggesting a remarkable transition. Since opening its borders, China has become one of the largest recipients of foreign direct investment (FDI), totalling US$78 billion in 2006. Additionally, the country's agricultural sector has seen a significant rise in both exports from and FDI into the industry, with food exports more than doubling from 2001, to reach US$30.7 billion in 2007. Wu and Dingtao undertake a comprehensive empirical analysis to comprehend the degree that total factor productivity (TFP) has contributed to agricultural growth. They find that while the level of TFP differs between China's regions and has shown a trend of slowdown since the early 1990s, the average level has nonetheless been a considerable 3.8 per cent for agriculture during 1979–2005, with technological progress the major contributor. Wu and Dingtao also find that despite agricultural productivity in the region showing vulnerability to internal and external shocks, the level of TFP suggests that growth should continue into the near future.

Chapter 8 explores the globalisation of agriculture and its impact on the Association of South East Asian nations (ASEAN) countries, with a distinction made between the ASEAN4 and ASEAN transition economics (ATEs). Siddique shows that the ASEAN region has experienced considerable recent growth, with average growth rates across all the countries being 5.93 per cent for the period 1984–2007, a possible indicator of increased openness of the region. Various policy reforms implemented in the region have caused an increased openness of the respective countries. FDI has also increased, further indicating a turn to globalisation. Siddique continues the chapter by showing an extraordinary increase in the absolute levels that agriculture is contributing to GDP in the region, and describes the sector's importance for the wealth and well-being of developing nations. In addition, many of the ATEs have benefited from importing technologies relating to the so-called 'Green Revolution' explored in previous chapters, while others have possibly had some increases in productivity as an outcome of government intervention.

In Chapter 9, Shaw explores the impact of early colonisation on the geography of Southeast Asia, and finds an evident influence on rural–urban migration as well as intense population growth, from 25 million in the early 1880s to a staggering excess of 500 million before the end of the millennium. Rapid urbanisation has continued through the second half of the twentieth century to the present day, alongside political sovereignty and then global integration, largely annihilating the rural idyll. Small-scale subsistence production was, and continues to be, replaced by that of a bustling city norm, epitomised by megacities such as Jakarta, Manila and Bangkok. Employment in farming continues to fall, as some seek the perceived opportunities in the urban life, while others are displaced by the ever-increasing land prices. In many instances the phenomenon of urban expansion, occurring at the expense of surrounding villages, produces a combination of circumstances characterised by a juxtaposition of urban and rural qualities, a distinctive regionalism evident in Southeast Asia.

Shaw depicts a Southeast Asian region largely unrecognisable from the days of the ancient cities. Where once people used to work largely in tune with the land, the collective impacts of globalisation and urbanisation have now caused a number of environmental concerns. As well as massive deforestation, there have been severe water shortages in the region, as the precious resource is stretched between farmers, industries and households. Incompatible and unregulated land uses have also contributed to the increasing levels of water pollution in the Southeast Asian region, with agricultural and industrial effluent flowing into fishing grounds and water sources. So it seems that while the increasing presence of the wealthy and foreign investors is escalating the level of disproportionate wealth, agriculture and the environment are struggling in a system equipped with limited resources.

In Chapter 10, Huddleston studies the impact of contract farming. He focuses on outgrowers in the Philippines and the specific consequences these farmers face once entered into a contract with the local oil palm processor, Agumil. Huddleston examines the role of, and variations in, technology used by the farmers, and looks at the effect that the technology transfer via contract farming schemes has had on the outgrowers. His findings suggest that concerns about adverse impacts, such as cultural, social and economic costs, from the transfer of certain technologies to the developing world, are not founded in this particular study. In contrast, he finds that 91 per cent of the studied outgrowers believe they have benefited from the contract, through for example the direct training processes inherent in the contract as well as the transferability benefits of technology transfer. Indeed, it seems that the farming agreements did in fact foster agricultural

development, and that the outgrowers were able to utilise their training further by applying it to improving their other farming practices.
Essentially, it seems, outgrowers are prepared to surrender some of their
independence in order to realise such benefits as acquiring new facets of
production, agricultural inputs and management processes. Furthermore,
strict contract requirements on factors such as product quality and safety
often mean that these aspects also improve. However, Huddleston emphasises that contract farming systems are very transient, differing in both
their implementation and success rates.

Huddleston also expresses his concern for the environmental impact of
such contractual agreements, and emphasises that the success of contract
farming schemes should be measured in terms of their environmental sustainability. The oil palm contracts in the Philippines certainly place less
emphasis on environmental sustainability than other facets of the industry, and lend credence to the argument that land care training needs to be
more uniformly implemented.

In Chapter 11, Clifton explores the concept of globalised conservation,
a perspective whereby globalisation is defined in terms of international
conservation programmes. With this classification, he looks at the effects
of the Lambusango Forest Conservation project, a four-year programme
co-financed by the UK-based Global Environment Facility (GEF) and
implemented on the developing Indonesian island of Buton. The island
was targeted for this conservation effort as it is home to a diverse and rich
ecology that is under threat from a combination of agricultural, economic
and population growth, as well as institutional weaknesses prevalent in the
national and state governments.

Clifton scrutinises the international presence in Buton, investigating
the programme's impact on the socio-economic and political environments of the region, as well as its effectiveness in advancing conservation
in the area. He finds that, intentions aside, a number of the programme's
features were not appropriate for the island of Buton. First, regulations
imposed on rattan were deemed to be incongruous to the transient need
and use of the good to households in the region. Second, the programme's
introduction of ginger, as an alternative to the reliance on income generated through illegal logging, created unrest. Ginger can have positive
economic returns and does not require irrigation. However there are considerable agricultural and economic risks attached to the tubers' production, some of which caused the limited success of the resource in Buton.
Hence, Clifton warns against achieving conservation through the use of
new markets for capital investment and accumulation. The third example
cited is the programme's ban on deforestation within the area, an enforcement that was to be realised at the village head level, where technically the

law in this case stipulates that it should be a state-controlled area. There is uncertainty therefore as to whether the proposed ban will see fruition, despite conservationists highlighting its fundamental importance to the integrity of the forested area.

In Chapter 12, Callow and Clifton consider the environmental impacts of a globalised agricultural system. They point out that while land degradation has long been associated with agricultural development and production, other environmental changes have also occurred including pollution, loss of biodiversity, and changes to waterways and water quality. Callow and Clifton emphasise that unless environmental systems are sustainable, then the economic viability of agriculture must remain in question. Moreover, the degradation of natural systems is argued to impact directly on social development.

CHALLENGES AHEAD

Although agriculture has traditionally played an important role in the development of the Asia-Pacific region, it has advanced its role dramatically since the quickening of globalisation processes in the 1970s. However, there are a number of challenges, both current and emerging, that will likely have an impact on the structure and performance of the sector, as well as having both social and environmental implications. Here we briefly suggest that there might be three major challenges, amongst many, that require attention: (1) environmental degradation and population growth; (2) production systems, and particularly the emergence of genetically modified crops; (3) population growth.

As Clifton and Callow pointed out in Chapter 12, there have been some important steps in the right direction as regards environmental management under globalised agricultural systems (see also Clifton in Chapter 11). However, the reality is that agriculture continues to have a problematic relationship with natural environmental systems. Soil erosion and degrading soil quality have become severe problems in the Asia-Pacific region and will likely continue to be a paramount challenge if exploitation of the resource beyond its means continues. Soil exposure to water and wind erosion is heightened by certain agricultural factors such as overgrazing. Additionally, acidification, depletion of soil nutrients, soil compaction and chemical use, among other factors, directly damage soil quality and health. Given that the agricultural sector finds its roots in the soil, so to speak, ruin of the resource has the potential to undermine not only agriculture, but also wider processes of rural development. As Callow and Clifton emphasise, if soil health is to be regained, modifications to production methods are required, in addition to the introduction and application of more effective ameliorants.

Extensive agriculture-driven deforestation in the Asia-Pacific region, particularly the tropical regions of Southeast Asia, is also of major concern. The conversion of natural habitat for agricultural expansion has had a significant impact on the biodiversity of the region and will have massive implications into the future. Conversion has intensified in recent decades as a result of extensive population growth, coupled with corporations avariciously and recklessly converting limited inputs for the sake of an insatiable demand. This has caused habitats once rich in flora and fauna to disappear, as seemingly endless tracts of agricultural monotony take their place. While estimates vary on the rate to which deforestation and diversity loss will continue, Sodhi et al. (2004) estimate that Southeast Asia could lose up to three-quarters of its original forests by 2100, and up to 42 per cent of its biodiversity (ibid., p. 654) unless some drastic changes are made.

Water is another major environmental challenge that faces the Asia-Pacific region as a whole, and the agricultural sector specifically. The agricultural sector traditionally relies heavily on water, using approximately 70 per cent of the world's accessible water supply every year (UN 2006). And, with its extensive use, a number of major problems have emerged, including pollution of lakes, rivers and underground water sources. Pesticides and other pollutants that run off from agricultural areas often find their way into water sources, having a negative impact on fragile ecosystems and the people that rely on them. Additionally, there are serious water shortages in much of the region, which have in part been caused by the agricultural sector. Wasteful methods of production as well as the cultivation of so-called 'thirsty crops' such as rice are not suited to the environment, using large amounts of water. Better water and waste management and legislation are needed in much of the Asia-Pacific region, particularly the tropical countries of the Southeast Asian region. Additionally, more efficient methods of agricultural production and perhaps greater emphasis on less water-reliant crops would be wise to ease the water shortage problem.

While there are those who suggest that there might be benefits associated with genetically modified (GM) food crops, such as decreased dependence on pesticide and insecticide use, there is serious concern over the unknown long-term effects the crops will have on both the consumer and the environment. There is certainly some evidence that these crops will offer higher yields and a range of other benefits, but there are also concerns about farmer dependence on the large corporations that control the supply chain for such organisms. As mentioned by Argent (Chapter

2), some farmers are already concerned that their GM-free crops will be cross-contaminated by modified crops. Whether one is 'for' or 'against' genetically manipulated agriculture, however, it is clear that the agricultural sector in the Asia-Pacific will be impacted upon by its advent, and as modification and research in the area continues, the sector will likely face new challenges.

Of course, many of the challenges described here are, in one way or another, linked to the dynamics of population growth. As Shaw pointed out in Chapter 9, parts of Southeast Asia continue to experience high rates of urbanisation and population growth. The pressure this places on agriculture in terms of food production and environmental impact is considerable. In China and India, the combination of large and/or growing regional and urban populations also place pressure on agricultural systems, and have the potential to undermine agricultural development. Linked to this is the tendency of growing and urbanising populations to utilise agricultural land for urban expansion. Such debates are not limited to developing countries. In Australia, for example, debates have re-emerged about the country's carrying capacity; that is, the number of people that the environment can sustain. In a continent with a fragile environment and limited water, agriculture places considerable pressure on natural ecosystems. Yet, it is also critical not just in terms of the national economy, but also in sustaining rural jobs and communities. Of course, the issues surrounding population are more than just 'how many' and 'where'. Also important is the socio-economic structure of the population. As levels of development increase, so too does consumption. Thus, the danger is that agricultural environments are placed under ever-increasing pressure as prosperity within the region increases. Better understanding these dynamics, as well as their broader environmental, social and political dimensions, is crucial for securing more sustainable agricultural and rural development in a globalised world.

REFERENCES

Sodhi, N.S., L.P. Koh, B.W. Brook and P.K.L. Ng (2004), 'Southeast Asian biodiversity: an impending disaster', *Review*, **19**(12), 654–60.
United Nations (2006), Facts and figures extracted from the *2nd United Nations World Water Development Report*, accessed at www.unesco.org/water/wwap/wwdr/wwdr2/facts_figures/index.shtml.

Index